ALSO BY SPALDING GRAY

Swimming to Cambodia
Sex and Death to the Age 14
Monster in a Box

IMPOSSIBLE VACATION

SPALDING GRAY

IMPOSSIBLE VACATION

ALFRED A. KNOPF   NEW YORK   1992

A NOTE ON THE TYPE

The text of this book was set in a digitized version of Bembo, a well-known Monotype face. Named for Pietro Bembo, the celebrated Renaissance writer and humanist scholar who was made a cardinal and served as secretary to Pope Leo X, the original cutting of Bembo was made by Francesco Griffo of Bologna only a few years after Columbus discovered America.
Sturdy, well-balanced, and finely proportioned, Bembo is a face of rare beauty, extremely legible in all of its sizes.
Composed by The Haddon Craftsmen, Scranton, Pennsylvania
Printed and bound by Fairfield Graphics, Fairfield, Pennsylvania
Designed by Iris Weinstein

TO MY MOTHER,

the Creator and Destroyer

"You will not know . . . what these acts are until you have performed them all. And after you have performed them you will not understand that they were expiating any more than you have understood all the other expiation that has kept you in such prolonged humiliation. Then, when these final acts are complete, you will stop trying to die because of me."

— WILLIAM KENNEDY, *Ironweed*

I would like to express my thanks to my faithful agent, Suzanne Gluck, for saying, "I think you have a novel in you," and then selling that idea to Knopf; also to the MacDowell Colony and the Edward Albee Foundation, for giving me a supportive and creative environment in which to write; then to Ron and Donna Feiner for their lovely gift of that grand writing table on which I finally finished it. Thanks to Gary Fisketjon for his edit of the original nineteen-hundred-page monster and to his assistant, Garth Battista, for his nuturing ordering of that sprawling hand-written mess. And last of all, my loving gratitude to Renée Shafransky, who put up with five years of my anxious complaints about this book and at last added her talented red pencil to it all.

IMPOSSIBLE VACATION

A ND I HALF DREAMED and half remem-
bered Mom's never-ending passion for the sea. We were
all on our way to Gram's summer house in Sakonnet,
Rhode Island, in our wooden-slatted '38 Ford beach wagon. What a
car! I see it now in my mind like a gloriously varnished antique: the
long stick shift jiggling on the floor; the dark tan leather seats that
smelled so good and felt so cool against our thighs; and the windshield
with its slightly blue discoloration at the very bottom near the crank
that opened it to let the fresh air in. The air was fresh then. The air
was so fresh that it burned like a pure white fire in our lungs. To be
in that car with all the family on the way to Gram's house was to be
alive. I was one and whole; I was right there and nowhere else in my
mind.

As soon as we were out into the country, which didn't take long,
we'd begin to count cows until we got to the most awe-inspiring place
of the trip, the landscape that signaled our proximity to the sea:
Windmill Hill (though it had no windmills on it that I can remember).
It was the only large hill near the coast of Rhode Island. It was the
first and only large hill that I had ever experienced, and coming onto
that hill was like flying for me. Going over Mount Hope Bridge on
our trip to Gram's was pretty spectacular; but Windmill Hill was *very*
special, because it ran along the edge of the Sakonnet River, and there
below the hill, built on a flat bank along the river, were all these little

summer bungalows. And to me at that height and at my age those houses did not translate in my mind into actual-size real beach houses but instead stayed exactly as I saw them—a settlement of tiny toy beach bungalows, or as I realized later in life, something like Monopoly-game houses. They were like the entire Lone Ranger town that Tommy Atwater assembled from the back of Cheerios boxes until there was no place to walk in his room without stepping on the little bank, the jail, or the post office. It was a view that at age five absolutely agreed with me. It was a little world that made me feel like a giant.

Then Mom, nosing the open crack of the windshield as she rode in front next to Dad, would cry out, "Do you smell it? Do you smell it? Do you smell the sea?" Coleman and I were bouncing in the leather seat, all excited; and Mom was right, we could smell it, we could smell the sea from miles away on top of Windmill Hill as we rolled down the hot asphalt highway, our little wooden Ford headed for the sandy edge of the world.

Then came our momentous arrival: the parking of the beach wagon and the running through white sand dunes scattered with wild beach roses, the hot soft sand underfoot and between our toes, running into that little protected beach which was the world, which was the only world, the world of totally protected pleasure. Mom chose a place for us to settle down, and there we'd spread our towels on that perfect little beach, that perfect little desert of white sand with beautiful high rocks that defined the beach on either end. There I'd lie feeling the sun all over me, idly watching one distant freighter move like a toy as it marked time and defined the horizon, the edge of that perfect world. Beyond that horizon was only an inkling of some faraway place of a war where Mom's brother, my uncle Jib, was.

Gramma North would sometimes come join us for lunch. And at the end of the day—after all the swimming in the surf, the sand castles, the peanut butter and jelly sandwiches, and Dad diving off the high rocks—Mom would call us in and we would go back to Gram's house, which was near a field with a haystack, and everyone seemed all together and happy. In the night there was deep sleep, and in the morning there was fog, so much fog that you couldn't see the haystack; and Gramma North would say, "But it will burn off before noon," and she was always right. Soon we could see the haystack while we ate fresh blueberries and cantaloupe melon balls. Dad stoked the wood stove and Mom made sandwiches as the fog lifted. Then we all went back to the beach again.

One day in July when I was five years old and standing in my little paradise, a part of me was swept away. It was a dazzling blue day with high white cotton clouds, and I was on the beach standing in front of Mom, who was in her bathing suit, lying stretched out in a blue-and-green-striped canvas beach chair. And suddenly my Mom's brother, my uncle Jib, had come home from the other side of the horizon. He was dressed in his pure white sailor's uniform, so white against the blue that he seemed almost absent, like a window to blank white space at the edge of the rolling waves. Jib was just standing there with his hands behind his back. He was barefoot, and the slight summer wind was blowing his white bell bottoms, and I knew from Mom's enthusiastic celebrating that the big war had ended and that her brother, Jib, had come home from it, and he was all new to me and born now for the first time in my eyes that day, born full-grown as some white hero. It was as though he had walked in on the water from the other side of that horizon that stretched before me. Dad was not there; he and my brother Coleman were somewhere else—perhaps about to dive off the distant high rocks. Topher had not been born yet. That was the day I heard the word "Bali" for the first time.

Mom was saying, "Your uncle Jib has just come back from Bali and he brought you something," and then Uncle Jib pulled out a crazy wooden monkey mask from behind his back and gave it to me. It was like no other mask or toy I'd ever seen or touched before, and I couldn't figure out what it had to do with the war. Had Uncle Jib been fighting monkeys in a place called Bali? Bali in my mind was like some funny beach ball on the other side of the earth from where we were all so happy here. Was this the sacred head of the enemy brought back to this beach in Rhode Island? I took the monkey mask in my hand with fear and trembling. It was made of painted wood and had a movable jaw that was tied to the face by little leather straps. Jib helped me to put it on. He guided a larger leather strap over my head and I was suddenly in a foreign, faraway world that smelled of rough smoky wood and weathered leather and I felt the animal spirit of the monkey go into my face and body and through those little wooden eye openings. I suddenly saw things as different and faraway. I could hear Mom laughing in her distant beach chair. I could see Mom's laughing eyes tear up as I became half child and half monkey in her eyes, and I began to spin and spin around and around until the beach and the distant rocks, the ocean and Mom and white white Jib blowing in the wind became like a solid spinning smear of colors. Mom's laughter mixed with the sound of waves breaking and I spun and spun in the protection of Mom's gaze and I was not dizzy because in my eyes there was a new abstract world and I knew I was safe spinning in Mom's eyes and Mom's laughter. I was her monkey boy spinning and spinning until the hard wet sand of the beach came up and slapped me. I was down, while that whole Garden of Eden that I had known for five endless summers spun on around me and the waves rolled in over my toes and Jib's big hand came into my monkey's-eye view and he lifted me up. Mom cried, "Brewster, Brewster, my monkey boy, my little monkey boy!" That day another place was born in my body and in my mind, which then was all imagination and no thinking.

Then that night, or one night shortly after Brewster the monkey boy was born, Mom was sitting by my bed on a summer night at Gram's house and she was reading to me—no, not so much reading as guiding me through my favorite book, which was almost all pictures and no words. I don't remember the name of the book, but I remember the story and Mom guiding me through it again that night under my new other self: the strange wooden monkey mask from Bali that hung on the wall above my bed. The story was about a little penguin who lived in the South Pole and was oh so very dissatisfied because he was always so cold and he desperately wanted to escape from all that snow and ice, so he took his few belongings, which included his toothbrush and his bathtub, and he cut away a large piece of ice from the solid ice of the South Pole and began to float off for the South Seas, where I knew Uncle Jib had come from. When that little penguin's ice block at last got into warmer waters, it began to melt until there was nothing left of it, and the penguin was forced to jump into his bathtub to save himself; and so, jumping into his bathtub, he turned the shower around so that it could take in sea water and spit it out the shower head, and that acted as an ingenious little motor that propelled him to his perfect paradise island, where at last we see him lying in a hammock between two palm trees, sipping a large glass of lemonade made with fresh lemons, and he's sweating and fanning himself and he is so dissatisfied because now he is too hot.

I remember being there in bed thinking, or imagining—because back then there was no difference between thinking and imagining—that the island he went to was Bali and that this book, this story that Mom was showing me, was somehow, although I had no words for it then, a lesson about dissatisfaction and the impossibility of ever attaining any earthly paradise. At the same time that monkey mask on the wall was calling me away from our island of roads to some other palm-treed island in my mind. That monkey face was calling me away from Mom.

We all had fun as our wonderful summers blended together in Sakonnet, although I could never lie on that beach again without thinking of Bali. Then after a while I just accepted that as a part of my life, accepted that forever I would always be a little bit in the place that I was not, a little bit in my body and a lot in my imagination.

W
E KEPT RETURNING to Sakonnet for the summer because Gramma North kept renting a house down there, and then one summer she didn't, so we stayed at home and swam in the Barrington River, which was not in any way as exciting as the ocean but still it was fun. Dad joined the Barrington Yacht Club, not because we had a yacht, or any boat, but because the yacht club had a little beach and a raft we could swim out to. By then Topher had been born and was two years old, and Mom would lie on the beach and watch us wallow in the water. Mom was always relaxed and happy then. She was the best she ever was whenever she was on a beach. She was even more relaxed than after church. It was as though the water was a god for her. It was as though the water was as important as Jesus, but she'd never admit that. She'd get real nervous and pent-up if she couldn't make it to the water in the summer.

Although I still had my monkey mask on the wall I had pretty much forgotten about Bali. I made a secret promise that I'd get there one day, and that secret promise allowed me to swim in the river and have fun in the ocean during all the special times we went there. But sometimes in the winter I'd have fantasies of Bali and how when I was old enough I would join the merchant marine and work my way there on a freighter and then return triumphant with monkey masks and all my dirty laundry in a duffel bag over my shoulder. And Mom would be there at the front gate to greet me and I would tell her about Bali and shower her with gifts from Bali. I would shower her with shawls and cloth of every color and there would be monkey masks for everyone.

Then one summer things went strange. I think I was about nine years old, and that was the summer that I noticed Mom didn't go to the beach all that often anymore.

That was the summer that Mom first really started to go crazy. I don't remember it starting slowly that time, all I remember was that it was hot and my brothers and I were in the playroom with our friends from down the street and we would hear Mom cry out from the kitchen. She would cry out all these wild and crazy things. Sometimes it was words or Dad's name, or she'd cry out, "Jesus save me!" Other times it was just moans and cries. All of a sudden she'd burst into singing Christian Science hymns real loud and all out of tune. It was a cry of madness that seemed to come out of nowhere, and our friends would look at us with this panic in their eyes. Later on in the day she'd be all right. But what was strange (and I don't think we thought of it as strange then) was that no one ever talked about it. That's what seems strange now. No one ever mentioned it. Not a word. Neither Dad nor Gram North, who lived with us then, ever took us aside and tried to explain. I guess they were as confused as we were.

Mom was then a fairly devout Christian Scientist, and I suppose this to some extent was causing her to deny the fact that anything was wrong. It was some time during that summer, someone came to tell me—but I don't remember who, maybe it was Dad or Gram—that the three of us, Topher, Coleman, and I, had to be split up for a while because Mom was real nervous and couldn't stand us fighting all the time. I didn't remember us fighting all that much, but if some adult came and said it, it must have been true.

I do remember that I used to hit Coleman a lot in the balls, and when he ran to tell Mom she would tell me, "Never hit Coleman there! Never hit him in that place again!" But I did it over and over again; no matter what she said I still did it, and Cole never hit me back. But he was a lot bigger and heavier than I; and at last one day that summer, he pinned me to the ground and wouldn't let me up. It was an awful feeling because I couldn't move and I remember I was kicking and screaming. He said he wouldn't let me up until I stopped screaming and kicking. And that made me scream and kick all the more. I felt like I was going to explode. I thought the veins in my head would burst. When I stopped moving at last I felt like a statue of myself. I felt like a dead boy—I felt dead! Finally Cole let me up and I went and shut myself in the bedroom and moved my bookcase against the door because we didn't have any door locks. When Cole came to bang on the door I screamed, "Stay away or I'll jump! I'll jump out the window." I ran to the window. "I'll kill myself like Milton Berle's wife!" is what I yelled at Cole that summer that Mom couldn't stop crying out loud.

I remember standing in that second-story window and looking down, wondering if I really had the courage to jump and if I did would it kill me from such a small height. I think I figured I'd just break a leg or something and end up in a cast for the rest of the summer, and that would be much better than dying because of all the attention I'd get. But then I also realized that Mom wouldn't be able to give me any attention, because she was cracking up and needed all of it for herself.

Anyway, one day, somebody came to me and said, "You boys are going to have to go away to different places." I remember that I was sitting alone on a chair on the front porch because it was real hot and you could hear the cicadas (which we called "heat bugs" then). You couldn't see the heat bugs and yet they were very loud. I was sitting there, dressed only in my blue shorts with white stripes on the side. I was just sitting there picking honeysuckle blossoms from the great honeysuckle vine that covered the whole front of the porch. I was snipping the base of each blossom with my thumbnail and pulling the little stem to try to fill up my father's one-ounce shot glass with honey, one drop at a time, until perhaps hours or days later I'd have enough honey for one little sip. I wasn't fighting with Cole or any-thing. I wasn't even trying to jump out the window. I don't remember where Cole and Topher were, but I do remember that someone came up behind me and said, "You boys are going to have to be separated for the rest of the summer because your Mom can't stand it anymore."

Cole went down the road to stay with Gramma Benton. I was to go stay with Gramma North in Sakonnet, where she was living for the summer with a friend. Topher got to stay at home with Mom and Dad. Mom drove me as far as Mount Hope Bridge. And then to save on the two-dollar toll we walked across together to meet Gramma North and her friend Anne. I'd never walked over that bridge before or even dreamed I ever would. We'd driven over it many times on our way to Windmill Hill and the ocean, but no one I knew had ever walked over it. It was very exciting and frightening. About halfway over we heard the voices of men talking underneath and it turned out that they were bridge painters suspended on little swings, painting the bridge just under us. Mom must have been in an all-right mood, because she was real chatty and made joking conversation with them and they whistled and called back and told us to have a good day. The view from that bridge made me dizzy, and the boats looked like toys far below. We met Gram North and her friend Anne on the other side; then Mom walked back across the bridge alone.

I spent the rest of the summer with Gram and Anne and I didn't like it that much. I didn't like being all alone with myself and I didn't like being told what to do by Gram, and most of all, I didn't like being told what to do by her friend Anne, who was almost a complete stranger to me.

Even going to the ocean with them didn't help. I missed Mom and Mom's eyes on me. I would lie on the warm sand with my eyes closed, dreaming of my trip to Bali and, most important, my return from Bali and how Mom would be there at the gate to greet me.

Then when I would go into the ocean I would just lie there at the edge like a limp drowned boy and let the waves wash me in and out. My body would roll into the surf and wash back up again just like a piece of driftwood. This would upset Gram and Anne so much that they would come and scold me. "Don't do that, Brewster," they'd say. "Do not do that. We don't like it. It frightens us," they'd cry, each waving a finger at me.

The next thing that I remember was that it was September and I was back home and Mom was not there because she had gone away to a Christian Science rest home. After that, when she had gotten all rested up, she went to spend some time at Gram and Gramp Benton's down the road from our house. I think she stayed in bed there a lot. When I came to visit her she was in bed in the guest bedroom in the middle of the day. I thought it was strange that Mom would be in bed in the middle of the day when she didn't even have a cold or a fever or anything like that. She just needed a lot of rest, someone kept saying, and please be quiet, don't raise your voice. "Your mother got very overtired and she needs a lot of rest to get well."

It was sometime between October and Thanksgiving when Mom came home again, and that was the time she had something real big and important happen to her. She had what she called "a healing." She all of a sudden got healed by a vision of Christ coming down into the living room on a shaft of late-morning sunlight. We were all away at school and Dad was at work. I don't know where Gramma North was, but Mom told me that she was lying on the couch reading from *Science and Health* and then she got all of a sudden very calm and very clear, like the clear calm before a storm, she said. But the storm didn't follow. Christ came instead. Christ came down a shaft of sunlight almost like he'd slid in on one of those bright, rolling autumn clouds off of Narragansett Bay. He came in on a shaft of light and touched Mom's feet and touched the palms of her hands, and she was instantaneously healed and filled with joy.

She got so very, very high, she said, like the time she once told me about watching Arturo Toscanini direct the New York Philharmonic in Providence. She said they were playing Tchaikovsky's *Pathétique* Symphony and she just floated right up out of her body. She floated right up to the ceiling like a ghost of herself looking back down at it all, and saw herself watching the Philharmonic play. So Jesus came and touched Mom with all of his electric love and left, never to return again.

Mom told me this story. And she told me that right after she was healed she made the mistake of telling Dad about it. It was a mistake to tell him because he doubted it in such a big way that she was poisoned by his doubt and fell back into a nervous collapse, and she had to fight real hard to know the truth again and remember how Christ had touched her. She had to fight hard to keep things to herself, to keep her newfound secrets from Dad.

T HE FOLLOWING SUMMER Dad decided that one way to be sure Mom stayed rested and relaxed was to rent a little beach bungalow down in Jerusalem, which was a small fishing village just across from Galilee on the Rhode Island shore. This made Mom very happy. She was back to her old lively self again, that good old "7UP Kid." Because Mom never drank anything stronger than 7UP at the parties Dad and she went to, people would often refer to her as "The 7UP Kid." And often she'd end up doing cartwheels and standing on her head, and many people who didn't know she was an abstainer would say, "Hey, wow! What has Kit been drinking?"

And once again she was all full of spirit and pep and raring to go. She couldn't wait for summer to come. Dad had told Mom that the house on the beach had a sun deck on the roof, and Mom was so excited about that she used to pretend that she was going up to the sun deck when she would go up the back stairs of our house. "Okay, guys," she'd yell, "just going up to the deck to get a little sun."

Dad had rented a sweet little boxlike house right on the beach. In fact, when big storms came the waves would wash under it. We heard that it had even been picked up and turned around by the sea during a hurricane. It had two little bedrooms, just large enough for a bureau and a set of bunk beds. Then there was a small living room, where Mom and Dad slept on a roll-away bed. Also there was a tiny kitchen. I slept in one room on the top bunk and Topher slept under me. Coleman and Gramma North slept in the other bunk room. It didn't matter how small the beach house was because we had the whole beach just outside. Also, the roof was flat and it did have a sun deck.

I wondered why anyone would want to lie on the roof when they had the whole beach to lie on. But Mom would go up there anyway and read her *Christian Science Monitor.* She loved to lie in the sun.

My brothers and I would spend most of the day in the water bobbing like corks, riding the waves until our skin was shriveled. We lived like fish in the sea. When Dad came home from work we'd all go swimming again with him at sundown. We had no radio or TV. We only had the sound of the sea making us all happy and well again. On rainy days we'd go into Wakefield, or race empty coffee cans on the neighbor's boardwalk. We had three fantastic summers in a row at that little house. Those were the summers when I laughed a lot for the last time.

AFTER THE YEARS of summering in Jerusalem we moved from inland Barrington to water's edge in West Barrington. We moved to a house right on the edge of Narragansett Bay. Then because we were right on the water there was no reason to travel to the seaside. We just stayed home on the bay, that fantastic ever-changing bay. We could see great freighters coming and going from all over the world—from Bali, maybe—coming to unload at the docks of Providence. We could see the lighthouse in the distance at the end of Nayatt Point, and far beyond the lighthouse on a clear day we could see Patience and Prudence islands. For the first time in our lives we were living with a view, an ever-changing view that stunned and mesmerized. On a clear winter night we could see the sparkling lights of Mount Hope Bridge twenty miles away blending with the stars twenty million light-years away. The sunsets were enough to make a strong man weep. There was hardly a need to go out of the house or out of the yard; all you had to do was give yourself to that view and your head would empty out and an odd peace would come, a peace and joy that were never there before among the cozy lawns and hedges of inland Barrington.

When I was in college I would come home on weekends just for the view. On vacations I would come home alone and spend much of the day sitting in Dad's easy chair by the bay window, slowly sipping beers to Bach on the hi-fi, just sipping beers and watching the freighters coming and going; dreaming of shipping out on one, watching the light change, watching the sun rise and set over the bay.

But there were times when I thought that the view was almost too much for Mom, perhaps because she didn't wash that raw beauty down with drink the way Dad and I did. Mom used to stamp her feet. I remember the way she would try to stamp out beauty as she watched the sunset from the sea wall. She'd stamp her saddle shoes and moan as she did her anxious beauty walk at the edge of Narragansett Bay, sometimes singing the song that went:

> Down on Narragansett Bay
> Where we watched the gulls at play
> It was on that Jamestown strand
> That I won her hand
> Down on Narragansett—
> Oh, you lovin' 'gansett—
> Down on Narragansett Bay . . .

Mom would just stamp her brown-and-white saddle shoes at the sunset, and wring her hands, and almost wet her pants, she said. It was as if she couldn't stand being separate from it all, couldn't stand not being a part of it no matter how much she tried.

On those weekends, I fell into being on that bay with Mom and I couldn't leave. I wanted to get to Land's End: Provincetown, Massachusetts, where the whole of the United States ended in a sort of clenched fist—the terminus of the flexed arm of the mighty Cape Cod. But I never went.

Mom lived for Narragansett Bay and the walks along its shore. She would have loved to walk on the water if she could; and in fact she did once, one winter when great winds came off the bay and froze our plumbing and brought a great white snowy owl down from the far north to roost. She went out and walked on the frozen bay.

That summer, though, that last summer on the bay, Mom and I would sit together by the water's edge and empty out. In the distance we could hear Topher practicing his Chopin in the dark basement below. Topher had become obsessed with the piano and would practice most of the day, surfacing occasionally only for a quick dip in the bay. At noon Mom would make him a tuna sandwich and bring it down to him to keep him going. If she didn't feed him he'd forget to eat. I was a little jealous that he could be so disciplined and obsessed. He lived through that piano and Mom encouraged him to keep at it.

So, with Chopin in the distance Mom and I watched a sea gull fly over and drop a quahog on the sea wall; the quahog smashed and the bird dove in for its sweet sea meat. Another sea gull took all afternoon to swallow an eel. The gull just sat there, stunned by the presence of the live, protesting prey in its throat; the eel's tail flipping out of its open mouth, as though the bird were choking rather than eating. And then the helpless eel slowly slipped down to curl up and drown in that belly of digestive juice. We watched it all together, Mom and I, our eyes like one common eye or sometimes even with Dad's binoculars, which were like the eyes he had left at home while he went off to work.

We also saw a tan boy come each day with his inflated inner tube and ride out in the bay all alone, kicking and splashing until his body glistened like dark brown gravy. Maybe he was me at a younger age, I thought as I watched him through Dad's binoculars, which made him look as though he were emerging from the head of the gull that was trying to swallow the eel.

Mom and I would swim together before lunch and after lunch. That's what we'd do whenever silence sometimes felt like death and the gull swallowing the eel became too gross, or the boy in the inner tube felt like he had to be touched to be real.

That summer the bay was clear, with no algae. We could see all the way down to the bottom as we swam, and Mom and I would swim together. If I couldn't see everywhere, in all directions at once, which was of course impossible, I would go into a sort of panic. She was a good, relaxed swimmer, as if she belonged to the bay. Mom never noticed my panic. She swam, strong and fearless, ahead of me.

Then we'd dry off in the sun and eat lunch together side by side. Mom always had something simple for lunch, like a glass of milk and a tuna fish sandwich or, for variety, peanut butter and jelly, or even sometimes peanut butter and marshmallow or cream cheese and jelly on white Pepperidge Farm bread. I was more baroque. I needed to have what I thought was the best, perhaps because it was the most prized. I wanted Dad's meat. I wanted steak for lunch. Dad had a whole bunch of frozen steaks wrapped in white freezer paper in the basement freezer, and I'd go fetch a small, rock-hard one at night just before bed. I'd sneak down after Mom and Dad went to bed and I'd take a small steak out and I'd put it in a glass Pyrex dish under the couch in the basement den. By lunchtime the next day, the meat would be perfectly thawed and lying there in its cool red pool of blood. Mom always called the blood "juice," but I'd always say, "No, it's blood, Mom, it's not juice. It's *blood!* It's the blood of an animal!" Our next-door neighbor was a vegetarian and no one understood that. I couldn't even think of him as a person, only as a vegetarian, and at the time I thought he must be the only vegetarian in the Western world.

So I would cook red meat at noon in July and eat it in the sun at the red card table next to Mom, who ate her simple sandwiches with gusto and washed them down with milk. *Gulp, gulp, gulp*—I could hear her swallow and see her throat expand and contract like that of the gull swallowing the eel. And I felt like Henry VIII eating Dad's meat. I was feeding myself rare meat and I was drinking red wine and I could feel my whole body blowing up like a big sotblob. I imagined myself to be the sea gull that swallowed the eel that swallowed the fish that swallowed the crab that ate the clam that lived in the bay that Mom and I swam in.

And after eating I'd lie there in my chair and digest it like the sea gull, then maybe doze for a bit in the sun. Or, just to get away from Mom, I'd go upstairs to my bedroom, where I'd peel off my wet Speedo swimsuit and let my damp eel loose and watch it grow out of my scrotum, which rolled and rippled like the patterns of a beach at low tide. The sun through the window warmed my balls. I'd bring myself off quickly, and fall into the welcome relief of a body spent, without any apparent complication or ramification, only the uneasy thought of Mom still stretched out and waiting for me there below my window by the bay in that sea yard.

But I really wanted to fly the nest; a big part of me wanted to get out of there. I wanted so to go to Bali, or at least to Provincetown, where I couldn't go any farther and I would know where and why to stop because it was all ocean from there on out. I wanted to go to Provincetown to sow my wild oats, whatever that meant. I knew that "wild oats" was just an expression, but still it had some secret meaning to me then—I don't know, to get in trouble, maybe even fall in love, whatever that was. I needed to get away from Mom. It was too sticky and warm to be right.

So in the morning I'd load up Mom's big tin-bread-box Ford wagon with all the goodies I felt I needed to survive on the beach in Provincetown. I was just going to go down there and try to learn how to hang out—you know, just be. It was in 1963, and people all around were starting to learn how to do that, to just hang out and just be in the moment. I'd load up Mom's car with all the provisions: my L. L. Bean sleeping bag, Mom's Metrecal and Instant Breakfast, and Dad's rock-hard frozen meat, which I'd put on ice in the cooler. I'd say goodbye to Mom and head out for Provincetown. A few blocks from home I'd end up turning around and heading back, unloading the car, and swimming and eating lunch with Mom on the lawn. One last swim, one last lunch. Then the next day I'd load up the car again with my sleeping bag, Mom's Metrecal and Instant Breakfast, and Dad's frozen meat and say goodbye to Mom and drive a few miles farther this time and then just end up turning around and coming back. Mom never asked me why I kept coming back. We'd just swim and eat lunch together and sit there on the edge of Narragansett Bay. I never made it to Provincetown that summer.

BUT THEN, as always, things began to change. The factory where Dad worked in Providence got too old; that's what they said, anyway—they wanted to update it. They wanted to build a new one; they wanted to keep up with modern times. So they decided to relocate inland, to the countryside across the bay. Mom and Dad began to talk a lot about this relocation problem.

I can remember Dad was quite upset, because this relocation

meant a big commute for him. As the sea gull flew, it would have been a short gliding trip, but a car would have to go all the way up through Providence and around the other side of the bay and then inland as well. *Inland*—that was the worst thought.

By then Mom had gotten deeper and deeper into Christian Science and the full-blown love of Christ. She wanted to do the Christian thing and move inland to be closer to Dad's new place of work, she really wanted to do the Christian thing and not be selfish, even though somewhere in her she knew that to leave the bay and move inland would be something like death. And much as she believed in heaven, I don't think she was ready to die yet, because being on that bay was sort of a heaven on earth for her.

I was away at college that fall and didn't know exactly what was going on. No one told me and I never asked. When I came home on weekends or holidays Mom acted fine. And she would be my date. I'd usually take her to the latest Bergman film and then we'd stay up late talking all of this real serious talk about loss of faith and wild creeping doubt, and God, and religion. We'd talk about how all of Bergman's characters had lost touch with God.

I had brought my own date home from college just once, the year before, and never did it again. I could feel it sort of disturbed Mom. It was difficult for Mom to feel right about having Kathy in the house. Oh, she was polite to her, but she was also uneasy about having her there, and after Kathy left Mom sat me down at the kitchen table and gave me a long talk about how important it was to abstain from sexual intercourse before marriage. I can't remember the reasons she gave. I don't think there were any, or maybe I didn't give her a chance to say them. I just said, "But, Mom, what if I never get married?" This response just seemed to confuse her.

What I couldn't tell Mom, or anyone for that matter, was that I hadn't really fucked a woman yet. I'd come in them, but I hadn't *fucked* them. "Fuck" was still only a word for me, not an experience. The experience of coming was still like a lame, stifled sneeze.

I had lost my virginity, not to Kathy but to Pam, and it had been so traumatic that I'd sworn off all sex for a year except for elaborate masturbation, where I could have myself safely. I'd never allowed the animal in me to come up in the presence of a woman. Besides, the only animal in me I'd ever known was the monkey boy spinning on that beach in Mom's eyes so long ago.

I had met Pam at a party and picked her up there. We never went home together. We just did it in an empty bedroom at the apartment where the party was. It was all so strange. I remember finding a big damp open place between her legs and then trying to fill it up with my almost numb erection. I was licking her breasts, not because I really wanted to but because for some reason I thought I should do it. And out of the clear blue she said, "What do you think I am, your mother?" and that's when I came, just like that. I hadn't been in her two minutes and I shot off and it didn't feel any different than a sneeze, from my crotch instead of my nose. After it was all over I had no idea what I had lost or what I had gained. I just wanted to get out of there, and I did.

As the days went by this incredible guilt took over. I had not used any birth control and was sure that I had made Pam pregnant. There was no one for me to talk to about it then, except God. I guess I still believed in God at age twenty. I would roll and roll on my floor in my dormitory room and promise to God that I would never have sex again if only He would stop Pam from getting pregnant.

It was almost a year after I lost my virginity that I met Kathy, and I have to say that I think a good part of my attraction to her was her name. She had the same first name as Mom—Katherine—only I called Mom Kit. For as long as I could remember I called Mom by her first name. Both my brothers called Kit Mom, but I called her Kit and I was never really aware or self-conscious about that until I was almost eleven or twelve and my friends would remark, "What did you just call your mom?" Those were the old days when no one, at least in our town, ever called their parents by first names, and I'd just sort of blush and get embarrassed and say, "Kit—I called her Kit."

So I don't know. Maybe I couldn't really fuck Kathy because of her name being so close to Mom's name. I wanted to fuck her but I couldn't. Sometimes I'd even come before entering her, and once I shot a good twelve feet from the bed and I was so overwhelmed by the power of that seminal discharge that I made Kathy trace it with me all the way from the bed to the wall. She may have been impressed, but she sure wasn't satisfied.

We broke up on New Year's Eve, 1963. I invited her home to spend New Year's Eve with Mom and Dad and me. We watched the Times Square ball drop on TV and drank cheap champagne. But after Mom and Dad went to bed Kathy told me that she'd found someone else—someone who could give her more. I didn't ask her, "More of what?" I had an idea what she was talking about.

She left the following day. I kissed her on the cheek and waved goodbye as she drove off in a light snow. I remember how her old green Chevy looked so beautiful cutting tracks in that new snow. Then I went inside, got out a bottle of Dad's vodka, and began to drink.

I drank almost the whole fifth. I was sitting there alone in Dad's easy chair by the window that looked over Narragansett Bay. As I drank I could hear Mom and Dad arranging furniture in the guest bedroom upstairs. After I got very drunk I got it in my head that I needed to drive to Providence to see a production of Chekhov's *The Sea Gull*. I thought that if I could just focus on a staged drama of someone else's dilemma I could somehow be saved from the sad drama of my life.

When I got up from Dad's easy chair I was staggering and I went upstairs to where Mom and Dad were frantically pushing around furniture and I asked Dad for the car keys so I could go see *The Sea Gull*. I was very drunk, and quite amazed that I could even talk.

Mom and Dad both stopped and looked at me. Mom said, "Well, Brewster, what's wrong with you?" It was as if she was annoyed, and I assumed she was annoyed about how she and Dad couldn't agree upon that new arrangement of beds and dressers and chairs. I couldn't hold back anymore and I burst into tears and cried, "I've lost Kathy and I'll never meet anyone like her again." Instead of hugging me, which I sort of expected, Mom pulled back and in a callous and distant tone she said, "Oh, that's what you said about the last one." This completely threw me. What "last one," I wondered. Then I turned away from Mom and asked Dad for the car keys again. To my amazement he let me have them.

Driving into Providence was like riding on a washboard. The whole road was like a liquid river in my eyes and every so often I would have to stop the car and open the door and throw up.

It was a miracle that I made it to the theater and that I was able to focus on the play. For the first act the whole stage was moving as if it was being performed aboard a ship in high seas. By the second act I had sobered up enough to get into it and that's when I began to think that maybe I would like to be an actor. It was not then a need for artistic expression as much as a discovery of a safe place to hide out in a state of controlled drama, knowing what the drama was going to be before stepping into it. The stage that night looked like a very safe place, and the actors seemed protected by the gaze of the audience.

It took me three days to recuperate from that hangover, and while I was recuperating I began to realize that Mom and Dad had been rearranging the guest bedroom so that Mom could use it. The time for their big move was getting closer and closer, and Mom needed that guest room as a place to collect her thoughts and prepare for the move. She used it as sort of a retreat.

Gram North said that she used to come over for dinner on Sundays and was surprised to find that Mom wasn't there. She thought that was odd but she really didn't want to pry, so she didn't say anything about it, if you can imagine that. She didn't even ask Dad where Mom was.

Then at last, Gram said, she figured out that Mom was not away but upstairs. I don't think anyone had any idea what Mom was doing up there at first. They only knew that she needed her privacy and she wanted to be left alone. She was tearing her hair out and talking to herself. She was picking at the inside of her ears until they bled.

Dad was very upset by all this, because they had just sold the house on the bay and were about to move. How could he move when Mom was so crazy? But he did; he did the whole move himself while she was away at a sanitarium, where he finally had to have her committed.

That was a wild day, which I thank God I wasn't there for. It took two doctors to legally commit her; two doctors to agree on the fact that she was crazy. She didn't want to go and the more they tried to make her go, the crazier she got. In the end she was pulling her skirt up over her head and beating off the doctors with her Bible and *Science and Health.*

THIS AND ONE OTHER event that happened two summers earlier began to make me wonder if Christian Science might not be the right religion for some people. That was the summer that Mom had gone away for two weeks to take a Christian Science intensive class that was supposed to prepare her to become a practitioner. Mom thought she would be able to be a real healer through Christ. It was while Mom was away that Mrs. Bowdin came to visit. Sally Bowdin was Mom's Christian Science friend who lived nearby. We used to pick Sally up at her house on the way to church on Sundays. Sometimes she'd bring her two little boys with her and take them to Sunday school. Sally Bowdin always seemed normal to us. She was tall, thin, and graceful and really quite beautiful. In fact, I remember Sally Bowdin looking a little like Katharine Hepburn. But over the years Sally got, as they say in the Christian Science church, "a little troubled." We could tell she was getting more than a little troubled because of the letters she one day started sending to Mom. They were like the end of an Uncle Wiggily story, when Nurse Jane Fuzzy-Wuzzy says things like, "If the old tomcat doesn't slip on a banana peel and trip over the lobster pot and hit the broom and knock the po-po-potty down"—some wacky things like that—"we'll tell you another story about Uncle Wiggily." Well, that's the only time I'd heard *crazy* language like that until we got these letters from Mrs. Sally Bowdin and they read something like this: "If the piano doesn't stop hiding my driver's license we'll be able to put a new toilet on the front lawn under the willow tree my husband just cut down to turn into soldiers"—and on and on they would go. When Coleman read these letters, he got real upset. He said, "Mom, this woman needs psychiatric help!" Mom just ignored him because she didn't believe in psychiatrists and she was upset that Coleman did. As time went by and we got more and more letters from Mrs. Bowdin, Mom told us that Mrs. Bowdin was so disturbed they had to ask her to sit in the back of the balcony at church because she couldn't keep from shouting out loud during the service, and everyone wanted the service to be calm. After all, that's why a lot of people came to church on Sunday in the first place: they came to get calm.

Well, anyway, that summer when Mom was away at Christian Science class, that season when madness seemed to come often, I woke up real early one morning, and at first I thought I was dreaming. Then I realized there were indeed many people having some sort of row down in our living room.

I looked out the window and saw two police cars right in front of our house, and that gave me a real scare. Then I recognized Mrs. Bowdin's voice. I got up and stood in my underwear at the top of the stairs to try to hear it better. It was her voice but not her words, or it was more like her words in the letters she had sent us. She was talking real wild. Her husband was down there along with the police and Dad. She was talking wild and dirty to her husband, who she was calling Jack, even though he kept correcting her and reminding her that his name was Fred. Sally Bowdin was talking like a crazy drunk, saying things like "Hey, Jack, you old poop—Jack, you old chip off the Texas block—don't you remember those wild outhouse underwear times we had? Oh, remember how we used to run all bare-assed across the whole state of Texas? Oh, those were the days and don't you deny it, Jack, you big hunk, you big chip off the old you-know-what! You big stinker, you! Jack! You toidy-woidy!" And you could hear her husband calmly say, real calm and quiet, "Now calm down, Sally. I'm not Jack, you know that. I'm Fred. Try to pull yourself together."

Then I heard this big wrestling sound but no words, like everyone was gagged and playing musical chairs only without music. This was followed by little moans like sex sounds. Then I heard Sally screaming "No! No! No!" and I ran to the window to see her being taken away, dressed only in a black negligee, all wrapped up in a straitjacket. After they had taken her away and the police cars had gone, I went downstairs to find Dad straightening up the living room as if nothing big had really happened. That's when he told me that Mrs. Bowdin had come to the house at dawn and gotten into bed with him. She had called him Jack and began to strip his pajamas off. She was a very beautiful woman even though she was crazy, and I figured she could probably be very sexy as well. But Dad said he just jumped out of bed and called the police and they came in ten minutes. I couldn't keep from wondering what went on in those ten minutes. But I didn't ask him. I think I was afraid to know too much. Or maybe we both had the secret sense that madness was not far from our door and that Mom might be the next to go.

I CAME HOME FROM my last year of college to a home that was now inland, or "relatively inland," as Dad would say. I would not have said "inland" so much as "in the woods." The new house was surrounded by trees at the end of a dead-end road that stopped at the woods. The name of the dead-end road was Shady Lane, a very apt description.

I don't know if Dad and Mom picked out that house together, but I assume they did, and with its view of nothing but woods it struck me as a very odd location to move to after living all those years on Narragansett Bay. But at the same time it was a sort of cute and very manageable house, something they could easily retire in, with two baths, a master bedroom downstairs for the coming of old age, two bedrooms upstairs for when we were at home, and a two-car garage attached so no one had to walk out of the house to get into their car during foul weather.

By the time I arrived at the new house Dad had pretty much moved in all by himself and was slowly beginning to unpack and start a new life in spite of the fact that Mom was away at the sanitarium. I had just graduated and had brought my sensuous college girlfriend Melissa home with me, but it wasn't working out very well. I think Dad was jealous. He made us sleep in separate rooms and kept a constant ear out for any odd sounds, which made me feel very inhibited. I kept trying to drag Melissa into the woods to make love but she would have none of it. She was not the outdoor type. I did manage to eat her once while she lay on a moss-covered rock, but the mosquitoes and Dad calling us in for a rare steak dinner cut it short before either of us could really complete ourselves. At college we had been sexually voracious together, but now all I was getting was Melissa's annoyance at how I was treating her like a sex object. She said, "You only pay attention to me when you want to get laid." I knew she was right. Now that I was home, or rather at Dad's new home, about to be Mom's new home as well, I began to realize that I didn't need Melissa as a friend because I still had Mom. I was just waiting for Mom to get out of that rest home so I could talk with her. I wanted Melissa for my physical needs and Mom for my emotional needs. And although Melissa didn't openly talk about that split in me, I think she intuited it and reacted accordingly by withholding her sweet body favors.

We said goodbye with no real plans to reconnect. We were just living our lives as if we'd go on forever, and ever be young. I drove Melissa to the Block Island ferry and she was off for a summer of fun and waitressing on Block Island.

The next week I was called up for my army physical. I made up my mind right away that I was simply going to act crazy, or because I had the perfect role model, I was just going to act like Mom. I had to start convincing myself that I was crazy, which was a tricky little game because if you're not careful, pretty soon you don't know if you *are* crazy or if you're just playing at it. I would actually go off into the woods and rehearse my madness like I was getting ready to play King Lear. As a kid I used to go off into the woods to hunt or masturbate, or on calmer days just to walk and enjoy and try to teach myself how to hang out. But now I was going off into the woods to shout and roll on the ground and act crazy. Besides preparing me to beat the draft, this became a wonderful sort of organic release, as though I was creating my own therapy. Sometimes I'd even bring a tambourine along with me and end up dancing in my underwear or naked like some demented shaman. That was only when I was deep in the woods and felt really alone. Most of the time I had the feeling someone was watching me. Maybe God was there watching me.

I beat the draft the morning Mom came home from the sanitarium. I almost didn't beat it, because someone who had a beard like mine went a little crazy right in front of me. I must say his act wasn't as good. He probably hadn't rehearsed it. I didn't know who was crazier, us naked guys with our cheeks spread or the men who had to walk up and down looking at our assholes, which at the time made me realize all I should have done was not wipe myself that morning and I'd be out of America's fight against communism forever. But that didn't occur to me until I was bent over and spread. So there I was in the line just after we'd had our holes checked and we had just reached the head sergeant and the guy in front of me started barking like a dog. This immediately triggered my wild-Indian act and we both started doing this naked dance together. We were immediately led away to a little room where we were told with great disdain to get dressed and go home. While we were dressing, we both recognized that we had created a great male bonding. We had beat the draft by dancing naked together, and we laughed a lot about this. He told me his name was Joe McCreedy and he was off to New Paltz, New York, to try to open a bookstore. It was going to be a fantastic "alternative bookstore," as he called it, and if ever there was a place for me he would give me a job. I wished him good luck and gave him a fond farewell and headed out to hitchhike home, but ended up walking most of the six miles, which was fine with me because I was in no hurry to do anything anymore.

That same day Gram and Gramp brought Mom down from the sanitarium in their car. Dad had spent the whole weekend fixing up the house so that it would be all nice and orderly for her. But I could tell as soon as Mom stepped out of the backseat of that black four-door Ford that something was never going to work again. It was as though she was trying to be happy, or acting happy, in the way I had acted crazy that very morning. It was as though she had sat there in that backseat all the way home from the sanitarium saying over and over to herself, "I'm going to be happy in this new house. I'm going to be happy in this new house." But there was a certain way she looked through me to the other side of nothing that made me feel I wasn't there. It was a certain frantic flicker in her eyes. It was as though a bird was in her head—a bird that wanted to get out. It was as though a bird had stolen my mother's soul or that her soul was a bird and I was only seeing it for the first time.

WHILE MOM WAS AWAY at the institution Dad, to his credit, had realized that maybe part of Mom's breakdown had to do with their moving away from Narragansett Bay. He even tried to buy the old house back from the new owners, but they would hear nothing of it. Oh, they were sympathetic, of course, but they weren't going to move. They told Dad that Mom's missing the bay was only a symptom of some larger problem. What could be a larger problem than Narragansett Bay, except for the ocean? I wondered. Perhaps a woman might miss a bay so much that it would drive her mad. Only the Narragansett Indians would know about that one, and they were all gone. Maybe Mom was a reincarnation of a Narragansett Indian, I began to muse. Maybe she tapped into that bay so much that she became the bay, but had no words for her condition. What does "I miss the bay" really mean? It all depends on who's saying it, right? And when Mom said it I trembled. We all trembled.

Dad had the good sense to rent a bathhouse for Mom down on the coast at Bonnet Shore. Of course that was not the same as stepping out on your lawn and having your head open up over the bay, but at least it was the ocean. We had to drive forty-five minutes to get there, which was a problem because we had to go down Route 2, by Rhode Island standards a rather fast and crowded highway. I could see how driving on that road could make Mom real confused, especially since she was on some sort of medication and had just returned from electroshock treatments. So I always drove her to the beach. She hadn't made any friends yet on this side of the bay, and I couldn't bear seeing her go alone. But the truth was, I was sure she wouldn't make it to the beach by herself.

On nice summer days we'd try to go to the beach as often as we could. At first the shock treatments seemed to be working pretty well, because except for that occasional bird flutter in her eye, she apparently was coping, which put Dad at ease. So Mom and I had a few days that were actually quite relaxed. We lay on the beach and dozed in the sun, both catching up with our much-needed sleep while the distant waves and children's voices played like lulling music in our ears.

But some time around the second week Mom was home, it slowly started up again. The effects of the shock treatments were wearing off. She turned on those old what-ifs, those old maybe-I-should-haves, the regret mechanism. She'd say things like "Maybe I should have been a better mother" or "Do you really think I did that?" or "Maybe I should have gone to Spain to visit Cole when he first went there and I had the time and money, when I had saved all that money to go and visit him" or "Maybe I shouldn't have stolen you boys away from your father." She'd turn to me and say, "Do you think I stole you away from your father? Do you think I was a good mother?" These questions made me very uneasy and confused. Deep down inside I thought that if she'd been a good mother I'd be able not to be there, I'd be off with my own woman. I would have been able to have flown the nest by then. I wanted in the worst way to fly, just fly this nest and get out, but I still couldn't.

When I was sixteen and Cole was nineteen, Mom would some-times take a bath in the upstairs bathroom and not lock the door, and Cole and I, instead of using the downstairs bathroom, would go upstairs to pee while we looked over our shoulder at her. It was like this odd kind of peep show. She'd let us look as long as we wanted, which was never very long: before we could get a good and steady look, Dad would come to the bottom of the stairs shouting, "Are you fellows"—Dad always called us "fellows" when reprimanding us— "are you fellows up there in that bathroom with your mother again? I don't like that one bit, and I don't want to have to come up there!" Dad didn't like it. That was one of the few things I can remember him ever thinking was wrong.

On those frantic summer nights after her return from the sanitar-ium, I would often try to calm Mom down by taking her to the movies, just to get us both out of the house and give Dad some relief. There were no new Bergman films around, and Mom had recently seen *The Sound of Music* at the sanitarium. So one night I made a big mistake. I took Mom to see the recently released film of *Who's Afraid of Virginia Woolf?* She wanted to go because she had this fascination with the life and death of Virginia Woolf. I'm not sure that she knew Virginia Woolf's books all that well, but she did know the story of how Woolf ended her life by filling her pockets with rocks and walking into a river. She seemed to know that story as well as she knew the story of how Hart Crane, one depressed morning, walked off the stern of his cruise ship in the Gulf of Mexico, never to be seen again. At the time I didn't know what effect that film would have on Mom. I did notice how quiet she was as we rode home, but I didn't find out how disturbed she really was until Dad told me the following morning. He said, "I think you took your mother to the wrong movie last night. She's so upset that we may have to take her back to the institution." At the time I felt like saying, "Well, why didn't *you* take her to the movies, then? *You* choose a good one for her to see." Outside of *The Ten Commandments,* which wasn't on the summer circuit that year, I didn't know what to choose. Some years back I had taken Mom to see *The Ten Commandments* and she had loved it.

Well, it did turn out that *Who's Afraid of Virginia Woolf?* was a real mistake, because Mom completely identified with the role of Martha, which was played by Elizabeth Taylor. In fact Dad told me that Mom thought she was Martha the next morning. She went into one of those funky tailspins. I had to spend that next beautiful summer day indoors with her while she flew around the house like a frightened bird again, like that bird that couldn't get out. That was a bad day. I remember it well because that was the day when she told me right out how she planned to do it, how she planned to do away with herself.

That whole morning she was pulling her hair and picking at her ears until they bled. She had a little bald spot now, at the back of her head, from tearing her hair out, just like people do in the movies when they're supposed to be going mad. I would try to calm her down by reading to her from my favorite book at the time, Alan Watts's *Psychotherapy, East and West,* but this didn't seem to help at all. She wanted to read from *Science and Health* but she couldn't sit still long enough to read. So at last, some time in mid-morning when she seemed about ready to pop, Mom began calling her Christian Science practitioner on the phone and she just stood there repeating after him what he told her, which seemed to be rather incoherent passages from *Science and Health.* I was never sure what it was he was saying to her because

Mom would repeat it all in halting confusion—things like "Error is unreal because untrue, all reality is in God and His creation harmonious and eternal. That which He creates is good and He makes all that is made." Then there was a long sentence which Mom was barely able to repeat back to him because she was too distracted, perhaps by the raving image of Elizabeth Taylor playing Martha in her mind, but she was able to get it out just once and she said it slowly back to him like a child trying to memorize a secret code. She said it once, all the way through: "Therefore the only reality of sin, sickness, and death is the awful fact that unrealities seem real to the human erring belief, until God strips off their disguise." The practitioner went on as Mom paced and pulled and stretched the phone cord until it almost broke, almost pulling the phone off the wall as she repeated the next phrase: "The science of mind disposes of all evil. Truth, God, is not the father of error. Man is not matter, he is spirit. Man is made in the image and likeness of God." Then the practitioner hung up and Mom held the phone and looked at it with this crazy scowl, like a little kid who finally managed after years to get in touch with Santa Claus on the telephone and, right in the middle of asking for everything she ever wanted, got cut off.

Then Mom hung up and began to pace again and tear at her hair and pick at her ears and tried to repeat the phrases the practitioner had told her. But they came out all mixed up and broken like, "Disposes of evil—man is not error—error is not man." I just sat there on the couch, I just sat there staring at her thinking, What the fuck is happening to this woman? The whole world was breaking down and falling apart. The whole house was shifting; I was getting dizzy and had to run outside, where I threw up green stomach bile that ended in dry heaves. When I came back in, this frantic birdlike creature was running from window to window as though she couldn't get out.

That was the day I clearly saw, once again, how like a sky hook that wasn't there when she needed it, the Christian Science wasn't working for Mom. It was one of those pull-yourself-up-by-your-bootstraps situations, but there were no more bootstraps. One part of the mind has to be the bootstraps for the other part, and all parts of Mom's mind seemed to have gone.

By late morning Mom had decided to take a bath. I wanted to

trust her but I couldn't stop myself from pacing outside the bathroom door, calling in every so often over the sound of the running water. The sound of light splashing in the tub produced even more fear in my mind. "Are you all right in there?" I called in. But there was no answer, just a little sound of water splashing. I was sure she didn't have a straight-edge razor. I knew we didn't have one in the house and I didn't think she was capable of driving anywhere to buy one.

After her bath Mom seemed calmer. She came out dressed in her pink robe looking just like a normal suburban housewife and curled up on the couch to read the *Christian Science Monitor*. I thought now that she was a little calmer it might be a good time to try again to introduce her to a few well-chosen passages from Alan Watts. But Mom would hear none of it. As soon as I started to read to her she lifted her newspaper up and made a kind of paper wall between us. I put all my anger into my index finger, curled it back tight against my thumb, fired, and hit that paper wall with a hard snap. Pop! My finger exploded against that newspaper like a shot, and Mom almost jumped off the couch. Then, quickly composing herself, she looked me clearly and directly in the eye and with that crazy bird gone out of her now, she said, "Oh, Brewster dear—how shall I do it? How shall I do away with myself? Shall I do it in the garage, with the car?"

I don't remember what happened after that. I don't know if I said anything back. I was amazed at her clarity. Something inside of me knew that for her it was time to go, that she had made a decision.

I made no effort to hide the keys to either of the cars. I did not tell Dad what she had said to me. It was as though Mom and I had made one last private pact together. Perhaps I was trying to help some sad sick part of her, which had now become almost the only part of her left, to die. But it was not as clear to me then as it seemed to be to her.

That night things got a little better before they got worse again. Every night around what was the traditional cocktail hour Mom would seem to get worse. She'd go into this double-bind behavior: by then she was looking at Dad as her keeper, and she knew that if she acted weird in any way he'd pack her off to the sanitarium again; but the effort to act sane only made her more insane. Every night, just before Dad was due home, she would go try to make dinner and end

up standing over the stove staring out the window into the encroaching woods like some fearful Pilgrim anticipating an Indian attack.
She'd just stand there stamping her saddle shoes, which made her look
like some weird cheerleader. She'd stamp and stamp and stare, trying
to get it together to cook frozen peas, saying over and over again,
"Don't let your father see me this way. I'm all right, I'm okay—perfect
reflection of God—there is no error. Please don't let your father see
me this way." Then Dad would come home and give her a peck on
the cheek and she would relax a little bit and ease into making the rest
of the dinner with her mad birdlike flutters of panic surfacing here and
there. Then Dad would fix himself a tall bourbon and, seeing that crazy
bird in her, would begin to realize things weren't going well.

It was just the three of us then. Topher was away with Gram;
Cole was away in Spain studying some dead existential Spanish writer.
The three of us remained in this strange kind of triangle. I was afraid
to pull out of it because I thought the whole thing would collapse.
Only a void would be left, some dark yawning impossible gap, only
darkness after so many years of shared history, of good and bad times
together.

Odd, or worse than odd, that it should come to this after all these
years: the mother bird gone mad. And yet that night after *Who's Afraid
of Virginia Woolf?* we were still able to rally after all the confusion
and madness of the day and Mom's confessions of wanting to do away
with herself. We were still able to rally around Dad's surprising
suggestion that we all go to the movies together. At last Dad had come
through, and with flying colors. Not only did he want to go to the
movies, but he wanted to go to a drive-in, to see, of all things, *Mary
Poppins,* which he probably thought would be a healthy antidote to
the horrors of *Who's Afraid of Virginia Woolf?* I laughed to myself at
the thought of Virginia Woolf meeting Mary Poppins on some stark
New England moor.

We went in Mom's car, a red Corvair convertible. It was a warm
summer night, and Dad even put the top down. At the last minute I
thought it might be fun for me to try to get in free. So I took a blanket
off the backseat, lay down on the back floor, and covered myself. I
could tell that Dad was proud of me in some way, almost like he
thought I was being enterprising or something. For a moment Mom

even slipped back into her old normal self, and suddenly we were all together again. Mom and Dad were sitting in the front seat like lovers, and I was wrapped in a blanket on the back floor like a child waiting to be born.

The following day things took a turn for the worse. Mom hadn't slept that night. She became like that anxious bird again, and when Dad went to pack up her little suitcase to take her back to the sanitarium, she got even wilder, running from room to room trying to avoid being caught and put back into the cage for those awful old shock treatments she couldn't bear.

At last, completely exasperated, Dad asked me to help round her up and get her into the Corvair, which by now had the top up. She tried to call her Christian Science practitioner, but Dad wouldn't allow it. He made her get in the front seat between us so she wouldn't try to jump out. I was as firm as I could be with her but my words sounded hollow and distant, as if I were doing a bad reading of someone else's script: "C'mon, Mom, we are only trying to do what is best for you."

The trip to the sanitarium was one of those rides that take no time and forever. At last, when we were right outside the heavy stone gates, so different from the happy gates at the drive-in movie the night before, Mom pulled her hand away from mine and, putting both hands over her mouth, looked up at the gates of the sanitarium and cried out in horror, "Oh, my God, my God, why hast thou forsaken me?"

DAD AND I didn't talk much driving home, just a few words about the weather and how there wasn't a whole lot of traffic for a Saturday. Dad stopped at the liquor store to stock up. When we got home we watched the Red Sox game on TV and got quietly drunk together.

The following day I knew I had to get out of there. I was in a total panic, as if the house were on fire. I thought of fleeing to Melissa on Block Island, but when I called her she sounded all cranky and whiny. She said she had a bad case of poison ivy on her left thigh and

really had no place of her own to put me up, so I decided very quickly
to just hitchhike to New Paltz, New York, to see Joe McCreedy, the
man I'd shared that mad, life-saving dance with.

It only took me four rides to get to New Paltz. Not bad. But
I was younger then, and those were the old days when people would
take chances picking you up on the highway.

My first ride was in a red-hot MG convertible. There were two
guys in it, and they shoved me in the back behind their bucket seats,
where I knelt with my head above the windshield like a dog in the
wind until they let me off on Route 128 just outside of Boston.

I stood there for quite a long while, but it didn't matter how long
I waited; it just felt good to be out there in the middle of nowhere,
in the middle of time. I thought I was beginning to learn how to hang
out. I was suspended between Rhode Island and some unknown future
point waiting for me in New Paltz.

Then I saw this big, bright powder-blue Cadillac, which was
going in the other direction at first, make a sweeping U-turn and
slowly cruise back to pick me up. The car reeked of perversion. It
smelled of cheap cigars and puke. All the windows were up, and all
the electric controls were on a central switchboard to the right of the
driver, who looked like a combination of an Italian butcher and a
Greek barber. He was enormous and gross and he had big, hairy
forearms and a big moon face with a set of lips that looked like they
could suck you whole. He also had three or four gold chains around
his neck with black hairs bristling out between them. And what was
worse was that he didn't really speak to me—only "Buckle up" and
"Where ya off to?" I think I said something like "Upstate New York,"
in a dry and nervous little boy's voice. I was dressed only in cutoffs
and a sweatshirt, with the rest of my stuff in a knapsack on my back.
I could feel his dark black eyes go all along, up and down my thighs.
Then he began to throw some of those electric switches on his control
board. My seat was a separate bucket seat, something like a modern
dentist's chair. *Buzz, buzz, buzz,* the seat went flat out and all I could
see was the plush ceiling. And then *buzz, buzz,* up it went again.
Strapped into my safety belt, I began to feel a little claustrophobic.
"Just tell me how you like it," he said in a thick, fat, heavy voice, like
he had a clump of warm mashed potatoes stuck in his throat. "Oh,

that's fine, that's good," I said. "I like it just up and normal, so I can see out, you know? I love to see out. That's why I travel in the day. I like to see where I'm going." After ten miles or so, he just stopped and let me out. Without a word. That was that. He made another U-turn and headed back toward Boston.

The next ride I got was a Chevy van with two guys in the front and one guy in a wheelchair in the back. The guy in the wheelchair had just come home from Vietnam, where he had received some horrid spinal injury, and would most likely never walk again. He said that when he shot his first "gook" he was so freaked out that he forgot to take his finger off the trigger of his automatic and he cut the guy right in two.

My last ride was with a man who sold Tupperware, and that was all he told me about himself. He had an easy-listening channel tuned in on his radio and after I got in he never looked at me once. He brought me right to the outskirts of New Paltz.

I had no problem finding Joe McCreedy's bookstore. There it was—Wyoming Books—right in the middle of town. I walked into that beautiful little bookstore to find Joe involved with a very intense woman. They were standing by the front window arguing over an idea for a window display and had reached a standoff. Joe was saying, "It matters to me," and she was yelling back, "But don't you think it matters to me?" And back and forth it was going like that as they fought like two kids, each trying to get their way; only I could see that she had already won just by how much more passionately she was expressing her needs.

I was immediately drawn to her strong, angry face, beautiful in its rage as she stood there with one raised blue vein on her forehead, screaming one final time, "But it matters to me, Joe! It matters to me!" Joe turned away from her and walked into the back of the bookstore. I didn't move. I stood there smitten, watching this woman, now suddenly empty of rage, carefully arranging the window display exactly to her liking. I just stood there feeling my whole being focus through hers. I stood there thinking that I'd made the trip just to meet her.

Joe and I had a shaky reunion in the back of the bookstore. He was happy and surprised to see me, but I could tell he had not fully recovered from that argument. We sat and talked. Joe told me things were going fine for him since he had escaped the draft. He was running the bookstore with his girlfriend, Diane, and that passionate woman at the window was her sister, Meg.

Joe and Diane let me stay in the back of the bookstore on a little cot until they could figure out how to put me to work. Then after a few days they decided that I could help Meg make the weekly runs to buy books at a wholesale house in lower Manhattan. I liked this idea a lot.

I loved the long drives down to New York with Meg. They really gave me a chance to space out and get uncomplicated again and try to learn to hang out. I also liked Meg's company. On the other side of her rage, I found a calm center that I could be quiet with. It was as though there was an unspoken understanding between us. When we got to New York we'd spend the whole day in the book warehouse, browsing in what was essentially a giant library. We would get lost in the aisles of books, only to meet by chance to share ideas and information instead of kisses. It was like spending a rainy day with a friend in a giant library that contained as much as you'd ever want to know about the world outside. It was a windowless protected world of its own where I felt safe at last.

After we finished buying the books for the store, Meg and I would go stay at a friend's place on Seventh Street on the Lower East Side. At the time, Seventh Street was the ultimate hippie haven of the East Coast. Everyone on the street seemed to have perfected hipness, to be able to live their lives totally in the moment, while I was only reading about it. But one of the things that I liked about Meg and Joe's friends up on Seventh Street was that they still liked to read, which was something that a lot of hippies weren't doing much of. In exchange for letting us crash in their pad, Meg would often steal them one or two books from the warehouse.

When we'd get to Seventh Street, I would cook chicken hearts for Meg and drink red wine. Most of the people at that pad were vegetarians and kept insisting I was paranoid from eating dead meat and drinking cheap Spanish wine, but I just laughed, or sort of laughed, and tried not to let it affect me. It seemed that everyone was in competition to be hipper than the next person. Also, the fact that all of them at Seventh Street smoked marijuana to relax was a big threat to me. When I tried to smoke marijuana with them I never relaxed; I just got real wired, and couldn't sleep. But Meg seemed to be naturally high. She didn't use any drugs at all that I was aware of, except an occasional sip of that Spanish burgundy with her chicken hearts.

It wasn't long before I was falling for Meg in some new strange way that didn't have to do with sex as much as it had to do with friendship and just being comfortable together.

This new experience of friendship with a woman other than Mom was a little confusing to me. I didn't know if I was falling in love or looking for a new mother or what. But I realized that Meg looked somewhat like my mom at that age. She had a very angular New England face, with a strong jaw and high cheekbones and very clear hazel eyes. She was the kind of woman who, in the old days when everyone got married, would have made a very beautiful bride. Also "Meg" was short for "Margaret," which was Mom's middle name. I'm not saying I didn't miss sex—I really *did* miss it. But I didn't miss the anxiety that sex produced. Good sex was like a drug for me and it could not be had without some unnerving side effects.

The whole world seemed crazy to me then in 1966, what with the Vietnam War, people taking drugs, free love and sex, and the constant image in my mind of Mom at the asylum getting another electric shock treatment. Or the image of Dad at home alone, drinking bourbon until he fell on the floor. It was a crazy time for me and I felt perpetually wounded by all that came at me.

As time went by, things got more settled and ordered into a nice routine that made me feel centered, which I felt was all I could expect at that point—the grace of habit. I got attached to the simple habits of my days: I still lived in the back of the bookstore, and I had started doing yoga in the morning to calm down. After yoga I'd eat a simple healthy breakfast, and then reread my little bible, *Psychotherapy, East and West,* underlining certain passages in red. Nothing all that mind-shattering happened. My life just went by without much passion, emotion, or despair. I wasn't depressed and I wasn't elated; I just was. It was like the life of an old rabbi studying his Talmud.

The only person who disturbed my peace was Joe. He didn't

think I was in the best of mental health, and he wanted to shake my habituation by converting me to Christ. I didn't realize that Joe had become a born-again until I saw him reading the Bible a lot. Joe, I soon found out, was a born-again Christian who took LSD as the Holy Eucharist.

At last, after much effort, Joe talked me into taking LSD with him, alone. I discussed the idea with Meg. She didn't really seem to think it was a bad idea as long as I was aware that at some point on the trip Joe would probably want to read to me from the Bible and try to convert me to Christ. She warned me not to get too paranoid when it happened.

It was a beautiful, clear Saturday afternoon in late summer. Joe wanted to drop the acid at his house and take it all real slow and quiet—just mellow out as it fell into place. I was extremely nervous and couldn't stop falling asleep. I felt as if I were going to die or something, like the dread before you take off on a roller coaster. Then all of a sudden we just did it. Joe took out a whole sheet of blue blotter Holy Eucharist LSD and cut off two small dots that seemed to glow in the nervous focus of my eye. With a trembling hand I did what Joe did: I put the dot on my tongue and washed it down with a big gulp of Dr Pepper. Then we just sat there smiling at each other like two cats that had just swallowed two mice.

But soon Joe got up to fetch his Bible and began to thumb through it. It was then that I asked him if we could please go up into the mountains. I wanted to be outdoors for the trip and I thought I knew a beautiful place to go: it was the stream on top of a mountain that flowed down to a waterfall that cascaded into a deep pool where everyone swam naked on hot days. If we could just get to the beginning of that stream, I thought, everything would be fine. I also thought if I didn't get near some water real quick I'd go mad. But I didn't tell Joe that. I kept wondering what madness would be for me. What would my crazy activity be if I really let go? Then I suddenly knew that madness was only a smoke screen to keep us from looking all the way down into the pure bottomless pit of death. What came to me then was the full and complete realization that we were all going to die and beyond our personal death there was only one thing larger, the end of all human history, when at last the sun would go out. But

I didn't tell any of these thoughts to Joe because I thought they would provoke him into reading to me from the Bible. I was sure I didn't want that. At the same time I was happy to know what I did want, and that was water. We went to the water.

Joe drove, telling me that the acid would probably just be coming on strong by the time we got up there. We reached the edge of the woods in about twenty minutes. Neither of us had watches, so time was just a sort of conditioned feeling by then. Not seeing any real path into the stream, we bushwhacked for a while. Then we found a path and came to a little clearing by that rushing stream. We stood there for a minute and then separated without a word. I followed the descent of the stream which led to the waterfall. It wasn't long after that I felt the acid coming on quite strong. Since I was a virgin to it all, I didn't know what to expect, but I felt like my whole mind and body was on this roller coaster just as it was starting up its first giant rise. I just stood there and watched that clear stream flow and break around some small rocks that sat out in the center. The clear water made silver rings around the rocks, which shimmered to blue as the water reflected the late-afternoon light. Then I hopped out and landed, with what felt like perfect balance, on one of the flat rocks in the center of the rushing stream. I felt the whole stream as one big snaking, ever-changing body all around me.

Out of some need to define myself against that stream, or perhaps out of some feeling of being born again for the first time, I just opened my arms and cried out, "I am!" My voice seemed small and low against the sound of the rushing water. I stood there waiting for something to happen, but nothing did. So I tried it again, a little louder this time. "I am!" I called to the sky and trees. Still no answer; nothing happened. The water continued to flow on, and the sun sank a little lower into the lush green all around me. Once more, I thought, and this time I really shouted until I could feel it down to the base of my balls: "I am!" It was only then that I suddenly got self-conscious and wondered if in fact I might be disturbing some of the campers in the area. This new feeling of self-consciousness, coupled with a touch of loneliness and curiosity about what Joe was up to, sent me back to where I had left him.

Joe was standing tall, beautiful, and glowing by the stream. His smile was the most open, completely relaxed smile I had ever seen on any face anywhere. He was even more beautiful than the drugstore picture of Christ Mom kept as a bookmark in her Bible. The sun set behind his head, creating a sort of red halo that fired up the edges of his beard. I couldn't get enough of all this in my eyes.

I chanted over and over again to Joe, "This is too much. This is too much to stand. I can hardly stand this beauty anymore." I saw a wild and crazy bat flying over Joe's head. I saw two bats with long peacock feathers coming out of their tails and I saw that the whole sky above Joe's head was filled with glorious, ornate, spectacular, almost suffocatingly baroque waves of peacock feathers, which I now tried to negate with Mom's old familiar pattern of escape. I couldn't stop assaulting Joe with what-ifs.

"Joe, this is really great here, tripping in the woods," I said. "But what if we were at the ocean? What about tripping at the ocean? What if we were down on Seventh Street now? What would it be like to be tripping on acid with all those Seventh Street hippies?" No sooner had I asked Joe that than out of the woods came this band of East Village hippies. I swear. I could immediately tell by the way they were dressed and the way they moved and talked that they were genuine East Village hippies come up to the country for an acid weekend. I thought Joe had set it all up. I thought that he had rehearsed the whole thing and had brought them up to hide in the trees until I gave them their cue so they could come out and play their Seventh Street hippie antics on me. Then I thought maybe I had conjured them. I thought that this was all a big theater and I had conjured these spirits to teach me a lesson. I felt some higher forces were speaking to me, telling me that I had the power to get exactly what I asked for, so be careful. I felt that I had the power to create my own reality. At the same time I tried to realize that these hippies who surrounded us in the dark were not phantoms but real human beings. I could only see them as a group of actors playing out some scenario that had been put together in some place I could not yet comprehend. I had the dark feeling of being completely and absolutely lost, stupid and blind and lost, and I knew that my only connection to meaning would be to tell Joe this. So I did. I said, on the verge of tears, "Joe, I feel lost." It was so dark now that I could hardly see his face. I wasn't sure if I was talking to him or one of the phantom hippies. Then I heard him laugh back at me his easy, comforting laugh and say, as if his words were smiling, "Yes, that's because we *are* lost. I didn't bring a flashlight and there's no moon tonight."

I was amazed at how quickly the sun had gone down. We were indeed lost. We were lost in the dark. If there was a path back to the road we had no idea where it was. Then Joe, who seemed more in control, asked these crazy hippies if they knew the way out of the woods. They seemed ready for a great adventure and cried out, "Follow us." They had a couple of kerosene camping lamps that they held high over their pale-blue demonlike faces as they led us into the thick of it. Every so often one would take a little hatchet and stoop and begin to hack at a tree root and scream, "Die! Die! There, it's dead! That's the fifth poisonous snake I've killed tonight!" But I only saw the snakes they hacked as tree roots and was never sure what they were seeing or if they were just trying to scare us. The funny thing was that in spite of all their mad antics I trusted them completely to lead us out onto the road. As we walked, Joe kept whispering to me in my ear, "Let the little children lead you. Let the little children lead you."

At times the woods turned into a gigantic jungle tangle and at other times it seemed like we were on some sort of path, until at last we were miraculously on the edge of the highway somewhere near where we had left Joe's truck. As soon as we got onto the road, the hippies left us as they laughed and sang, "We are the happy wanderers . . ." and they staggered on down the road swinging their lanterns like a band of happy gypsies, all disappearing into the night as magically as they had come out of it.

Relieved to be on the solid asphalt, I walked into the middle of the road and looked up and gazed upon that gigantic night sky. I was seeing the night sky for the first time in my life. I just plain *saw* it, just saw it directly without any mediation of thought or comment. I saw the stars for the first time and they were just *stars*. There was no word for them in my mind. I saw it all not as hallucination but so clearly and powerfully and directly that it brought me to my hands and knees right there in the middle of the road. I could feel the warm asphalt still radiating the heat of the day, like it was a warm body under me. I lay down and clung to it with all my might. When I rolled over and looked at the sky again I was amazed not to be looking up; I now had the sensation of looking *out*. I could feel the complete roundness of the earth and I knew I was looking out into the universe. This view of the stars as "out" lasted for some time, and was always on the edge of being unbearable. It was awful, in the sense of inspiring awe. There was no longer any room for fear. It was all just one big AWE.

When I stood up I saw that Joe too was looking at the stars, and I went over and hugged him and his whole body felt like a great warm loving bear as I wondered how I would ever live my life after this trip into the mountains.

"Shall we head down?" Joe asked.

"Oh my God, whatever. Let's go get a beer or whatever, I don't care." I felt no need for anything. My body was in total harmonious motion as we sauntered to Joe's pickup truck and got in. It never occurred to me that Joe might not be able to drive. All things seemed possible. Why, we could even fly down to town if we chose. Joe made a U-turn and we started toward town. Not far down the road we came to a spectacular turnout, one of those scenic overlooks, and he pulled in to let me out while he sat in the truck and waited. I walked to the edge of the lookout and there below me the whole Hudson Valley was stretched out with its scattered streetlights and farmhouses, and New Paltz sparkled like a gem in the distance. Looking down on it all, I could see that it was breathing—the entire Hudson Valley was breathing, and not only the entire valley, the entire earth, and my breath was in union with it, or its breath was in union with mine, I couldn't tell. The waving swell of my diaphragm was also the swell of the valley below. There was suddenly no me, or I should say no complication of me. There was no Brewster with a history anymore. My body was filled with a colored liquid, like the mercury in a thermometer, and then it all went down until it drained out my feet and left only an empty outline, like a Matisse drawing. Now I was the landscape, which was all liquid and flowing through my outlines. I don't know how long this lasted or what it meant. I only know that I never experienced anything like it before or ever after.

At some point I turned to see Joe glowing behind the wheel of the pickup. I climbed in beside him and everything in that cabin was as liquid and interesting as the valley below. As we drove down the winding mountain road toward New Paltz I began again with the what-ifs. But this time it wasn't Seventh Street. "What if we were in Vietnam tripping right now, Joe? What if we were in the middle of that war? What if we couldn't get our fingers off the triggers of our machine guns?"

Joe didn't answer. He just smiled and drove. As the what-ifs spun by in my mind, I knew I could stop the Ferris wheel at any point and take the thought out and examine it. Or I could let the Ferris wheel keep spinning. Then the Ferris wheel turned into a stream just like the one I'd been standing by and its seats were now wooden boxes floating down the stream and every box, I knew, contained a thought. I could drag it out and open it up. Or I could let the boxes go—and I did. I watched them flow by.

That night I pledged myself to Meg. "I think we should try to make a life together," I said to her at the diner over a BLT. "For better or worse, let's try to make a life together." Meg seemed a little surprised and then took my hand while I turned to her and said, "I like you, Meg, because things matter to you."

M EG AND I had made love once or twice, but I didn't like that out-of-control animal feeling. I liked that all-over spiritual feeling I got from the LSD better, and I began to feel that my little room in the back of the bookstore was meant to be a monk's cell, not a sex pad, and I wanted to keep it that way. I had had the sex pad with Melissa; now I wanted something else with Meg.

One day I found a way to re-enter that joyously transcendental state without using drugs. Actually, Meg found it. Meg came up with the idea that I should try modeling for her life drawing class to make some extra money. They were looking for a model, so I took the job. I had never modeled before but I knew I'd be right for it. I was in good shape and had an almost classic body. I had no objection to being naked in front of an art class, although a jock strap was required. I hated jock straps and had never owned one.

I bought one at the college athletic store and then, repulsed by the horrid white clinical aspect of it, I decided to dye it red. On Monday at nine in the morning I showed up at Meg's life drawing class with an old bathrobe I had bought at a thrift shop and my new scarlet-red jock strap. I think the drawing teacher and the whole class were impressed and thought of me as a real professional.

It all happened on that first day. I made the wonderful discovery within an hour. I found that I could empty out and turn into an outline again. I could disappear without fear because I knew that the whole class was keeping me in that room with their eyes. The more people looked at me, the more I was present, and I was also free to come and go from that presence. If there were ten students looking at me, times two eyes, then I'd feel twenty times larger than I usually felt. It was their constant gaze that kept my body in that room, while my imagination flew to Bali, then out into the cosmos, getting ever closer to a state of nothingness. It was a way of constantly dying and being brought back from the dead, resurrected once again by the voice of the art instructor, which was like the voice of God bringing me back into the world of the living when he'd say, "Let's take a break," and *whoosh,* I'd be back in my body and putting on my robe and talking with Meg about all the places I'd been in my imagination.

They paid me very little, only $3.50 an hour, but that was fine, because I was getting paid for just standing still, or sometimes sitting, and that left my mind free to roam and soar. The only thing I had to be careful of was not to roam into any sexual fantasies, because it would lead to erections that would swell up and try to peek out of my red jock strap like some sly snake with a mind of its own. Then I would have to relax the snake by saying the simple phrase over in my mind: "Remember, Brewster, you are going to die. One day, you are going to not be—forever." That would pretty much take care of it.

Then I'd look around, or rather my eyes would look around, because I couldn't move my body—I had to remain very still—and I would see Meg and all these other students looking at me and drawing me, and I would feel my whole body fill up with substance again in their eyes. I'd come and go from that. I would come and go; it was like a game of hide-and-seek.

I liked the long sitting poses in a comfortable chair best of all, just sort of lolling there, stretched out and lounging, for forty-five minutes until I turned into a soft, languid statue, like one of the figures on Keats's Grecian urn. I'd sit in the most delicious of places, the place of greatest hope, the purest, most delicious place of suspended desire and anticipation, that place just before action destroys perfection and leads to the completion of desire and the inevitable corruption and disappointment of consequence.

These long poses not only brought a stillness to my body, they also brought a stillness to my mind. It was no longer racing over the past in a manic state. My mind came to this still place until, at last, the room and I were one.

After a three-hour session of modeling in those long poses, I would be stunned by how vividly I saw the world around me. Colors and sounds vibrated in me. It was as if I had the eyes of a ten-year-old. I didn't mind the low pay. I would have done it for free because it was for me a special kind of meditation. It was about being alone and not being alone all at the same time. But most of all it was about my body being consumed by those eyes.

After a while it was not enough just to have my body be seen, I wanted my mind to be seen as well. I wanted to move it in some more creative direction, and that was when I got interested in theater again. I began to wonder what it would be like to get my body and mind together, so that both aspects were being seen simultaneously.

There was a little theater group in New Paltz then. They were staging real straight, traditional plays. All around me the whole world was falling apart. There was nothing straight or traditional about it. The Vietnam War was boiling, Mom was cracking up, everyone seemed to be spaced out on some psychedelic drug; and in the middle of all this I found myself gravitating toward a conservative community theater, composed of people who imbibed little more than scotch or cheap sherry. I mean, they'd just sit around sipping cheap sherry and say, "Why not do Shaw's *Heartbreak House*?" or "Why not do *Long Day's Journey into Night*?" And then they'd just up and do it. They would put on the three-and-a-half-hour uncut version of *Long Day's Journey into Night* in front of ten people.

They called themselves the New Age Players, and that was odd, because there was nothing new age about them. But I liked working with them because it gave such order to my life. Having to rehearse and learn lines was so focusing. And I didn't have to be me. Not that I felt that there was a real me to be. I mean, taking the LSD had showed me that I was really empty, so I was perfectly happy to be filled up with someone else's words and someone else's personality. That's what I liked about acting in plays. I felt like no one; and I guess that in some secret way pretending to be someone else saved me from the giant fear of death. It allowed me the fantasy that I had to be someone in order to die, and that as long as I was no one, or just an actor, death would never find me; death would somehow pass me by.

So I played small roles and big roles. I even got to play Edmund in *Long Day's Journey into Night.* When Mom heard that I was in *Long Day's Journey,* she immediately wanted to come up and see it, which made me think that she was getting better. But Dad didn't want Mom to see *Long Day's Journey* because he felt it would be as disturbing as *Who's Afraid of Virginia Woolf?* had been for her. So he brought her up to see *The Knack* instead, a very silly, sophomoric English play where three very cool and crazy kind of guys try to learn the knack of picking up women. I was cast in the role of Tolen, a kind of cocky, strutting stud. At the time that was a real big stretch for me as an actor.

So Mom came up with Dad and they stayed at a motel. You can imagine how disappointed she was having wanted and expected to see me play the role of poor tortured Edmund in *Long Day's Journey into Night* and ending up instead seeing me strut my wares as Tolen in *The Knack.*

After the show, Meg, Mom, Dad, and I all went back to their motel for drinks. I could tell that Mom was annoyed. I think she was beginning to perceive that she'd been brought up there on false pretenses, and she was just sort of clamming up at the table. She was polite to Meg, but that was about it. She sat there like a nervous little bird sipping her 7UP. Dad, on the other hand, got slightly drunk on bourbon and kept dropping hints about how nice it was to be back in a motel with "your mother" (that's what he always called Mom in front of me) after all these years. She didn't respond to his motel innuendos. She only got annoyed.

Anyway, that was the night that I broke it to Mom and Dad that I had gotten a paying offer at the Alamo Theatre in Houston, Texas. Some sort of talent scout for regional theaters all over America had seen me play the role of Boss Mangan in *Heartbreak House*. He asked me to come down to New York City to audition for two major regional theaters. One of them was in Wisconsin and the other was the Alamo Theatre in Houston. I chose the Alamo because they were planning to do Chekhov's *The Sea Gull* as one of their plays that season. I loved Chekhov and loved that play ever since I'd seen it through drunken eyes in Providence. I had always wanted to play the role of Konstantin Gavrilovich because of the way I often acted so tortured and hung up on Mom. That's exactly how Konstantin was: tortured, sensitive, and very much hung up on his mother. Also, and best of all, Konstantin gets to commit suicide at the end of the play—every night! over and over again!—and for some reason I thought that would be really neat, to be able to kill myself every night and come back to life the following evening to do it again.

I broke the news to Dad and Mom over motel drinks that night. Meg and I had spent a long time discussing it. It was her plan to finish school and then join me for the summer in Mexico, where we would have our own perfect vacation after I'd finished my first season at the Alamo Theatre. That was to be our first vacation together and our first time out of the United States. Dad's response was "How much are they paying you?" And Mom just looked sad and said, "I wish you'd get a job acting in Providence so we could come and see you there." That was it. That's all they said.

After Mom saw me in *The Knack* Dad had to send her to Fuller Sanitarium again. I think it had to do with the fact that he had brought her to see me in *The Knack* and not *Long Day's Journey*. She was most likely angry at him but kept turning all her rage back on herself. It was going in instead of out. In the old days when something was bothering her and she couldn't talk about it she would often fart at the dinner table. That would drive Dad wild. He'd jump up and go read his newspaper. I don't think he really read the paper; I think he just held it up in front of his face like a paper wall or a Japanese screen. And there he would sit in the living room just steaming and fuming behind the headlines of the *Providence Journal.*

Now instead of just farting, Mom got real crazy. She had what they call irrational behavior, and Dad would not put up with it and packed her off again to Fuller Sanitarium.

Then shortly before I was due to leave for the Alamo Theatre, I got this letter from Mom:

Hi Darling!
I'm home and all well and deliriously happy to be here! I called Cole a few nights ago and broke the news to him. He was overjoyed as are Dad and Topher. I wanted to talk with you but Dad says you can't be reached by phone so will you please call me right away quick!! I can hardly wait for us to be all together for a while anyway. What a reunion that will be! I feel as though I have been reborn. They call me the miracle patient at Fuller Sanitarium. The doctor said he had never seen anyone get well as fast as I did. The other patients there couldn't understand it. They kept asking me what I had that they didn't have.
Love Ya!
Mom

Just reading this letter made me nervous. I could hear Mom's old frantic voice in it. I didn't trust her miracles anymore. I wanted to believe she was healed but I feared the worst. I knew when I called her I had to be careful not to let that fear show.

On the phone Mom sounded really high and told me all about this big family reunion she and Dad were planning to welcome Coleman home from Spain and to send me off to the Alamo Theatre.

I went home with more than a little trepidation, but it turned out to be fun, almost like going to the drive-in to see *Mary Poppins.* I was amazed that Mom had made such a miraculous recovery. She seemed to be back to her old "7UP Kid" personality again. Dad was in good spirits, cooking his big fat steak on the portable barbecue in the middle of the driveway. It was good to see Coleman back from

Spain, and Topher, who had taken a brief break from playing the pipe organ, which he had grown obsessed with, going through a pair of shoes a month just working those pedals like a maniac. It was really a wonderful family reunion.

Cole brought Topher and me wineskins from Spain and we filled them with Almadén burgundy and danced around the picnic table squirting red wine into each other's mouth. Dad laughed once or twice and didn't even get angry with Cole when he did his crazy version of a Spanish dance around a full glass of wine in the middle of the driveway until at last, quite by accident, he stepped right on it and smashed it to bits. I really expected Dad to blow his top on that one, but he didn't. It was as if Dad was so happy to have Mom home that he was really trying to turn over a new leaf at fifty-six.

I T W A S T H A T happy reunion that let me think it was all right to fly off to the Alamo Theatre to pursue an acting career.

I didn't know it at the time, but that was the last time I would see Mom forever and ever. You see, you never know; you never know when it will be the last time forever.

Upon arriving in Houston I was at first a little stunned and overwhelmed by the newness of the place. It was almost tropical and I'd never been to the tropics before. It was hot, very humid, lush, and there were palm trees everywhere, the first I'd ever seen. But after a while things began to settle into a routine and I began living a rather isolated life. I played small roles and kept to myself, occasionally going out to smoke dope at the homes of Houston locals. I didn't get on that well with the other actors, and after a while I wasn't really sure why I was there—if I was just doing time to earn my Equity card, if I was trying to escape from Mom, or waiting to see if I would get to play the lead role in *The Sea Gull*. I didn't have a telephone in my apartment, so I only wrote letters to Mom and Dad, but rarely. Mostly I wrote letters to Meg. Some time in early winter, which really wasn't winter for me down there in Houston with all those palm trees and swimming pools and muggy warm days, I got the following letter from Dad:

Dear Brewster,

I have not been a very good correspondent lately, have had to write twice a week to the Bentons, get my house-work and meals done and I suppose it's somewhat due to lethargy. Mother is not doing well at all. Not long after you left for Houston she had a relapse. I had high hopes that she might get better at Fuller, but, if anything, I think, she is worse. While in the beginning I phoned her twice a week, there was very little to say and I only seemed to upset her. Hence I infrequently call now. I did talk with her last Tuesday, but it was very discouraging—she is now certain that she is insane and that she can never recover. This is a very difficult frame of mind to recover from. While I keep avoiding the thought, I find myself more and more wondering if maybe this is so—it does happen to people—but I can't believe it is really happening to us.

There had been some thought of Mother coming home with a Christian Science nurse if one could be located—at least to get her out of the institution atmo-sphere—but nothing definite as yet.

Friday night when I came home I went into the bed-room and found glass all over the floor—then discovered that the storm window and one 8 by 10 pane next to mother's bed had been smashed. I was about to call the police and looked around for the stone or other object, but found nothing—then discovered feathers and after looking further found a partridge, dead on my bedside table. It's hard to believe that a bird which weighed one and a quarter pounds could go through two windows, brush through the curtain, knock over the TV aerial and, without losing any altitude, zoom across the room hitting the corner and dropping dead on the table without even disturbing the lampshade.

It took me about two hours to clean up the mess and, I might add, dress the bird for the ice box. Gram North came for the weekend and we had a delicious partridge dinner Saturday night. So far I have not been able to get hold of the storm window man but have the window covered with a sheet of cardboard and masking tape, which does a pretty good job considering the temperature this morning was five degrees.

Would love to hear further from you when there is time.

Love,
Dad

It was as though the mad bird in Mom had at last burst out of her and broken free like a heart with wings flying out of that sanitarium, to find its way to home to crash and die on Dad's bedside table. Then, after all of that, to at last be eaten by Dad and his mother . . . well, it was all really too much.

And what was happening in Houston didn't make it any better. The role of Konstantin in *The Sea Gull* was given to an older, less sensitive actor named Brian, who was not at all right for the role. But he had tenure, which means he'd been suffering down there for five years, and I, after all, had only just arrived. And to add great insult to injury, the director of the theater decided that because of my obviously tortured sensitivity, Brian should use me as a life study. He should observe me in my daily routines. What he was really observing was my disappointment at not having the role of Konstantin. I went home and cried alone for one whole day.

The director, who was this very histrionic, flamboyant woman named Thelma, decided that I should also "create" (I think that was her word) a very imaginative collection of sound effects for the final dinner party that is going on offstage while Konstantin has his last sad unrequited love meeting with Nina. She wanted me to organize the other actors to sit around me in chairs offstage while I conducted them like some demented symphony orchestra in the jangling of silverware and the striking of empty glasses. I was to give them cues for laughter as well as maintain a constant improvisational mumble of "rhubarb

rhubarb rhubarb" or "peas and carrots, peas and carrots." All of this
had to be orchestrated around Konstantin's and Nina's onstage lines.
What was worse was that I agreed to do all this. So there I sat backstage
during each show conducting all these ridiculous, meaningless sounds
while Brian as Konstantin spewed and strutted his badly performed
sensitivity for all of Houston to see.

Good God, what was I doing? I wondered. Maybe I was trying
to punish myself for something. It seemed like I had run away from
Mom's insanity to come to an even more insane world. The whole
situation was producing great anger and rage in me, but for some
reason I could not express it. Instead I judged it as being bad and tried
to purge it by going on what I thought would be a purifying diet of
soybeans. Trying to escape Dad's corrupting legacy of meat, I was
eating soybeans morning, noon, and night, and those soybeans were
causing enormous intestinal gas. Wherever I walked I was leaving
those silent but deadly slow hot burners. But I was not taking responsibility for them. I just kept moving and wafting and letting them drift
in, reeking hot invisible waves behind me. You see, I'd not learned
how to express my anger through the proper orifice yet.

The only time I held back, and with great pain, was when I was
conducting the backstage sound effects. I was afraid I would be discovered as the volcanic source of those perverse stinkers, so there in the
wings while conducting Russian party sounds I would squeeze my
sphincter tight against those hot winds.

For the entire four-week run of *The Sea Gull* my rage grew.
Then at last on closing night I had a chance to vent it fully. The
closing-night party was held in Galveston, a short drive to the gulf
from Houston, at an authentic Greek restaurant where all the Greek
merchant marines came and danced when their ships were in port. We
drove down in three fully packed cars and I ended up with Brian, the
New York actress who played Madame Arkadina, the actress who
played Nina, and Thelma, the director. The woman driving the car was
a Houston native who ran the theater box office and often went
dancing that old Greek grapevine dance with the sailors who had just
come into port. It was her idea to have the party at the Greek
restaurant, and everyone else followed.

As she drove, she gave us all a preparatory lecture for the upcoming event, how to act or not act around a bunch of horny Greek sailors who had been out to sea for months. And somewhere in the middle of her precautionary notes she said, "Oh, by the way, just before we get to Galveston we're going to pass through some very sloppy low-lands, and I have to warn you that the smell is quite intense. In fact, it's almost overwhelming. So just before we get there I'm going to warn you all to roll up your windows."

I felt the car seat burning under me. I couldn't hold out any longer and let out the longest, hottest, most silent slow burner ever. As soon as that cloud reached the sweet little turned-up nose of our lady driver, she cried, "Oh my God! There it is! I didn't know we were there yet. Roll up your windows! Everybody, roll up your windows!" And up all the windows went tight, real tight, while everyone wept and gasped and cried, "Oh my God! Oh, help! Step on it, let's get out of here!" I sat still, weeping with the silent angry laughter that was buried so deep. There I sat, tears rolling down my cheeks, with no idea that this was a fun version of Mom's soon-to-come exit from this world.

A FTER THAT closing-night *Sea Gull* party, I knew my relationship with the Alamo Theatre, or maybe all theater, was over, but I felt too inadequate to walk away from it all. I was determined to finish the season out so that I could save enough money to spend the summer in Mexico with Meg. That was my big celebration plan. I had been writing her about it, and she planned to join me as soon as she graduated from college.

I'd decided to relocate in San Miguel Allende, an American art colony high in the central plains of Mexico. I made arrangements to ride down there with two Houston locals, Axel and Odele. In my deepest fantasy mind it was a sort of trial run for Bali, just to see what it would be like to vacation in a foreign country.

The trip down was like a hallucinogenic dream. I rode and sometimes drove in Odele's VW bus while Axel rolled joints and took photos with his little Leica. I don't think we had one normal slice of conversation the whole way down. It was just driving, looking, smoking, peeing, and eating trashy hot Mexican food at roadside stands. I don't know how Axel and Odele drove stoned. I was incapacitated by the grass most of the time and lay on the back floor of that VW bus vibrating all over. When I was able to pull myself up to look out the windows, all I could see was endless armies of cactus that looked like they were fighting each other.

We got to San Miguel forty-eight hours later with very little rest or sleep. I was spent and very ready to be alone. Then Odele and Axel went their own ways, Axel off to the Michigan area to deal in pre-Columbian art and Odele hitchhiking on to Mexico City to visit a Dutch sculptor.

I walked into my little hotel room and stood in front of the tin-framed mirror and just stared at my gaunt bearded face. I didn't dare move. I just stood there watching my face dissolve and then re-form in the mirror. I felt out of touch and really away from home for the first time. And as I stood there, barely having arrived, I had that fantasy again of coming through the driveway gate with a duffel bag full of dirty laundry and presents, and Mom rushing out to greet me. I could see myself standing there, a brave independent hero, like one of those Greek sailors dropping in with gifts and stories just long enough to get his laundry done before heading out to the next port. Coming from Mexico would not be as great, perhaps, as returning from Bali, but it would still be triumphant.

The following day I found my own apartment up at the top of a hill overlooking the entire town and the wild purple central plains beyond. Far below I could hear church bells chiming and the sound of slow-rolling wooden wheels on cobblestones. It was old, it was beautiful, it was slow. It felt just right, and I immediately sent off a postcard to Meg with a little map to "our" new place in Mexico.

She arrived, and we settled into a comfortable routine of working, shopping for food, and just walking around looking at it all: going down to the *zócalo,* the public square, at dusk, with the long-tailed black birds cruising in at sundown to fill the trees, and fill the entire square with their mad cackling.

We discovered an art school for Americans there, and Meg signed up for a rug-weaving course while I did live modeling for food money. While Meg worked on her rug I'd go shopping at the open market to buy goat chops and vegetables.

The weather was always ideal, warm and dry, and there was no apparent reason for depressions, yet I kept falling into them. I began to figure out that some of them were connected to tequila and marijuana. Between the two of them I was not doing very well. I craved altered states of consciousness. I liked feeling good all day but was not able to take too much of it. Too much feeling good became flat and boring, and I'd want to push it a little. So at sunset I would sit on our little balcony and sip tequila and go into quiet raptures, waves of minor beatitudes. Meg didn't drink. She read, or sat beside me looking out. The marijuana was strong stuff, and I'd just take a few tokes and that would be it.

I stopped altogether after I had a very disturbing hallucination, or vision. I was alone in our apartment. Meg had gone down to the art institute to do some photo printing in the darkroom and I was alone and anxious. I was pacing a lot and trying to resist getting drunk when I heard this party going on in the apartment below. They were playing a cut from a Stones album over and over. It was "Ruby Tuesday," and the music pulled me out on the balcony and at last pulled me all the way down to their door. The apartment was rented by some Norwegian guy named Olaf who looked like a Viking god. Olaf drove a new white VW bus. Meg and I would often see him driving around town in search of a girlfriend. He was always checking out all the new single women who passed through town, and he had recently scored with a real blond beauty. They made a great couple to look at: a blond goddess and a blond god.

Olaf had a large apartment, which he had opened up to another extraordinary couple, who had been driving around Mexico in an old Chevy panel truck with California plates. He looked like one of those California free spirits, with shoulder-length blond hair and a full red beard. She, his traveling companion, was a slender Welsh beauty. She had long black hair and very beautiful pale skin, translucent and untouched by the Mexican sun. You could see the blue veins just below the surface. The man had contracted viral hepatitis on their travels and she was nursing him in the back room. By "nursing him" I mean she was pretty much keeping him stoned day and night on strong Mexican grass.

Olaf was having a wild get-well party down there and I was drawn to it. I came in and saw another couple from New York City who were down traveling around Mexico in a pickup truck camper. He was shy and she was real outspoken. She was in the middle of relating an acid trip she had taken in the Mexican mountains where she had split from her boyfriend to go off alone in the hills to masturbate with a green banana. I was both shocked and drawn to her brazen openness. She was talking loudly in order to be heard over the Rolling Stones and was telling, just as I came in, how the banana seemed to have a life and mind of its own and how it came alive and softened "like the flesh of the gods" as soon as it entered her. Her story set me off, and right in the middle of it her boyfriend passed me a lit joint and without thinking I took three deep, greedy drags as though I was sucking on that green banana and *whammo,* it hit me—I got instantly stoned. Everything was suddenly too much for me. Her story, the fire in the fireplace, the red-bearded man with hepatitis, it all closed in and beat on me. I felt wide open and devastated. I went out to the hall and began to pace.

The Welsh woman, who must have had a kind of built-in nurse in her, immediately noticed my anxiety and left her hepatitis-stricken lover to come out and try to comfort me. When I saw her standing there in that dim amber light I saw for the first time how beautiful she was, which made me even more anxious. I wanted her right there and then. I tried to ground myself by talking to her, but her spare black-and-white beauty distracted me so that I couldn't even finish my sentence.

But she talked me down by telling me about her hometown in Wales. It had the strangest, longest name and the way she spoke it was like pure music. I think it was the longest name of any town or city in the world. It was more like an entire song, or a Druidic spell, than a name, and each time she spoke it I got calmer.

Lulled by the sound of that Welsh woman's hometown I was able to re-enter Olaf's apartment. I went right to an empty chair by the fire and that's where I saw it, staring into that roaring fire. I saw it and, horrible as it was, I could not stop looking. In the middle of the flames was a woman sitting up in bed, and the flames were raging all about her, going in her ears and burning out of her screaming mouth. The flames enveloped the entire bed and the woman seemed unable to move and she screamed out my name and I thought, It's Mom—Mom is burning up somewhere.

I T   W A S   A U G U S T   by the time Meg and I took a train to the border and a bus from there to Houston, where we caught a flight to New York. From New York City Meg went to New Jersey to visit her parents and I took a flight to Providence. I gave Dad a call at work and asked him to pick me up. He sounded fine on the phone and was not at all surprised to hear I was back. He assumed a businesslike tone, which is what he always did when you phoned him at work. I would have phoned Mom at home but I assumed she was still at Fuller.

It was a hot, humid August day. I opened the bottle of tequila I had been carrying with me and sat on the lawn of the airport brown-bagging until Dad pulled up in his Ford LTD. He had the air conditioner on and all of the windows rolled up and as soon as I got in he said, "Tying one on, I see." Then he asked if Coleman had caught up with me and told me how Coleman, not being able to deal with Mom anymore, had finagled a drive-away car to El Paso and was going to take a bus down to Mexico from there. I suddenly had a deep, sad pain of regret. I was so sad to have missed Coleman.

We rode in silence for a while until I finally asked, "So how is Mom doing—how's Mom?" and Dad turned to me and said, "She's gone." He broke into convulsive crying as he drove. I just sat there across from him while he cried. I sat there with my open bottle of tequila in my lap staring out the window at that flat, hot Rhode Island landscape and all of the other air-conditioned cars with their windows closed. I just sat there and didn't reach out to Dad or say a word. I just sat there with the phrase going over and over in my head. "She's gone." She's gone. And over and over that phrase continued, like the

end of a story in a Grimm fairy tale, like when the princess or the queen
dies of a broken heart. And it played over and over again, that phrase
"She's gone." She's gone—died of a broken heart. She's gone. She's
gone. She died of a broken heart.

When we got home Dad led me through the house like he was
some sort of official tour guide in a museum. First, in the living room,
he showed me all the sympathy cards on the mantel. I was amazed to
see how many there were, all lined up like Christmas cards, but not
quite as colorful. Dad was angry that Mom's Christian Science practitioner never sent a card, after all the bills he'd paid for all those prayers.
Next he led me into their bedroom and opened Mom's closet to show
me all her clothes and a neat little row of all her empty shoes. Then
he told me about all the dental work Mom had done just before she
died. While Dad was telling me this I noticed a picture of myself on
the night table by Mom's bed. It had been taken at my old girlfriend
Kathy's wedding to the guy who gave her more. Then Dad showed
me the cardboard box that contained Mom's ashes, which sat on his
bedside table exactly where the partridge had landed and died. At last
we went out into the living room, where Dad made drinks at the bar.
As he mixed the drinks he told me what happened.

Dad did wake up the night Mom got up to kill herself, but he
went right back to sleep. He didn't pay attention to her absence because
she would often get up in the night when she couldn't sleep and go
out to the living room to read. Only this particular night she didn't
get up to read. She went out to the garage instead, and got into his
car and started it up. After some time Dad woke up to a sound which
he thought was the refrigerator at first. When he sat up in bed and
realized it was the car, he raced out to try to save Mom. He called an
ambulance and woke Topher, who was asleep in his room just above
the garage. The rescue unit came right away. Dad said he had to give
them credit for that. It made him feel like his taxes were doing some
good. They were fast, but not fast enough. They tried to revive Mom
in the driveway, but it was too late. I pictured Dad and Topher
standing over Mom, looking down on her. It must have taken its
wicked toll on both of them forever.

After we had finished our first round of scotches, Dad got up and went to his desk and brought back a bill from Pete's Gulf station to show me exactly how much gasoline it had taken Mom to do herself in. Then Dad told me about his plan to asphalt the driveway. He and Mom had always fought over this issue. She wanted to keep it gravel and he wanted asphalt.

We got quite drunk together and in the middle of it all Coleman called from Mexico City to say that he had just received the news of Mom's death through a Mexican business associate of Dad's. Dad didn't want to talk to Coleman. I didn't know why; he seemed angry with him for something. So I got on the phone. Coleman asked me what was going on and I told him, "Mom's gone, and we're drinking a lot, but otherwise I guess we're okay." "Well, I'm sorry about all of this," Cole said. "I'll be home in a few days. I'm taking a bus up from Mexico City." When I told Dad what Cole said about taking a bus up instead of flying, he went into a rage. He couldn't understand it and carried on for an hour about it, as though everything else that had happened was nothing compared to Cole taking a bus instead of a plane.

By nightfall Dad was so drunk he couldn't stand up, so I put two TV turkey dinners on and we ate in front of the television watching the latest episode of the war, live from Vietnam. After dinner I got a very bad chill and went up to bed. Perhaps it was something I picked up in Mexico.

I turned out the lights and the chill became a fever and further into the night the fever led to a sort of delirium and I didn't know where I was. The blankets I'd piled up on myself felt like they were moving and shaping themselves around me into a hammock that turned into a straw Vietcong body bag. The bag wrapped itself tighter around me like a cocoon or straitjacket. I began to see on the wall what looked like black-and-white movies of all these Amish men all dressed in black coming out of a farmhouse door. They would come out and beckon to me like automatic windup toys. Back and forth they would go like hysterical cuckoos, beckoning to me with giant white blown-up index fingers that leaped out from the wall and beckoned me to come into their farmhouse. They kept opening and closing the farmhouse door. Open, close, beckon, beckon, open, close, beckon. There was another door on the other side of the farmhouse and there I could see Amish men carrying coffins outside. It was a macabre assembly line of death: open, beckon, close, coffins. The rhythm started to go in my head like some crazy out-of-control train. And as I watched this I could feel the blankets bind my arms even tighter until I couldn't move. The whole bed began to rise slowly up like a giant gun on a battleship with me inside the barrel. The gun turned into a long, deep, dark, endless well. And I was falling backwards, full-speed down this tunnel in an extreme state of panic, but in the center of that panic was an absolutely clear place where the simple fact occurred to me that I was dying, and that if I kept falling, I would never, ever come back. And it wouldn't matter, because there would be no one waiting to come back to. Then at the top of the well, I saw an overwhelmingly dazzling white light. I knew it was brighter than the star that the shepherds followed to Jesus. It was like that star, only brighter and closer, pulsing like a big fluid diamond, and the sight of that light reversed my fall and pulled me right up, as fast as I was falling, right up out of the dark. I flew to it like a moth and stuck, and the next thing I knew I was back in my bed and what had been that diamond light was only the reflection of the streetlight at the end of Shady Lane playing through the shadows of blowing leaves across my bedroom wall. Soaked with sweat, I fell asleep to the sound of that summer wind in the trees around Dad's house.

AFTER A FEW DAYS, when I felt better, I wrote Meg a letter:

Dear Meg,
My mother has killed herself, and I caught some sort of flu. I'll come to New York as soon as I'm better.
Love,
Brewster

Meg responded with a sympathetic letter and a report that she planned to go look for an apartment in New York City. She wanted to know if I was going to join her.

There seemed to be no choice. What else was there to do but move in with Meg? I had no real love for New York City, but I desperately needed a nest, a sanctuary in which to separate myself from my loss. One thing I did know was that I couldn't stay in Rhode Island.

I left Dad to take that sad boat ride with Uncle Jib. They went out in Jib's little power boat to spread Mom's ashes over Narragansett Bay, the bay Mom had loved beyond words and, without words, died for. By that time I was safely ensconced in New York City with Meg.

As soon as I arrived in New York I knew Meg was exactly who I needed to give me direction and motivation. She was moving books and chairs into the new apartment and she was doing it with such determination, going up those stairs and down those stairs like a little dynamo. She gave me a quick kiss on the cheek and told me to keep an eye on the car so nothing got ripped off. That much I could do. Beyond that I felt incapable of anything. Meg was this great organizer and mover, a new mother of sorts.

She had found us a small railroad apartment up in Germantown on Ninety-third Street at Third Avenue. The rent for four very tiny rooms was only $37.55. I never understood how the landlord rounded it off to fifty-five cents. I was secretly glad that Meg had not chosen to settle in the East Village, because I really did not want to be living with a bunch of drugged-out hippies. I longed for some sort of stable, conservative environment, and that was exactly what we were in.

We lived among the families of all the service people of New York City, the firemen, plumbers, and police. There was no one in the neighborhood like us, so there were no comparisons, no others to steal my being away. At last I was not threatened by my neighbors. They were not trying to live constantly ecstatic lives. They were living in a kind of fifties workaday world, carrying their basket of coupons to the local A&P.

The apartment had a bathtub in the kitchen, which was a real novelty for me. Dad couldn't believe it when I told him. "What?" he said. "A bathtub in the kitchen? How could this possibly be?" Our little bedroom consisted of a mattress, which we found on the street, and a bookcase behind it, which held my little KLH radio. We did not own a television, and neither of us missed it. At times it was like we were living somewhere back in the thirties or forties. The toilet was in a water closet at the end of the hall and we shared it with our neighbor, a very old German bachelor. The odd smell he left behind was so pungent and ancient that at times it made me feel like we were living in postwar Berlin. The toilet seat was made of old wood and there was a pull chain with a wooden handle to release the water from its sweaty trough above. We were slumming it, and it felt good, like a kind of penance for all the soft middle-class living that had gone before. We were the new WASP refugees in New York City. We fell into living a simple life together.

The apartment was on the top floor of a five-story walk-up, and our two living-room windows, which were grated with black metal accordion gates, looked out over the defunct Jacob Ruppert Brewery, whose great empty brick edifice also reminded me of postwar Germany. On cold winter nights the wind would blow through it, tearing old metal and copper loose, and I'd wake to those foreign sounds of metal ripping instead of elm trees blowing in the wind. Also, the brewery was affined with my name, Brewster, which I always equated with brew ever since my father fed beer to me in that little one-ounce mug with the cork on the bottom. I was a hophead and no longer ashamed to admit it, living in the heart of Germantown. Nothing pleased me more than to be sitting at the table with Meg in our little kitchen sipping a fine German brew, a nice thick dark one, while the winter winds swept through that giant empty brewery and Meg warmed up a pot of our ongoing stew. We were like this odd couple grown somehow old before our time.

As for sex together, or making love, like in Mexico I don't remember it. Usually I remember sexual positions I get in with women so that I can play them back in my memory as a turn-on, but I don't remember any from those early days with Meg. It must have been going on between us, but I don't remember it. Night was always the time of warm snuggling while the radio played in the dark, after many beers, which relaxed me enough to allow me to fall into a childlike sleep, free of all desire.

Next to Meg, beer was my best friend. I loved to look at it in the simple glass that I drank from. I loved the musty autumn smell of the hops as I lifted it to my nose. I loved the tickle of its foamy head as it left a white mustache on my upper lip, and the feeling of its smooth thickness going all the way down. Yes, it's odd to say, but I have to admit it: I remember more how I made love to my beer than how I made love to Meg.

There was another reason that Meg and I did not make love at night and that was our cat, Phil. We found Phil as a stray kitten in the hall of our building. Our friend Barney was working in the kitchen of Maxwell's Plum, a fancy Upper East Side restaurant, and after work he used to bring over big plastic bags full of leftover meat which he'd hang on our doorknob. I had a great ongoing stew made from that meat. One morning I opened the door to find this sweet little emaciated tabby kitten crying and licking the bottom of the meat bag. We took him in and Meg named him after her brother who had died as a child of leukemia. So Phil grew up with us and actually slept between us at night, and stranger still, Phil slept on his back with his little paws over the edge of the blanket. The only thing that was missing was a pillow for his head. So on our first Christmas together, Meg made a little pillow for him. Phil was like our only child and we treated him that way.

Our night rituals were clear and set. Everything felt in control. There were the beers and Phil, there was classical music on the little radio, there was Barney's stew and hot baths in the kitchen. Whoever was not in the tub would read to the other from *The Collected Poems of Wallace Stevens*. It was a good life as lives go. It was a life of moderation and in-betweens. It was a settled, regular life.

I was collecting Texas unemployment from the Alamo Theatre and lived off that as well as what I made from modeling. During the days I would walk. I would walk and walk. I would walk the city and get to know it that way. Walking was my therapy. Some days I would walk the whole length of Central Park, or just sit on a park bench and watch people and listen to them talk.

Meg got a job selling postcards at the Metropolitan Museum gift shop and also made money by selling some of the rugs she had brought back from Mexico. When she wasn't at work in the day she was doing her own artwork at home. She was getting into extremely dense charcoal drawings, which she called "landscapes," although they were like no landscape I'd ever seen before. They were a foreign land to me and a home to her.

Meg would start with a blank piece of white paper about two by three feet, and then lay a piece of masking tape across it like some artificial horizon. She'd proceed to fill in the whole piece of paper in gradations of charcoal. When she finished, she would tear away the masking tape to reveal startling white areas that were in such dramatic contrast against that black charcoal landscape.

It was amazing to watch the way Meg worked, with the absolute focus of a pure obsession. I was witnessing a living, moving act of sublimation. She would take that piece of charcoal in her right hand and make endless little marks like streaks of black rain. She became that black rain. She could do it for hours. It was a beautiful world Meg created, a beautiful ordered world that reminded me of my favorite poem of Wallace Stevens, "The Idea of Order at Key West," which has the line "Oh! Blessed rage for order. . . ." Meg had that rage for order and she created it wherever she went.

This was when I was most deeply in love with Meg, when I would watch her go into these drawing trances, these sketching fits, and I would be her sound track while she created her black rain. I would sit and slowly sip my dark German brews and tell her stories of all the people I'd seen and phrases I'd heard while on my daily walks. At the time it never occurred to me that I saw Meg as the woman Mom could've been, had Mom been able to complete art school and do something with it. Mom had dropped out of art school to marry Dad, and during her nervous breakdown she tried to get started again. She took painting classes, but she had a rough time because her concentration was so low and she kept slipping into the past.

Now I was helping to create a space for Meg's art to flourish, as if I were doing something my father had never done for my mother. It was a wonder and delight to me that Meg could find such passionate meaning in such strange and frivolous work. I secretly longed to find passionate meaning in my own life, but I couldn't imagine what it would be. I had only the sad, soft, ancient legacy of the bog people, the old inheritance of the soft, pulpy Irish in me, telling stories while drinking beer.

The stories I told Meg, the stories that came at the end of every day, were my art, my rage for order, my way of mastering the night, but I couldn't see it at the time, because the words just disappeared. They never took a form I could look at. I would have had to write them down, and yet it never occurred to me at the time to do so. What did occur to me was that I wanted, or thought I wanted, to go back to acting. I liked Meg as an audience, but I also craved a larger one.

So on my walks I began to buy the trade paper *Back Stage* and see what shows were being cast. I now was a member of Actors' Equity and I had my Equity card; that much I had salvaged from the Alamo Theatre. So I'd check the paper and go to all these hopeless open-casting calls the out-of-work actors called "cattle calls." I would show up and there would be all these other actors waiting who probably could have done the role just as well as I, or better, and I hated them. I fantasized about giving up on the whole art thing and sacrificing myself to help the needy—which made me think that I might be drawn to the less fortunate in a sick way. Maybe I could only live among sick people in order to feel well. I couldn't be among normal, healthy people without feeling drained or stolen away by them, without feeling like I was disappearing. It really terrified me. I couldn't take responsibility for these feelings and I would begin to get angry and blame them on Mom, on some failing in the way that she had raised me. This would be the darkest of paranoias. I would think Mom was like some sort of Medea who had killed her children, that somewhere along the line Mom had realized that if she couldn't have her children for herself completely and forever, she was going to lay the ground-work for their self-destruction and then, after laying the groundwork, kill herself, just like in the Greek tragedies. Her children would be left with the curse, the fear of intimacy with other women. Because Mom was insatiable and couldn't get enough intimacy from her family, she was going to make very sure that we couldn't get it from someone else.

Now I'm not saying that Mom did this consciously, but some

dark unconscious shadow was operating through her, a shadow that she never came to recognize because of her constant search for the divine transcendent life. That shadow was a part of her, but she could not see it, because in Christian Science she was taught only to look for the light side, only look for the good.

Those were dark times when I blamed Mom for my not being able to get closer to Meg or succeed in the theater. Then, just as I'd get swamped in all of that dark psychologizing, I'd try to pull out of it by getting a larger overview. I'd try to understand my failure in theater by taking a look at the plays they were casting. None of them really had to do with me. They were all so ethnic—you know, things like *The Indian Wants the Bronx*. Directors were always looking for courageous tough ethnic types, young antiheroes, not neurotic New England WASPs. They were all plays about tough ethnic guys bucking the system, not about people who disappeared when they came into a room of strangers.

The big break came along out of nowhere. I read in *Back Stage* that Robert Lowell's play *Endecott and the Red Cross* was being restaged at St. Clement's Church. I had no idea what *Endecott and the Red Cross* was about. I assumed it was not about the guy who founded the American Red Cross but probably had to do with some dark Puritan heritage, of which Robert Lowell was still one of the great autobiographic voices. I loved Robert Lowell at a distance. I didn't want to get too close because he represented that New England overbreeding which led to hypersensitivity and periodic madness, as well as wicked bouts with alcohol. He was a noble, beautiful man to look at, but deep in his writing I could feel him like an overbred Irish setter; nervous, quivering and shaking, constantly on the edge.

Not only had Robert Lowell written the play, but he had chosen a man named John Hancock to direct it, and I thought: This is perfect. This play was made for me.

And I was right. I went up for the audition and was immediately cast in the role of the King of the May. The play was based on a short story by Nathaniel Hawthorne called "The Maypole of Merry Mount," which took place at the Merry Mount colony in Massachusetts and was basically about the punishment of the colonists for taking pleasure in the celebration of the pagan May Day festival. The whole colony was punished by a horrible oppressor named Endecott, who carried a flag with a red cross on it. In our first rehearsal, we all sat and listened to Robert Lowell read the play all the way through. He read in one long monotonous drone. Every character seemed to be speaking in the same depressive New England tones. He mumbled it through in a resigned way, with very little passion. I felt right at home. The play was all about my people, my repressive Puritan people.

The Queen of the May was played by a beautiful blond actress, and I played the King, all dressed up in a fine white peasant shirt, long flowing auburn wig, rough brown leather pants, and high-laced suede boots. We looked great together, the Queen and I. She was dressed in pure white, with flowers in her hair. We got to dance around the maypole with some Puerto Rican actors who were playing American Indians and some other odd assorted colonial types. Then, right in the middle of our sensuous revels, we get busted by Endecott and his big red cross. The Queen and I get tied up and punished along with everyone else. And that was about it. It was like a "let's pretend" backyard children's game, only it was played in an Off-Broadway theater which doubled as a church on Sundays.

But the experience of acting in that play did not, as I had hoped, lift me into some transcendent state. I hardly had any lines at all, and I felt like a prop. I wanted more out of theater, or I was going to give up on it and try to do something else, maybe become a poet even, if one could will such a thing.

But as they say in show business, things lead to things, and indeed they did. At the opening-night cast party of *Endecott,* I met a weird and interesting theater director named Rex Duffy who took a liking to me. Rex was extremely dramatic-looking. He was very pale and angular, with a little goatee. He was about my age, but twice as intense and very passionate. He seemed to possess the male equivalent of Meg's passion, and because of this I was immediately drawn to him. He was dressed completely in black—black pants, black shirt, black leather boots—and he smoked a filtered cigarette in a cigarette holder. He drank, I noticed, only straight Polish vodka. Most of all I was drawn to Rex's mesmerizing stories about Bali and some crazy, unorthodox

French actor named Antonin Artaud, who had gone there to study Balinese trance dance long before my uncle Jib went there to buy my monkey mask.

The cast party was held around the maypole on the set of *Endecott* and suddenly I was back on that distant Rhode Island beach where Brewster the monkey boy had danced in front of Mom with the Balinese mask on. Robert Lowell had replaced Mom and was standing there like a great wise New England patrician in his tweed jacket and horn-rimmed glasses, palliating his shaky madness with tumblers of straight scotch. And Rex, in black, had replaced my uncle Jib, in white, telling wild island stories to an awestruck boy. I stood there between them having a déjà vu. I stood there, this innocent Boy-King of the May, dreaming once again of Bali, that faraway other side of my cold dark New England heritage. *I'd found my way to a lost trade route into a lost time.*

It was on that glorious night that Rex invited me to his experimental theater company, which he called the Rex Duffy Laboratory Theatre. I was ecstatic about what Rex told me at that party. His idea was that theater was action to heal the split between language and the body. He called the body "the flesh," which at the time sounded even more exotic to me. I couldn't get that word "flesh" out of my mind, as well as the word "heal." And I thought that we were in the perfect place to talk of healing the flesh, here around the maypole at Merry Mount, where we had been punished for trying to celebrate the senses.

Rex and I hit it off. I would almost say we bonded, which was rare for me because I had so few male friends. I was never attracted to real male men. But Rex had a nice blend of male and female in him and I was attracted to that quality. At the end of our conversation he invited me to come visit his theater.

I showed up at Rex's Laboratory Theatre early Monday morning. It was really just a hole in the wall in a basement room on West Nineteenth Street, no more than twenty-five by thirty feet, with one bare light bulb hanging from a very low ceiling.

After a short coffee break and introductions to three very striking women and two less-than-striking men, the laboratory got down to work. Rex wanted to show me a run-through of an original theater piece they'd been rehearsing. It was called *The Tower* and it was based on the Tower of Babel story: how all humankind—who, at the time, spoke one language—tried to build a big tower tall enough to reach heaven and how God knocked the tower down and confounded their language and left them all alienated and speaking in many tongues.

They planned to tour wherever and whenever they thought they could. Rex assured me that they were in no hurry and did not work under any kind of deadline. They were, he said, an organic theater group.

As soon as Rex went to the little dimmer on the wall and turned the light down, the group abandoned their coffee cups and scattered. Now the room was dark and silent except for the distant grind of trash trucks. For a long time I sat in the dark thinking nothing was going on and maybe that was the whole point, that I was supposed to get in touch with that nothing.

As my eyes adjusted to the darkness, I began to see various leotard-clad bodies stirring in and around the four corners of the room, accompanied by low moans that grew into one shared tone as the group slowly came together under the single light bulb in the center. The bodies began building a body pile in which they seemed to be crawling up each other to turn out the light. Soon the pile (which now resembled a sort of spastic rendition of the Flying Wallendas) stood still for a moment, then collapsed. As soon as this happened, the uniform voice drone went into wild dispersions and everyone crawled off growling, barking, and grunting into the various corners of the room, until once again there was only the sound of distant trash trucks grinding.

Rex turned the light bulb up to full and everyone slowly got up and came over to sit in a circle. Someone made space for me. I was more than a little nervous, because I was sure they would ask me what I thought, and I really didn't know what to say. I had a sense that it was art, but that it would be more fun to be in it than outside of it, which seemed to me to contradict at least one of the definitions of art.

But Rex simply asked me if I wanted to join. Without hesitation, I said yes. What they were doing was original and like nothing I'd ever seen before. I wanted to learn how to perform with equal commitment.

That night it worried me that I was not able to come up with the words to describe what I'd been through to Meg. But she let me off the hook by saying that it was most likely a nonnarrative, visceral experience, not easily lending itself to linear translation. Thank God for Meg.

A FTER MANY WEEKS, somehow, and I don't know how, Rex and his company got invited to bring the production of *The Tower* to play in grade schools outside St. Louis. We were so happy that someone wanted us somewhere that no one questioned it. Rex divided the company between two rental cars and we were off with our show to St. Louis.

The first school we played at was a rambling single-story clapboard building in the middle of a cornfield about forty-five minutes outside of St. Louis. It looked, on that gray March day, like a combination of an Edward Hopper painting and a set for a new Alfred Hitchcock movie. There was a dirt playground with a baseball diamond and a couple of old tires hanging by a rope from the limb of a giant spreading oak tree. As soon as we stepped out of our cars we saw the school kids flying to the windows of the classrooms, pressing their faces and wildly waving, their teachers pulling them back to their seats, shooting us disdainful glances.

We were all taken in to be shown the sacred performance space. It was the school cafeteria, with the tables and chairs pushed aside. The floor was cold, hard concrete, but the ceiling was quite high, so at least we had a grander heaven to reach up to.

We changed into our leotards in the girls' and boys' toilets and came out to do our warm-ups. It was freezing, and that concrete floor felt hard and ungiving after working all those months on wood. Rex refused to give in to any of these problems and proceeded to carry on as if we were in our laboratory in New York City.

After our warm-up we were all led to a small empty office to wait. We could hear the excited commotion and yelling as the children were ushered into the cafeteria single-file by their teachers. When it was filled to overflowing with screaming kids, Rex guided us through the drafty corridor. I don't know about the rest of the group, but I definitely felt like a Christian being escorted into a Roman arena.

We arrived outside the cafeteria, got down on all fours, and began to crawl, making contact with our personal sounds as we crept. In the distance we could hear the teachers trying to discipline the children by blowing what sounded like police whistles to bring them to order.

We crawled into the cafeteria to almost total silence and awe, broken by a few hysterical whispers. There we all were, crawling in our ripped and tattered leotards, feeling the cold from the concrete floor leaking through to our warm flesh. Three men and three women making strange sounds, groveling on all fours in front of a mob of grade-school children somewhere on the outskirts of St. Louis. Don't think about it, I thought. Just don't think about it.

We crawled to the center of the room to build our tower. At first the kids seemed mesmerized. There was a very intense hush as we moved toward the center. And then it happened. It happened as soon as we began to touch each other to find our balance. As soon as the first one of us touched another, the entire room went wild. Anarchy spread like a brush fire. The children became hysterical. They went out of control and started jumping up and down and spinning like tops. They were screaming and spinning and running toward us and running around us. Police whistles began to blow again. Teachers ran to try to drive the children back, but they slipped through the teachers' arms and legs and ran spinning and shouting toward us. A very large, matronly woman was rushing toward Rex, waving her arms and blowing her police whistle, giving him orders: "Stop this show! Stop this show immediately!"

Rex touched us all like some gentle football coach and said, "Okay, people, clear the space. Clear the space," and we all jumped up and ran for the exit.

Rex was called down to the principal's office while we, completely humiliated, changed back into our street clothes in the girls' and boys' rooms. Then we went back to the empty office to wait. Twenty minutes later Rex came in to join us, his sense of humor still intact. He was smiling when he told us that we were to return to St. Louis to meet Mr. Tweedy, our sponsor.

In St. Louis Mr. Tweedy told Rex that the Missouri Arts Council, which had originally put up the money for our tour, was pulling out. As far as they were concerned the tour was over and they were not about to honor the rest of our contract. Tweedy said it was because we were exposing inappropriate naked flesh to minors and attempting to build obscene body piles in front of schoolchildren. The "inappropriate flesh" had consisted of the patches of skin that had shown through the small rips in our leotards. Mr. Tweedy had most likely lost his job, he told us, and we were banned from Missouri forever. It was, he said, a scandal.

We were totally humiliated. We were stunned. We were cast out of the Garden of Eden. We had lost all innocence about our art. The Tower of Babel had turned into the story of the Expulsion. We had come face-to-face with America and they had found us lacking.

I lost my faith in Rex and the Laboratory. I also lost my faith in America and the chance of ever bringing it art. I was depressed. I even thought that I never wanted to go to Bali.

Meg laughed when I told her the story over beers, and that helped. That made me feel good; once again, telling a story saved me. But where was I to go from there? I knew I no longer had a group I could thrash with.

The Rex Duffy Laboratory Theatre was never the same. Before we went to St. Louis, we never even noticed the holes in our leotards. Now we made jokes about them. Before we went to St. Louis we thought our body configurations as we built our Tower of Babel were sacred and beautiful; now it felt like a group grope. We had not converted Middle America. They had instead oppressed and broken us. We were down and out—at least I was. I now saw myself as a fool for spending so many days rolling on the floor in a dark room when I could have been doing Chekhov.

AFTER MY DISILLUSIONMENT with art I turned to fantasies of Liberation. The idea now was that I would give up on art and just lead a regular life and become liberated by learning how to live it in the moment. The word was clearly out that "being here now" was all there was and you better live now or fall prey later to hellish regrets like Mom's what-ifs. It could drive you mad to wake up to the fact that your whole life has been about chasing some false goal. I wanted to learn how to just be. I wanted now to take a regular job and work toward accomplishing some personal salvation in my life. I wanted to learn how to hang out in the blissful present. After all, if I was eventually going to Bali someday, if I was ever to try to take a perfect vacation, I knew I had to have a life from which to take it. After all, a vacation doesn't exist without a life that you're vacationing from. So I had to have a regular job; but also I wanted to let go of my past, and let go of Mom. I thought that the right way to do this was through Zen meditation, a relatively popular but rigorous route to the blissful present.

Ironically my attraction to Zen was historic. I could see how it was mirrored in Mom's father, my grandfather Benton. He was a man who led a middle-of-the-road life of peaceful New England centeredness. He did nothing in excess. You could almost say he did "nothing in excess" to excess. He was excessively unexcessive. Grampa Benton rarely talked about the past. For that matter, he rarely talked. He was a living example of New England Zen. He was also an example of what we might call the Zen miracle.

The story about the Zen miracle was always one of my favorites. It goes something like this: Some very sensational Hindu miracle worker is having a competitive discussion with a Zen master about various miracles, and the Hindu is discussing how he can fly, walk on the water, and materialize diamonds, rubies, and pearls out of thin air. The Zen master listens quietly, with stern enthusiasm, and then replies, quite simply, "But that's nothing. Listen to the miracles I can perform. When I'm hungry I eat. When I am tired I lie down and sleep."

Grampa Benton never got overly excited. Grampa Benton was a sailor, and the whole way he sailed was a reflection of his calm stability; he was always, as they used to say around the Barrington Yacht Club, "steady as she goes." How he ever fathered such a manic daughter as Mom, I will never know.

To sail with Grampa Benton was to become completely relaxed. Every move he made on that boat was done with New England Zen, with perfect attention and care. He would row the dinghy out to his sailboat, which was named *The Stout Fellow*. Grampa Benton would row his dinghy out to the side of the sailboat, hold it fast and steady while we all climbed aboard. Then he would slip around to the stern of the boat, tie the dinghy on, and come aboard himself. Once all of us were aboard *The Stout Fellow* he would, with some help from Uncle Jib or Dad, prepare the sails and rigging. At last we would motor out of the harbor, with all of us shouting over the sound of the engine, crying out things like "What a beautiful day!" and "Not a cloud in the sky!" and "Couldn't be better!" Grampa Benton would hoist the sail and cut the engine and we'd all pass from that noisy mechanical world into the silent world of wind and sail. There was only the sound of wind in the canvas and the halyards whipping against the mast, and the water rippling along the gunwales as Grampa Benton pulled the mainsheet in, bringing the *The Stout Fellow* onto a high heeling tack toward the great clock tower on the distant Warwick shore.

Around lunchtime, Grampa would let me take the tiller. He would choose a landmark like the Warwick clock tower or Popersquash Point off Bristol, and he'd say, "Just hold it there—steady as she goes." The salt water would spray up in my face and over my bare legs and arms as I sat straining in the shadow of the sail, holding it, steady as she goes.

Then, exactly at noon, as we heard the Warren groaner blasting, Gram Benton would break out lunch. There would be peanut butter and jelly (the grape jelly leaking through the doughy holes in the bread) or egg salad or tuna, all made on Pepperidge Farm bread and wrapped in waxed paper. There would be orange pop and Hires root beer for us kids, and for the adults there would be beautiful frosted cans of Schlitz beer. Gram Benton would pull them out of the cooler, perfect white cans with that strange word "Schlitz" on the brown label. Beads of moisture would drip off the cans as Gram opened them and passed one to Jib and one to Grampa Benton, who would always have only "just one." I loved to watch Gram open those cans of Schlitz for the men. Gram was a Christian Scientist, so she didn't drink, but she was great at opening cans of Schlitz. She pressed the metal church key into the top and then there would be a hiss of foam that sounded just like the name of the beer itself. I always thought the beer had been named after the sound it made while it was being opened. *Snap, hiss, schlitz!*—and up would rise the smell of hops, mixed with the salt smell of bay foam and the spume racing along the gunwales, and for a moment the whole bay was beer. Then Grampa lifted the can to his slightly trembling-in-anticipation lower lip and sipped it down. His giant Adam's apple pumped in and out, letting the foam flood down into his belly. As he looked up from the can to check his navigating points on the Warwick clock tower his face was blissfully relaxed. When he was thirsty he drank, and when his thirst was quenched he stopped. He never confused his biological thirst with a metaphysical thirst, which could be, as in Mom's case, a bottomless pit.

Looking back now, I'd have to say Grampa Benton was a remarkable man, remarkable in the simplest and most unexciting ways; a little distant, but still remarkable. He had his own little advertising firm and only took on the most proven and trustworthy accounts, things like Hospital Brand cough drops. Grampa Benton prepared his only son, Jib, to take over the advertising firm so he could retire at fifty-five years old. He wanted to enjoy the money he made and not leave it behind for others. And he'd say that; he'd speak it right out: "I'm spending it all while I'm here." He also said that if he ever had a stroke and was in any way reduced to a vegetative state, a hammer should be placed by his bed so he could use it before he lost all the strength in his hands. It was a ludicrous scene in my mind, Grampa Benton left alone for a few minutes because Gramma had left him to go get him some cranberry juice or something, and him reaching over, taking that household hammer, and knocking in the side of his own head. What a mess. It didn't seem in his nature to do that, to leave a bloody mess on the pillow for Gramma Benton to clean up.

He didn't retire at fifty-five; he retired at fifty-six. He retired to work in his vegetable garden, where he grew tomatoes, and to take trips with the only woman he'd ever loved. He spent his money traveling with her. They took a freighter to Panama. They went to China to see the Wall. They sailed to Bermuda. They sailed, they walked, they rode bikes, they laughed. They spent all their money. Gramma Benton believed in heaven and Grampa believed that this fantastic accident on Earth was all we had or ever would have. He lived his steady-as-she-goes life with no regrets, and left nothing behind but memories and questions in my mind.

I will never know how manic Mom came out of the union between Gram and Grampa Benton. They were both such steady-as-she-goes types; and Mom, perhaps in reaction, before her dark days, before the sanitarium, was always acting up a storm: tap-dancing in the kitchen, singing, farting, and laughing, always trying to rock the boat.

There is no question but that Mom's suicide was an incomprehensible horror to Gramma and Grampa Benton. After it happened, Coleman and I had a quiet lunch at their house. Cole was always the more confrontational. He tried to speak of Mom's death in the middle of our fresh shrimp salad. Grampa Benton stopped him and said, "No more. I don't want to talk about it. No more." Gramma Benton quickly followed with, "She's better off in heaven now. We know that. She's better off in heaven." We finished our shrimp salad in silence, and I had this strange feeling that Grampa Benton was the only one who could taste his shrimp that day.

S O   I F   T H E R E   W A S   any propensity on my part to take up the path of Zen, it was that steady-as-she-goes quality of Grampa Benton's—coupled with a very beautiful book that had come to me by chance. The book was called *Zen Mind, Beginner's Mind.* It was utterly without pretense or style. If it had any style at all it was that of a very insightful ten-year-old talking. *Zen Mind, Beginner's Mind* read the way Grampa Benton sailed *The Stout Fellow*: beautifully, directly, without complication or unnecessary excitement. It cried out to me to let go of all the manufactured drama in my life, all the hype that I felt I had to make in order to feel I was living, really living. I wanted to be done with that once and for all. Zen was about concentrating on everyday routines, becoming calm and ordinary, making everyday life into a state of present enlightenment.

I began to practice meditation at a Zendo on the Upper West Side, just a short walk across Central Park from my apartment. It was a neat little parquet box of a place, relatively quiet and without dust, which is a rare phenomenon in New York City. I'd go over there two or three times a week, sit for an hour and count my breath while I looked at the blank white wall. It was good. There were only two things I didn't like. One was the smell of incense. It made me sneeze. The other was the fact that you were required to count your breath from one to ten, over and over. When you got to ten you'd go back to one and start again, and this made me feel completely hemmed in by numbers. I could see the number attached to each breath. I could see a 1, then a 2, and so on rise up from my diaphragm and go up and out of my nose. The room filled with numbers, numbers everywhere, hundreds of 1-to-10s. Except for the numbers and the incense, my Zen sittings were all quite relaxing and centering.

On the other hand, my new sort of regular job was not so relaxing and centering, which I guess is often the case. It was not a regular job so much as a full-time part-time job, in the recently finished Gulf & Western Building at Columbus Circle. I was in charge of making sure all the right office furniture was placed in all the right offices. And each day I could see my job heading toward termination, because each day we'd be on a higher floor, working our way to the top.

It was an absurd job, because all the furniture looked exactly the same. The movers, who were very aware of this, kept trying to shove any old generic piece of furniture into any old generic office. My job was to stop them from doing it. My job was to get the properly tagged desk and chair into the properly numbered office. Visually it didn't matter, so I completely sympathized with the furniture movers, and I'm afraid they knew that. But I could in no way behave as if I did. I had to use all my old acting techniques to pretend that I was very very concerned that all the tags on the furniture matched up with all the office numbers.

It really was a horrid job, but I didn't have much money—nothing outside of the little modeling I was doing on the side. And the worst of it was that the building was hermetically sealed. None of the windows would open, so we had to breathe that same foul recycled air all day. I was constantly drowsy. When I couldn't fight the sleep anymore, I would go up to one of the empty floors of the building, pick one of the empty offices, stretch out on the gray industrial carpeting, and take a quick nap. In most cases such naps would be disastrous, because I'd come back to all the wrong furniture in all the wrong rooms. Then I'd have to act angry and say things like "Okay, you guys, hey, come on, don't tell me you guys are fucking up again! Can't I go make a phone call to the boss man without you messing up this goddamned furniture?" They would just laugh and whisper behind my back. They could see right through me, and we all knew it, but I went on with my act anyway, and they grumbled as they proceeded to rearrange the furniture.

As for my nights with Meg, they were strained and strange. When I wasn't out meditating at the Zendo, I was reading books on Zen. Thinking that it was destroying my meditative consciousness, I cut back on my beer intake, and it was like losing a relationship with my best friend. The evenings with Meg were sober and quiet. I'd also given up telling her stories about my day, because I felt that it was bad to dwell so much on the past. It wasn't very Zen. Meg missed the stories most of all. She missed them more than I did and tried to convince me that to be able to tell a good story about the immediate past and be very present in the telling of it was to be very present in a very Zen way. "After all," Meg said, "aren't there hundreds of little stories about Zen, little Zen anecdotes all over the place? Aren't the stories told to illustrate the philosophy of Zen?"

"Oh yes, yes," I agreed. But I was not one who could tell such Zen stories, because I was just a novice and I knew nothing of the subject. I thought I'd better shut up for a while and meditate until I got closer to some insight. So at night I would read *Zen Mind, Beginner's Mind* and Meg would read *A Brief History of the Oriental Rug.*

I really don't know why we continued to live in the big city. I think it was just our inertia. I was using the Gulf & Western Building as a sort of thermometer and figured we would move once it got filled up with furniture—that is, if Meg was ready to give up her museum job. Ever since Bobby Kennedy was shot and Phil, our cat, ran behind Meg's first framed piece of art and smashed it, she had been shying away from art. She saw these disasters as a kind of sign, I think. She was suffering from despair and mourning the loss of Robert Kennedy. I wanted her to go back to art. "Please," I said, "why don't you start drawing again?" I'd begun to realize that all this time Meg had been doing a kind of Zen with her charcoal landscape drawings. I didn't see how she could give them up to study rugs, of all things—*rugs!* But she wanted to travel now and saw those Oriental rugs as the magical flying carpets that would get us out of New York City. I think she secretly saw, as many of us did then, the decline and fall of America, but was unable to talk about it. She just wanted to flee from it and have a foreign experience. And she saw order in the patterns of those rugs beyond anything she could ever accomplish in her drawings. They were patterns that calmed her, ancient patterns.

As for me, I was planning to take a big retreat at the Dogen Zen center in the Poconos as soon as we filled the top floor of the Gulf & Western Building with that god-awful gray-and-chrome furniture. In order to get it done I'd even taken up smoking cigars. This seemed to make the furniture men trust me more, or at least respect me and listen when I'd act angry. I was smoking those cheap rum-soaked crooked cigars and suddenly the right furniture started ending up in the right place without me even having to be there.

We finished filling the top floor in early spring and all of us celebrated with a few bottles of André champagne. I've never been more happy to be out of a job.

I rode up to the Dogen Zen center in the Poconos with a bunch of fellow meditators from the Upper West Side Zendo. Everyone was jabbering away, because we all knew we were going to have to stop talking for seven days as soon as we got there. The thought of seven intensive days of meditation with no talking had me more than a little claustrophobic.

There was a long dirt road that led into an old converted hotel next to a trout stream. It was spring and trees and bushes were just budding.

The hotel was divided into separate dorm rooms for men and women, as well as a kitchen and a main recreation room that had now been converted into the meditation chamber. It was all done in a blend between a sort of Japanese restaurant and an American hunting lodge.

Best of all, there was an authentic resident Japanese Zen master to guide and instruct us in our meditations. I was longing for enlightenment. I was hot for it, and couldn't wait to begin sitting.

Sitting was exactly what we did. We sat and sat. We sat for fourteen hours a day. We were up at five-thirty in the morning and were sitting by six. After a short morning sitting there was breakfast, then a sitting until lunch, then a short rest, then an afternoon sitting, then dinner, then an evening sitting, and to bed by nine. I never dreamed I would do such a crazy thing to myself: to sit with my eyes open staring at a white wall while counting my breath from one to ten over and over again. I never could have done it without the others, and of course our Zen master, who seemed to be the most highly charged and awake man I'd ever come across. He was vibrating.

His name was Hara Sho Roshi and he was a fiery little speedball with a shaved head, dressed in the most colorful Japanese robes. He looked like a big bullet, like a decorated bomb, like something you might load a big circus cannon with.

We wore only plain brown cotton monks' robes, which felt kind of sexy to me. At first I didn't wear any underwear under the robes, but then I realized that might detract from my concentration.

There were about thirty of us, men and women, all sitting in a row cross-legged on round black cushions, just staring at a white wall, counting our breaths. I sat there counting my breath, watching my thoughts flow, watching the numbers come up out of my nose. There goes a number 7, there goes a number 6, there goes a number 5 floating right across the room. Now, when I say I was "watching my thoughts," they weren't exactly thoughts so much as they were images and memories that would come in from the storage in my mind. In fact, I'd say that everything I have told you so far about myself came to mind in one form or another in the first two days of that seven-day sitting.

The best time at the Zendo was mealtime. No one was allowed to talk, so all you could do was chew and taste, just chew and taste your food. It was a simple vegetarian diet with lots of brown rice, but I'd never had such a pure and intense taste sensation before. Original sin, I began to think, was not Adam eating the apple but Adam not eating it slowly enough to really enjoy it. We couldn't do a running commentary about how things tasted; we just tasted. It was the same when we walked outside for our fresh-air breaks. No one said things like "Oh, what a beautiful spring day! Oh, look at those red buds!" or "My God, isn't that silver shine on the trout stream just wonderful?" Instead we became the silver stream and the red buds. Just like it said in the books, it happened. Without words or commentary we became a part of it all and blended with those spring breezes and the land and the light around us. It was all new and glorious and very confusing. At times I thought I was getting closer to enlightenment.

Then around the third day of sitting things began to get more than a little claustrophobic. I was stuck in my past. Memory felt almost like a substance now. Memory felt like the only thing that was real. I was trapped with myself and wanted desperately to get out, but had no idea what there was outside of myself. Memories of my past played over and over again. Memories flowed into horrors of hindsight and regret, thoughts of how I would do things differently if only I could relive them, if only I could come back with the knowledge that I had now. That would truly be heaven. Then I'd realize I'd forgotten to count my breath and I'd be back in the numbers again.

Every morning Hara Sho Roshi would give us a little talk after breakfast, just a little talk to help fuel our meditations. The first morning he said that to study Zen is to study ourselves and to study ourselves is to forget ourselves. This was wonderfully paradoxical, I thought, but I was frustrated that I couldn't quite figure it out. He said only then will we be free to return to what he called "Big Mind." He said before we were born we had no feeling and were one with the universe. He called this "mind only" or "Big Mind." Then at birth we are separated into individual minds, but we can still have the experience of Big Mind as we sit here in small mind. We can still experience the ground from which we came. He told us that many sensations and images would come and go, but they are just mind waves from our small mind and we should not get attached to them. We should just let them come and go until we reach the calm of Big Mind at last.

I had no idea what Big Mind could look like, would look like or feel like once it came, but I sure was hankering for it. At the same time I knew that if I wanted to come into it, I'd have to give up all my hankerings and just sit and count my breath from one to ten.

And so it went into the third day: a torturous review of my small, sad mind, my small life with no Big Mind in view, nothing larger than myself and my memory over and over. Then, some time on the afternoon of the third day, the black-and-white porn movies began.

I had no sense that I was creating them. It was as though they were being projected on the wall, and for a while I wondered if the two people sitting on either side of me could see them, too.

They started with images of the most splendidly erect penises and full, rolling balls. I hadn't seen many penises in my life outside of a few photographs and that one time at the Boston bus station when I absentmindedly looked down while urinating and the man at the next urinal was fingering his giant erection while smiling up at me and winking. I stopped peeing. My dick shriveled and I got out of there real fast. Why, I wondered, could I take so much pleasure in looking at my own cock but be completely repulsed by the sight of someone else's? And here now on the Zendo wall were these giant disembodied erect cocks with balls with little fluttering wings like butterfly wings growing out of them. These cocks were flying and diving all over the place. They were soaring on the white plaster walls of this Poconos Zendo, and I didn't know what to make of them. I think because they were disconnected and kind of fetishized things unto themselves, I could enjoy them. If they were attached to some big hairy male body I might have been repulsed.

But I couldn't figure out who was making them up. I didn't feel like I was doing it. And the more I tried not to hold onto them (sure that they were small-mind ephemera), the more baroque the images seemed to become. Soon the wall was also full with vaginas, as though my mind were creating a weird Garden of Eden, inhabited only by sex organs. The vaginas looked like fleshy butterflies in flight. They were deliciously swollen, pink, puckering vaginas, with a little edge of black hair around them. They would fly and then stop and flutter and pose and then start flying again all around the zooming cocks. The whole wall became a film of a springtime meadow of cocks and cunts. The cocks were soaring and diving into the butterfly vaginas. When they got to one, they'd glide in and pump real hard for a moment and then fly on to another vagina, like bees pollinating a flower. The cocks never seemed to come or spurt or wilt. They remained erect, like hot buttered corn, just pumping in and out. In and out, in and out they'd go.

After a while the cocks and cunts got connected to bodies. Then things really got hot, let me tell you. I'd never seen anything like it in my life, so I knew I wasn't recalling it from some pictures I'd observed in the past. A body pile of naked men and women, the most outrageous combinations ever imagined, began to appear on the white wall in front of me. They were gobbling and pumping and gobbling and licking and sucking and pumping, like the sounds of a toilet plunger. No, *hundreds* of sucking toilet plungers. And I got so excited by this that I had a beast of an erection popping right up through the fly of my underwear, straight up into the brown cotton meditation robes, turning them into what looked like a Bedouin tent.

I have to say I'd never encountered anything like what I saw and heard on the walls of that Poconos Zendo. And I had no interest in transcending it. As I watched this, all my feeling, as well as my mind, drained like a giant waterfall, down, down until it filled up my cock and balls. It felt all right and good and I didn't want to go beyond it. I was no longer experiencing small mind, I was sure, or my past history. I was experiencing for the first time in my life pure cock mind. I was stuck there, very much stuck there.

During the course of our daily meditations we were allowed one three-minute audience with Hara Sho Roshi in which we could discuss our particular meditation problems. We were asked not to discuss anything psychological, because he was not trained or versed in such matters. We were only to discuss the quality of our particular meditation practice. I really didn't want to tell him about the flying cocks and cunts, yet at the same time I felt drawn to participate in at least one session with him just to see what he was like face-to-face. So on the fourth day I went to see him.

Everyone who wanted to see him would pass in silence to a small room just off the main meditation room and sit until we were touched on the shoulder by one of the resident American Zen monks. Then we were to go in and sit cross-legged directly across from Hara Sho Roshi and speak our Zen minds directly to him.

As I sat there waiting, I reviewed what I was going to say. Should I describe the porn films, I wondered, or reduce it to a simple statement

like "I'm seeing a lot of strange things on the wall"? Then I decided
that I would just try to be in the moment and take it from there, just
see what came up while sitting across from him.

I was touched on the shoulder and led in and I was overwhelmed
by what I saw. There he sat before me, Hara Sho Roshi, dressed in
Japanese robes of silver, cream, and crimson. There he sat rock-hard
in full lotus, like a beautiful Zen statue, like a Buddha. He sat with
his back to the window, which looked out to the trout stream. The
window emitted the most incredible white spring light, which spread
and emanated like a silver aura off of Hara Sho Roshi's robes. It was
as though his robes were radiating that light, and as I looked closer
I could see it growing out of the back of his head, like a silver halo.
I just sat there stunned, looking into his dancing eyes, and for a
moment the whole room seemed to be filled with love; and yet how
could it have been? I hardly knew this strange head-shaved Japanese
man.

Hara Sho Roshi said sternly and directly, "Sit! Speak! What do
you have to say to me?"

I sat, feeling like this humble little boy back in Christian Science
Sunday school. My whole body felt like the body of a young boy and
I said softly, hearing the odd sound of my voice for the first time in
four days, "I'm seeing a lot of strange things on the wall."

And he, speaking now in the low, deeply centered voice of a Zen
roshi, said, "Those are only small-mind waves that will pass. Soon you
will be in Big Mind. Continue your meditations with vigor." And
then he dismissed me and I went back to the endless porn films on the
wall.

Then on the fifth day it happened. It came completely unexpect-
edly, as I assume something like that must. It came like a great clear
sky at the end of a storm. I was just sitting there on my Zen cushion
with my spine and cock fully erect watching a particularly complicated
daisy chain of naked men and women all intertwined in the most
complicated pleasure connections. They were all moving together in
one mindless pumping motion, as though they'd taken off their minds
along with their clothes and checked them at the door. They were now
engaged in this mindless superhump—the way we all might be in this
meditation room, I thought, if only it was a hotel for swingers. (I was

beginning to think that that's what it might have been before it was turned into a Zendo. Maybe I was seeing leftover energy on the wall from the history of that place.) And just as I was contemplating that idea, everything suddenly broke and went clear—just as clear as that time I had seen the stars on LSD. Suddenly there was no me observing. There was only the room and bare essential presence. It was as though I was the whole room and the whole room was me, and we were all sitting breathing together. The room had breath, everyone had breath, it was one big swelling breath, and we were all one with it. There was no boundary, and as I breathed I could feel the whole room breathe and expand with breath so that now the room was breathing and there was hardly any me left, only breath and a room and all of us breathing together, and at the same time there was just enough awareness left in me to feel the magnificence of it all, the magnificence and beatitude of what I guess was Big Mind, and my God, how sweet it was. I don't know how long it lasted. It couldn't have been very long, maybe a few seconds, and then it burst, just like a precious soap bubble.

It was broken by some grasping analytic mind in me that leaped on it like a tiger, ripping and tearing. This beast of analysis leaped upon this precious moment and tore it to bits: "What was that? How do I name that? How do I explain it to Meg or to anyone? How do I tell its story?" And then, *poof,* the Big Mind moment was gone, gone into a new memory, the memory of it blended now with other memories from my past, which blended with the porn films on the wall. I sat there for the next three days longing for what I thought was Big Mind to come again. I felt so very sad; I had looked through a window into a landscape that seemed larger than me, and yet a part of me. I'd experienced it and it might never come again. I felt so very, very sad that I sat there with tears flowing down and dripping onto my perpetual erection which poked up under my Zen robes.

At the end of seven days of silence I was popping to talk. I was bursting at the mouth, and what amazed me was that no one else at the Zendo seemed to have the same need as I did. I came into the men's dorm room just after we were allowed to speak again and a fellow meditator was making his bed. As soon as I saw him I burst into a vivid description of all I'd seen, felt, and heard over the past six days. He would not even turn from what he was doing. I told him about Big

Mind and the hot-buttered-corn cocks with wings and the butterfly cunts, and he just turned to me very directly and said, "There are things to be done."

All I wanted to do was talk. It was as though the meditation experience had simply fed more into my storytelling library rather than bringing me the power of insight and value of focused silence.

It was the same driving home. All the people in the car seemed more interested in maintaining the silence they had cultivated than talking about what happened to them there. They just sat there and looked out the window, while I babbled on and on about the butterfly cunts and flying cocks and Big Mind versus small mind. All that silence had made me sad and a little crazy. The silence allowed the great and always present sadness behind words to rise up in me, and I didn't like it one bit. It covered me like a great gray web. For the rest of the trip I rode in silence thinking about Grandpa Benton, and I realized for the first time that I'd never known him beyond his style of control and order. That upright, uptight pillar of the community. That steady-as-she-goes man. And for one dark moment I wondered if Mom had gotten beyond that in him. Had they ever touched hearts? I wondered.

Meg was happy to see me and I was happy to see her and to be back in our nest again. Our apartment looked completely new and vivid compared to that empty wall I'd been looking at for so long. Well, not exactly empty, but certainly black-and-white. Our apartment seemed to shimmer with light and color. I was immediately struck by another reason I loved Meg so much. She instinctively knew how to make a neat, comfortable little place to get centered in. She could make a home anywhere. This is why she stayed in New York City, I was sure. She had settled in here for better or worse and realized that one place was no different from another once you made your nest in it. I was happy to be home in a place with colors, shapes, and forms and lots of small mind. It was as though now that Meg had given up doing her charcoal drawing, she had put her creativity into making the apartment perfect, like a work of art we could live in with our cat, Phil.

In a nonstop gush I told Meg all that had happened at the Zendo over the past seven days. She listened with rapt attention. She smiled, she laughed, and at times she laughed so hard I thought that, like Mom, she would wet her pants. I could tell she was happy to have her old storyteller back, and for a while I was happy to be telling stories, to be opening and pouring beers again after not having one for so long. And that old welcome fuzzy feeling returned, that beery fuzz that clouded all thoughts of mortality and creeping time.

BEFORE I WENT to the Zendo it had never occurred to me to pay money to see people have sex. It had never occurred to me to go to a porn film, although they were beginning to be more and more popular at the time. *Deep Throat* was the rage, and *Behind the Green Door*—things like that. I simply wasn't interested. But now that I was out of work, I was back on the streets walking again, and I found that I had become obsessed with women's bodies. Most specifically, I was focused on asses, particularly asses that filled out faded jeans. I could follow a dungaree ass for blocks and blocks until I'd find myself lost in neighborhoods I'd never seen before. Then the dungaree ass would disappear into a doorway and I'd just stand there totally frustrated, looking for another dungaree ass to follow out of that neighborhood to another one.

This was a major change in my life. I'd never experienced anything like this before, never; and I wasn't sure if it was a sign that I was becoming a man or if it was a symptom of some sort of growing obsessive-compulsive condition.

When I first moved to New York City in 1967 I had spent some time with a friend who had lived in the city for a long time. I considered him a pretty normal, meat-and-potatoes kind of guy. By that I mean he was married and watched a lot of baseball on TV. He drank a few beers when he watched it. The rest of the time, when he wasn't working as an actor, or wasn't with his wife, or watching a ball game on TV, he was girl watching. It was impossible to take a walk with him without him stopping every few feet to ooh and aah and ogle some new woman. "Oh, my fuckin' word, look at that piece," he'd say. And here I'd been trying to talk to him about philosophical issues, the meaninglessness of life, the shortness of time. It never occurred to me to ogle women on the street. I don't mean I was ignoring them or not noticing them so much as I was just taking them in as a part of the whole picture, along with men, children, trees, dogs, cars, and buildings; I rarely selected a fragment to fetishize in those days. And now I found myself in that boat, and I had no idea how I got into it, how to get out of it, or if I even wanted out. I was just walking around like a dog with his tongue hanging out. That was the way of the world for me then, and I tried not to judge it. I tried to be open.

Asses led to more asses. I'd follow them anywhere. I felt biologically determined, like those cocks on the wall, the way they flew from cunt to cunt like bees flying from flower to flower. I was a walking penis with no mind. I would spy a young woman in dungarees on the subway and just lock onto her rear with my eyes. When she'd get off the subway at her stop, I would get off and follow her. I would follow that ass again until some door slammed in my face, leaving me standing there on the street looking for another one. Eventually I would find an ass that would lead me home to Meg.

Soon it was not enough to see the asses clad in dungarees; I had to see them naked. Yes, nude. I had to see the way they were put together, the way they shook. I had to feel them. I was too shy, too embarrassed, too considerate really, to just stop women and ask them if they would, you know, take me inside and pull down their pants. Instead I discovered pornographic movies. I was not interested in the plot; I was interested only in the bare asses. I was just interested in seeing women naked. And as many as I possibly could see; so I'd go to the cheap porn films. I'd go to a theater on Eighth Avenue. It was called Eros II, and you could see four or five porn movies in the afternoon for a dollar ninety-nine.

Like any drug, it decreased in its effect over time. At first I was instantly mesmerized and turned on by the sight of all those naked bodies doing all those crazy naked things. I would just stand there in the aisle of the theater with my mouth hanging open and my eyes glazed and transfixed. This hypnotic condition was not unfamiliar to me. I had read about it in *The Tibetan Book of the Dead*. The book instructs that as you die and leave your body, you must keep your eyes on the clear white light and must not look away, lest you see the image of a copulating couple and get drawn back, sucked back into the womb, trapped and reborn in yet another life. But I could not understand how a clear white light could be more attractive than an open womb.

After my eyes adjusted to the movie theater and to those naked strangers doing it on a twenty-foot screen, I'd try to find a seat down front and away from everyone else. I preferred not to have other people's heads in front of me, so that I could imagine it was all being shown just for me, not for the obsessive-compulsive businessmen on lunch breaks and bums and street people catching up on their sleep. I didn't want to see them and I didn't want to be seen.

I was more than a little nervous about sitting down in the theater because I was sure that the businessmen were always slowly and silently working themselves off under their coats. As for me, I never masturbated in a porn theater. In fact I rarely even got an erection. I was all in my eyes. That's where the stimulation was going on. I was in my eyes, memorizing the images that I was seeing so that I could replay them while I was having sex with Meg. It may have been lack of imagination on my part, a need to collect other people's erotic images.

Meg had no idea why I'd come in off the streets of New York so horny, but she didn't question it. She had an absolutely fantastic ass, and she would leave her boots on for me. That was the only thing she didn't take off, her brown Italian boots, her high boots with the zippers on the side.

I'd never seen that in a movie. I saw this: Mother addressing daughter, "Gloria, your new flute teacher is just about to arrive. I'm going out for lunch with friends, then I'm going bowling, then I'm going shopping, and I won't, and I mean will *not,* be back for hours and hours and hours, so don't you get into any trouble, Gloria. You hear me? Don't you get into any trouble while I'm gone. You have a nice flute lesson, you hear? Give me a kiss now. Goodbye, dear." Mother exits; flute teacher arrives; then, "Hi, Mr. Flute Teacher, blah, blah, blah." Two or three scales are played on the flute; then, "Let's fuck."

After a while it got boring. You know, back shot of an asshole and tight scrotum pumping, pumping, so you got a chance to compare the size of your balls with his; a side shot of his long flesh shaft going in and out, in and out, accompanied by a generic sound track of moans and groans and a few select words like "Do it to me," "Oh, it feels so good," or "Don't stop now." Finally, there was the horrible per-functory cum shot in which the man had to pull out and bring himself off on the woman's belly, she pretending to love it and rub it into her flesh as though just feeling his warm cum was making her come.

I could not break through. I could not feel it. I could not get to the other side of the screen and be in it—and that's what I wanted. I wanted to feel what the sex I was seeing was like. I felt lonely, so lonely and outside. When I felt that way I'd flee the theater and try to fill myself with some other more wholesome images, if I could find them. That was rare, so I'd walk all the way home until I was exhausted and then would come on to Meg. I couldn't believe that all of this, this obsession for porn films, had come from Zen meditation in the Poconos.

Again, I longed for a way out and found it one afternoon at the Eros II. I don't remember the plot. I'd really given up on plots at that point. What I remember is that extraordinary close-up of a very tanned long-legged woman with a fantastic manipulatable ass. She was being fucked by two very long-donged guys, and I'd never seen anything like that, not even on the walls of the Poconos Zendo. It was like a sexual circus act. She was totally filled up. One cock was all the way up into her ass, just wedged there pumping, and the other was pumping away in the more traditional palce, and still to this day I don't understand how their bodies were arranged, because it was such a close-up, all you were seeing was two pumping cocks and one sucking cunt. I don't know how they timed it or what the director said to them or what the cue was, but both men pulled out and came at the same time, and the extraordinary thing was that she not only had her period but she also had a very bad case of diarrhea. So as the dicks unplugged from her and shot their white loads, an ocean of menstrual blood and hot brown watery shit mixed with semen gushed with such force that it actually sprayed the lens of the camera and turned the whole thing into an abstract Chinese landscape painting. The audience groaned. The bums woke up and moaned. I'd never seen such a responsive audience. They choked, they gasped, they got up and fled from the theater with more energy than they ever had coming in. For the first time the place was alive with vibrant energy. I stayed. I was mesmerized. If the smell was there I too would have retched and run. But I'd never seen such a beautiful work of art.

I never went back to the porn films after that. I felt like something inside of me had been completed.

T H E R E ' S   A N   O L D   Tantric idea that excessive indulgence in sex can take you to the other side and free you of a need for it. I thought I was going to have a chance to test it. I could see opportunity looming on the horizon in India, of all places. Yes, I was off to try to take a vacation in India, the place where Tantric sex began.

Meg had the great idea to import Kashmiri rugs and sell them at one of the New York City flea markets. She had saved some money and borrowed enough money from her father to pay for two round-trip tickets and buy the rugs. I had saved money from unemployment and my furniture-moving job to live there, so we were off.

One minute we were in New York City feeling like it was the center of the world and the next minute we were in Amsterdam, stopping over on the way to India, riding in from the Amsterdam airport, looking out the bus window at people skating on the frozen canals. It was a dark, cold, ancient Brueghel scene: small fires burning on the ice with lean, dark figures skating all around. When I could see it as a picture, I felt safe, but when I saw the people as living, individuated others, I felt undermined and depleted, uncentered and swept away, like that time on the beach with Mom at Jib's out-of-the-blue homecoming when I first perceived that there was a world elsewhere. Now, riding into Amsterdam with Meg, seeing all those people skating, I had a deeply disturbing thought: Why me here—why can't I be them out there? It was ludicrous, but at that moment I had the fantasy that there was a choice involved and I could have been some Dutch person skating out there instead of who I was. That feeling permeated my entire being, stole me away, reduced me to a frozen scarecrow, a heap of overstuffed winter clothing sitting beside Meg.

We got off the bus and looked for a taxi to take us to the home of our friends Hans and Sonia as a cold wind swept down. I could not visualize the place from which that wind blew. In New York I would imagine Chicago and the sweeping plains, or Albany and Montreal; but now I couldn't tell. I could imagine nothing of the landscape beyond that little patch of street on which we stood, all hunched in the cold. We were in Holland, the tulip capital of the world, and it was cold and gray and there was not a tulip in sight, but it didn't matter because it was all new and beyond tulips.

Hans and Sonia were a mime team. I had seen them doing a street mime in Washington Square a year before and offered to put them up for a few nights when they needed a place to stay. Meg thought it was real weird of me to drag them back to our apartment, because she knew how much I hated mime. But they weren't so bad; at least they didn't work in whiteface, and they seemed to be genuinely in love. They treated each other with mutual respect and concern, holding hands, touching each other in a nice simple way. We planned to spend the night with them and then fly out to Delhi on Air India the next afternoon.

Sonia was pregnant and looked radiant. Hans was his old tall, dour self. We ate thick Dutch homemade pea soup with little hot dogs cut up in it and drank room-temperature beer. Everything tasted good. The feeling in my eyes and mouth was like a child's. We were four kids all having our own little backyard party. The only reality that dimmed that fantasy was Sonia's pregnant belly.

Meg and I slept under an old cozy Dutch eiderdown in their attic room. I dropped off to the sound of the north wind blowing like it was coming from the cheeks and lips of a storybook Mr. North Wind cloud. The banging of old rusty iron shutters and the shivering of distant buildings turned my dreams into a great animated cartoon of winter.

I was awake the whole next night straining on Air India to see anything, any glimpse of the wildly imagined landscape below. Meg slept while I pressed my nose to the window and saw a portion of my face, reflected, which I first mistook for Turkey or Saudi Arabia.

Soon it was dawn, but we were too high up and over too many clouds to see anything of the earth below. Meg was still asleep. Almost everyone else was too, so I felt free to explore.

I stretched my legs near the cockpit door, and with that haphazard boldness that often comes from lack of sleep I just reached down and turned the handle, stepping into the cockpit, where there were three Indian men all dressed in pilot uniforms. No one protested or acted surprised, as it all continued like a waking dream. Slowly adjusting to the intricate, innumerable dials and panels, I zeroed in on two of the pilots, who were carefully taping a newspaper comic strip across the front window with two rolls of Scotch tape. I could see nothing but funny papers. "What are you doing?" I cried. Both pilots turned toward me, their heads bobbing like strange dolls. "We are flying directly into the sun now; we are on automatic pilot." I forced a smile and staggered back to my seat. There it was, spread below my window like an endless hot, colorless mud pie: India. I didn't want the plane to land. I felt like I'd already seen too much.

I was dazed in the airport. I followed Meg like a somnambulist. She turned and pointed and following her hand I was swept away into some other world. It was a strange family scene she pointed at—not a family waiting for a plane but a family engaged in communal repair work on a brick airport wall. They were mixing mortar in an old wooden trough. A slight man, dressed only in a loincloth, was squatting by the trough, playing with the mortar like a fascinated child. A woman dressed in a beautiful sari stood chipping at the brick with a little trowel. Surrounding them was what I took to be the rest of the family: an older woman in a sari pouring tea and two young girls holding babies in slings. The scene was slow and self-contained, like some strange piece of theater composed to usher travelers into the rhythms of ancient India. We watched and we sighed. We felt something together, like "Here we are at last."

Like the trip from the airport into Amsterdam, the ride into Delhi was confusing; but there was no time to reflect on it. We both held on for dear life as the cab careened through streets of chaos. I only had time for two thoughts: one, how Gandhi had ever imagined he could bring peace and order into such a place, and two, that I did not want to die here and that was what I felt was about to happen. Precarious, chaotic, whimsical anarchy is all I saw. Our driver leaned on the horn the whole way, which made a high-pitched, crazy, raspy, tinny sound as he wove from lane to lane, trying to avoid the huge cows that were standing docile in the road like stuffed museum pieces. People in the sweaty hundreds squatted by the edge of the road doing everything Western people usually do in the deepest privacy of their bathrooms. Motorcycles buzzed by with whole families balanced on them, Mom in her sari sitting sidesaddle behind smiling Dad, a baby in her arms, a child behind her, and another one balanced on the gas tank between Dad and the handlebars, and they were all smiling this crazy smile. It would not have surprised me to see one of them doing an Indian classical dance on Dad's head. Big, steaming colored dump trucks roared by; on one of them we saw a man dressed in shorts riding balanced on the front fender, one hand holding the side of the hood up while his other he adjusted the carburetor, working the throttle while another man steered his truck through flower vendors, crazy people, happy people, dying people. The scent of jasmine, and the smell, the great smell of streets mixed with cheap diesel fumes. This was an overpopulated world, and it immediately brought up those old colonialist attitudes in me: There must be some order imposed here immediately! There are too many people in the world! Humankind is a virus that must be stopped! . . . I never sensed my father in me more—that constant, almost fascistic craving he had for order and control at all costs.

Exhausted, we reached our little hotel. I just wanted to go upstairs, lock myself in our room, lie on the bed with the overhead fan on, and read about India. I never wanted to see that insane, chaotic vision in person again.

I tried to make plans to avoid the lack of structure that might sweep one or both of us into the country's irrational, crazy mouth. But I needed some direction; I needed to be in India for a reason. It was clearly no place to take a vacation.

Meg had direction: her rugs. I needed to tap into my own interests. I didn't want to live through Meg, to be led through the rug markets of India like a helpless child. We both decided that it would be good for our relationship to explore a little independence, to see if we had developed a center that we could come and go from. But my idea of freedom, although I didn't voice it, was sexual freedom. I was stuck in some adolescent mode and I could only equate freedom with the ability to get laid anywhere, with anyone I wanted.

I heard there was a new guru in India who dealt exactly with that problem. He had a huge following of Westerners. His name was Bhagwan Shree Rajneesh, and word had it that he advocated you could only get over your need for constant sex and get into greater spiritual realms by having so much sex that you got sick of it. His theory, or at least the way it came down to me, was that because sex had been forbidden by our puritanical parents, we all thought—as I did—that sex was what we wanted more than anything else in the world. Until we got past that, we would never grow up; we would never pass on to larger issues of commitment and meaningful labor. And best of all, what the Bhagwan advocated for getting through these sexual hang-ups was doing it—doing a lot of it. He preached a kind of homeo-pathic sex cure, fucking your way to the other side. And if there was anything I needed a cure from, it was those compulsive thoughts about sex. All I wanted was to get laid over and over again with a stranger. I had the notion that pure, isolated, uncomplicated, nonintegrated sex could cure me. Sex was best for me with Meg when I could manage to turn her into a stranger through fantasy, and that was getting more and more difficult. So I wanted to keep Meg as a comfortable friend and explore the rivers of anonymous Dionysian sex; that was my idea. I had to go to that island of licentiousness, that bastion of free love located right in the middle of the sexiest-sounding town in India, Poona. I was sure the Bhagwan had a great sense of humor and had decided to locate his free love ashram there just for the turn-on of that name, Poona. Can you imagine pooning in Poona? Just saying it gave me an erection.

Before we explored my sexual healing and her rugs, Meg and I made the mistake of deciding to see one or two of the sights together. It was the end of February and still pleasant, but we were told that within a month's time it would begin to get too hot to travel and by April it would be unbearable.

Our first side trip was Meg's idea. She wanted to see the Taj Mahal. I wasn't real interested; I'd never been keen on grand palaces. But Meg really wanted to see the Taj and I agreed, because after the

Taj I wanted to see Benares and Meg wasn't real interested in *that*. We made a deal to take turns.

On the train to Agra to see the Taj, Meg ate some scrambled eggs. Two hours later, just as we stepped onto a glorious walkway that led over golf-course-green lawns being cut by giant lawn mowers pulled by white Brahma bulls, Meg collapsed into a moaning heap. She had never been in such pain, she cried. I didn't know what to do. I was torn. There was one of the wonders of the world, a trumpeting edifice of white marble just crying out to be explored, and here was my girlfriend practically dying at my feet. I'm ashamed to admit it, but I did it: I left Meg in a heap and ran to the Taj to take a quick peek. Of course I couldn't enjoy it. With the thought of Meg lying out there in a sick heap on the lawn I could hardly see it. But I could hear it. It was crowded with Indian tourists all calling out and yelling to hear their echo, although there were Silence signs hanging everywhere.

By the time I got back, Meg had dragged herself into the shade of a flame tree and some sort of Indian holy man was bending over her, trying to force-feed her something. I could see her groaning and turning away from the Indian as he held a dirty glass of some vile liquid to her lips. He said, "Please, I am trying to give the madam some health." Meg was moaning, "No, no, no, take him away, Brewster. Please take him away."

By that point I was almost carrying Meg. She was doubled over in pain. I managed to find a bicycle rickshaw, and as we headed for town I screamed at the rickshaw driver, "Doctor! Doctor! Doctor!"

He took us to a small clinic in Agra. There was a long line outside, but when the people saw two Westerners, one of whom was in great pain, they stood aside to let us pass.

As soon as the doctor saw her he wanted to give her a shot. I said, "But do you have throw-away needles?" and he said, "Did you bring your own?"

Whatever was in that shot calmed Meg's stomach down. We took a room in a small hotel nearby and both of us fell right into a deep sleep.

We awoke very early the next day, and still in half-sleep, without breakfast, we took a rickshaw to the train and that's when it happened again: we went back in time. It was ancient, ancient, ancient. There were no sounds of motors, not a car anywhere, only thatched huts and shacks and people coming out of the shacks in multicolored robes only to lift them and squat in a soft morning haze of burning cow dung, amid the moans of cows and the easy, soft pedaling sound of our rickshaw. Both of us sat there silent and suspended in the newness of a place that had not changed its slow habits for two thousand years.

In Benares we decided we would splurge and stay in a Western-style hotel where I could buy Indian beer and we'd have a small swimming pool. We arrived at night, went to sleep early, and got up early. It was still dark when we woke a sleeping rickshaw driver and got him to take us to the ghats on those holy shores of the Ganges.

It was still dark when we arrived. There were very few people around, but there were several boat-tour men; so off we went for a rowboat ride across the black, swirling Ganges. There were no lights and therefore no way to get your bearings. Our boatman rowed in silence. The river rushed and swirled. We sat silent and dazed, waiting for the first light of day to show us the ancient river's edge.

As the light came, the sounds came with it. Now we could see that one side of the river was completely empty. The sun rose from that side, illuminating the other: a teeming sprawl of people moving like ants in and out of ancient domes and arches. The sounds of women squeezing and beating laundry on the stone edge of the ghat used for bathing, cowbells, finger cymbals, and chanting all mixed in the air; but no matter how cacophonous it all got, it was always soft, sweet, and human. Even the sound of handsaws cutting wood was like music to our ears. Ancient sailing ships that looked like they'd just sailed out of the Bible glided by.

Not far from us we saw another rowboat, much larger than ours, filled with eight or ten Japanese tourists who were all clambering to one side with cameras raised, while their Indian guide cried out to please trim ship. Then we saw what they were aiming at. A fully extended arm with a gnarled, clawlike hand extended out of the water, rising up into the air like a shot from a Hollywood horror film. Another boat between us was trying to lasso the arm with a rope so that they could drag it elsewhere, out of the view of that morning's batch of tourists.

We returned to shore. Walking along the ghats was like walking in the land of jolly death, a bizarre, haphazard carnival; people doing their washing, people selling food, beggars of every odd shape and form, some with extra limbs growing out of their heads or chests.

We kept on walking, stunned, through it all. We were walking on another planet. We walked until we got to the burning ghat at the far end of that holy-unholy spectacle. After a while I figured out that what we were seeing was a middle-class Indian funeral, or I should say the tail end of a funeral, because the body by now looked pretty well cooked. It was my first—I had never been to a funeral before this. I had missed Mom's because I was in Mexico, and now here I was at the funeral of a stranger.

I imagined that it would take a huge pile of wood and brush the size of a haystack to be able to burn a human body. That's how I'd pictured Joan of Arc being burned. But this was a very small, hot pile of logs not much bigger than a bonfire on a beach, and there, right on top, in the middle of the orange flames, was the body. I could only think of it as "cooking" because of the way the two slim Indian men dressed only in their loincloths kept poking it with long poles and turning it like a big barbecued pig. And it smelled like roast pig. For a moment I actually thought I perceived my mouth beginning to water. As we stood there watching and listening to that stranger's corpse burn, I was thinking how strange it was that I should be so protected from death, or at least the sight of death, for so many years. I also knew that because I'd been protected from death for so long, it had, for that very reason, always been on my mind.

We watched the body burn, sputter and pop and slowly melt into the flames. It would have been better, I thought, if Mom could have been cremated like this, out in the open, slowly, rather than being shoved into a white-hot oven on a cold metal slab. Nothing graceful about it. This was slow and organic. It was a clear meditation on watching the dead return to the elements: some parts to ashes, other parts as smoke into air. It was beautiful.

A member of the deceased's family came over to Meg and me, smiling. He was a tall, thin Indian man dressed in a long white robe. He introduced himself and told us that we were watching his brother burn. He said he was a dentist from Lucknow and the whole family had come to Benares for the cremation.

After Meg and I shook hands with him he offered us a sip of holy water, as he called it, from the Ganges. We both politely but quickly declined. Imagine, I thought, a middle-class dentist from Queens offering me a glass of the East River at a funeral in New York.

IN THE STATES, one would be put down for an interest in Tantric sex practices by being called a "swinger." But in India you could get away with what would be considered crass swapping back home. In India you could indulge your wildest needs with the fantasy that you were a Tantric monk in search of a female surrogate with whom to unite your cosmic polar opposites. I admit, this vague Tantric idea was just an excuse for me to become a rhythm pig, a naked animal coupled with another naked animal with some faint notion that we could in the end return to being our respectful, independent human selves. I'm sure this was the concept of most swingers' clubs, and Rajneesh's ashram in Poona appeared to be a swingers' club for the spiritually minded. It attracted a class of people who felt it was too tacky to swing in New Jersey. They had to go to India for spiritual validation. That was my cynical view of it at the time, anyway. Nevertheless, I was gravitating toward Poona. If I only lived once (not an Indian concept), I had to try it. Meg—good old wholesome, motivated Meg—still wanted to shop for rugs in Kashmir and learn traditional hatha yoga in Bombay. So we went our separate ways.

What frightened me on the train all the way to Poona was that I no longer knew the difference between an obsessive compulsion and an intuitive instinct. Meg knew the difference for herself, and I was envious of her for that. I was feeling completely dependent on her for this quality. In fact, I think I'd been running off her intuition for years. She held the power of her intuition over me and would only lend it to me when she felt the cause was worthy. Meg, my conscience queen. She obviously looked down upon the Rajneesh Ashram with disdain. And she said to me—just like Mom said to me when I, having been

raised as a Christian Scientist, decided to get vaccinated for polio—
"Very well, dear, it's your choice." Meg just said, "Do what you have
to, Brewster. I'm going to Bombay to study yoga, then I'm going to
Kashmir to buy Oriental rugs." Then she added with a smirk, "They're
disease-free and they last."

It was hot, very hot, when I arrived. There was no more room
for people to stay in the ashram, so I checked into the first hotel I could
find. It was a humble little place called the Ritz, and it served mainly
vegetarian food. Some of Rajneesh's followers, or sannyasins, were also
staying there. You could tell who they were immediately by their
long, flowing orange robes and the malla with the black-and-white
photo of Rajneesh hanging around their necks.

I was told by one of them, a German, that there were about four
thousand people spread out all over Poona come to be with the
Bhagwan. I was a little taken aback. Not only did I hate orange but
I also hated crowds. I got lost in them and always felt like a statistic
rather than a person.

I went to bed early and I got up early and headed down to the
ashram while it was still dark. It was a short walk from my hotel and
easy to find. There it was, a large ornate wooden gate with a big sign
over it that read SHREE RAJNEESH ASHRAM. There was an Indian
gatekeeper guarding it who looked like he'd been up all night. He was
stretched out in his chair, half asleep, with an empty bottle of wine
beside him and a copy of *People* magazine open in his lap. He directed
me back into the ashram to the dynamic meditation pavilion with a
loose hand gesture. "Oh yes, you will go just so straight ahead and then
when the sun rises you will hear the music," he said with a thick Indian
accent, his head bobbing back and forth as if he was actually telling
me, "No, don't go."

I walked back until I found the cement pavilion. It was a large
green area with a stone floor and a green opaque plastic roof covering
it. I squatted with my back against the cool cement wall and waited.
Then the sun slowly began to come up and the music began. It was
emanating from a number of huge rock and roll speakers and sounded
like a combination of Indian spiritual ragas and disco music. It was
almost too sexy for that hour of the day.

As the music got louder, the pavilion began to fill up with lithe young people all dressed in orange robes, coming from every direction. As they entered they would immediately wrap orange bandanas around their eyes or put on orange sleep masks like the black ones you get in first class on the airlines. Then they'd begin to swing and sway. Soon the room was packed with these beautiful lithe men and women all swaying in the most languidly sexy way. No one had any underwear on. I could see hints of everything through their orange robes. I could see pubic hair and breasts and the way the men were hung. And there I was, trying to dance in beige pajamas with underwear on. I was the only one in that room without orange robes and a blindfold, and I couldn't stop looking. I'd never seen such a collection of beautiful people in one place before.

It was the most sensual dancing I'd ever seen, and I felt completely undermined by it. I think I would have felt better if I was in a room filled with people in wheelchairs. I was too much in my eyes and head again, and I felt awful. I longed for the safety of my familiar relationship with Meg.

After the dynamic meditation dance was over, people filed out for breakfast at the cafeteria and I followed along, feeling even more alienated because no one was speaking any English around me, only German. And also, it was starting to get really hot.

After breakfast there was a brief break where people hung out and spoke German, and then it was time to line up to go hear the Bhagwan speak. I got swept into the crowd, but I didn't panic at the thought of disappearing. I was able to remember who I was: because I was the only one not dressed in orange.

We were ushered down a narrow passageway into a large open tent that faced an empty stage. After everyone got settled (I'd say there must have been close to two thousand people, all orange as far as the eye could see) there was a long silence followed by a small commotion of whispering, which was followed by an announcement over the PA system. The voice that came out over the system was smooth and hypnotic and spoke with an Australian accent, saying, "Would whoever is wearing the perfume or scented soap please remove themselves from the gathering." There was a silence and no one moved. Then everyone started looking around and whispering again. Soon five or six young men, all with beards, started up the aisles, bending over now and then to do what I can only describe as sniffing. They would lower their faces close to people's heads, take a sniff and then move on.

I could not contain my curiosity any longer, so I asked the young blond woman next to me what was going on. She told me, in a thick Dutch accent, that the Bhagwan was very sensitive to all smells and that the strong smell of any perfume could cause him to leave his body. I was not sure what she meant by "leave his body." I wasn't sure if she meant die, or astral-project, or what, but before I could ask I saw one of the languid sniffers discover the scented culprit and lead her out of the tent. As soon as this happened the whole atmosphere got very concentrated and charged. The focus of energy was enormous as two bearded men brought out a great white VIP executive's chair. As soon as the chair was set and the two men went to stand on either side of it, the Bhagwan swept out in his white robes and sat. Yes, I thought, the perfect guru. He was like Kennedy, the perfect president. He had the charisma. He had the aura. He had the look. He was a tall man with a balding head, long hair on the sides, and a flowing white beard. His face was open and expressive, but his eyes were the thing. I had never seen eyes like them. His eyes were anything and everything you wanted to read into them.

He was silent for a while, sitting there, taking in his devoted audience. Then, placing his hands in prayer position under his chin, he began to speak slowly. And what he said was even more threatening to me than watching all those orange people do their sexy dance.

"You are not asleep. You have chosen to do whatever you are doing now, and if you are in agony and anxiety and pain I want you to realize that it is because you have chosen it. Then you have to ask why—why you would choose a life of pain and suffering. There are reasons for it. You have to realize that only in sorrow can you *be*. When you are in ecstasy you disappear. Suffering gives you a definition. It makes you feel solid."

He went on talking about how we are divided by our pain, how misery separates and separation makes us more miserable. He told us that when we become happy the ego cannot exist. He asked us to take a look and see how when we are suddenly happy our egos disappear.

By now the man had really terrified me. I could not remember the last time I was suddenly happy. The most I ever got was a mild sense of well-being, and I wondered if I even had an ego to lose.

After more talk about ecstasy and ego and how the choice is ours whether to go deeper into pain or let it go and cry and laugh together so that we at last become one, he started explaining the initiation process. "All you have to do is tell me when you're ready and I will be ready to receive you. When you do this it is not throwing away your responsibility; it is giving up your resistance. If you cannot trust yourself, then trust me. Please, pass through the Master in trust, in love, in surrender, and things will start happening."

God, this was tempting stuff. If he didn't mean it, he sure knew how to say it well. Of course I felt everything he said applied to me. I was the ultimate self-help-book sucker. I was unhappy, and to some extent I suspected that I was engineering my misery, but I had no idea how to stop. It had become such an ingrained habit. To take it away would be to take away me. I'm sure that's the way Mom must have felt the night she got up, climbed into the car, and started it for the last time.

Yes, many things the Bhagwan said made seductive sense; but I was not yet sure if I trusted him. I had to get closer to him physically to find out.

When the Bhagwan finished speaking, he placed his hands in prayer position, bowed to his audience, and, gathering his white robes around him, strolled regally offstage. As soon as he was out of sight, the two tall, bearded assistants removed his great white chair. Instantly, about fifteen or twenty women rushed up onto the stage, threw themselves down, and kissed the floor where the chair had been. "What are they doing?" I asked the person next to me. "That," she replied, "is Bhakti yoga, the yoga of worship."

I filed out with the two thousand people dressed in orange and retreated to the Ritz to recuperate. I had to be alone. It was too confusing. I had lost my sex drive. It was too hot. I missed Meg a lot. I needed someone to talk to, someone not dressed in orange and in touch with irony. I needed to have a regular conversation with someone who was not smiling. The whole place suddenly reminded me of one big Christian Science camp, only everyone was dressed in orange and making love.

My wish came true. At lunch at the hotel I met another person who was not dressed in orange. Her name was Melvy, and she was a mime from France. She was very androgynous, and I was attracted to her immediately. Her story was this: She had been on tour performing in America and she had an affair with a woman in Seattle. In this relationship she had an experience of melding that was so cosmic, so overwhelming, and so unlike anything she'd ever had before that she asked her lover where she could find out more about it all. The woman told her to go to Rajneesh in Poona, and Melvy did.

I thought it was funny that she'd had a cosmic melding experience like that and fled to find out more about it when it was going on right there in Seattle. How French of her, I thought. She must have an analytic and inquiring mind. We became fast friends over a vegetarian lunch. I discovered that Melvy's biggest objection to Rajneesh was that he had been putting down homosexuality in some of his talks and she had discovered cosmic love in a homosexual experience. So her plan was that she was going to have an audience with him and confront him on this issue. She told me she'd get back to me with her report.

After lunch I went to sleep. It was too hot to do anything else. I woke in a sweat, feeling awful, lonely and confused. Nothing made sense. I wanted a scotch very badly. It was too hot to drink in my sweatbox of a hotel, so I walked down to the Blue Diamond, the only five-star hotel in town. I had scotch and a steak and everything made sense again. The Blue Diamond was dark and air-conditioned and I got into just fuzzing out. The booze worked as it always does: it slowed my head down. I felt like Dad.

Melvy showed up and we drank cheap Indian whiskey and talked about her experience with the Bhagwan. She was very discouraged by what he told her. He said being homosexual was just a rebellion for her and that if everyone became homosexual tomorrow she would immediately become heterosexual. Melvy was furious and wanted to fly back to France after she saw the Taj Mahal. We drank more whiskey and continued to dish Rajneesh. We were the only ones holding out on him, and we were only able to do that because we had each other. Melvy said Rajneesh didn't know what he was talking about with all this be-here-now crap. She kept raving about Proust and saying that Proust had demonstrated how the present always turns into the past before you can make any statement about it. She said that the French language was better equipped to deal with the space between experience and reflection. She was adamant about Proust and how well he'd written of how there can be no peace of mind when it comes to love because all love is only the beginning of more desire, which is endless.

I was amazed to see how she'd changed her tune from that afternoon, and to calm her down I said that I would apply for a meeting with the Master and then we would exchange notes. The following day I got to the ashram early to sign up. I put my name on a list and was told to show up at the back gate of the ashram at four o'clock. I was to bathe first, with no scented soaps, of course, or after-shave, and to carry no cut flowers.

By four o'clock the day had cooled down enough to be bearable, and I took a slow walk down to the ashram from the Ritz. About sixteen of us lined up at the gate, and again I was the only one not dressed in orange. The others were dressed in flowing orange robes, but because they had not been initiated yet they did not have the malla with the little black-and-white picture of Rajneesh around their necks. I assumed they were going in to be initiated. This made me think about why I was going in, outside of curiosity. I remembered something Rajneesh had said in his talk, about not coming to him out of curiosity but rather with a sincere and open heart.

While I stood there, I did my best to open my heart, but I had no idea who or what I was opening up to. Just to be wide open seemed a little risky unless I was looking to be Christ.

We were all led around to a little garden behind the house and told to sit. We sat cross-legged on the grass and stared with great anticipation at the big empty white chair. A young woman of about nineteen or twenty came out dressed in orange and sat cross-legged on the floor just to the left of the chair. I think this was one of his consorts. Then the Bhagwan entered and moved in a very direct and focused way to sit. He lifted his hands into prayer position, closed his eyes, and breathed.

Opening his eyes, he said, in a most sensual and hypnotic voice, "Now I am here to receive you." One at a time people were singled out by the bearded ushers to go up and kneel. As they did, the

Bhagwan would look at them with this great open smile and study them for a bit until he intuited the right Sanskrit name to give them. When he got the name he would write it on a piece of paper and hand it to the initiate while he spoke it to them and told them what it meant. After he put the malla, with his little black-and-white glossy picture on it, around their necks, he got out a little pen flashlight and shined it on their third eye, then dismissed them. Most of the people were joyful and ecstatic; it was a big event for them, I could see. But much to my surprise, I could also see that each initiation was being video-taped by one of the ushers off to the side and that there were two small microphones on the edge of the porch right at the foot of the Bhagwan's chair. It was all being recorded.

When my time came, the usher approached me and whispered, "Go up and kneel, but not too close or you may cause him to leave his body." At that point I had a great temptation to get in very close, but I could also see that one of the ushers standing just behind Rajneesh was really a big bodyguard.

When I got to him he smiled and, seeing I was not in orange, said, "What can I do for you?" At that point I felt very lost. Nothing came to mind, not even that I wanted to get laid. I just felt real lost and empty, and I told him I was confused and didn't know what to do. He told me to take a workshop, and he listed some of them. "You can take the Enlightenment Intensive, the Centering Group, or Interpersonal Confrontation. Or you could try Primal Scream, Let Go, or Art Therapy. You choose one, do one, and then come back to me and we shall talk some more."

When I got outside I saw that there was a little counter set up where they were selling audio and video tapes of the whole event.

Back at the Ritz that night I raved to Melvy. I was going into great angry diatribes, saying, "What does Rajneesh mean by 'Live in the moment, forget the past,' and then he goes and sells you video tapes of your past moments with him! All moments are not equal! There are some that will stand out in your memory, and we have memory for a reason. It's like that song: 'We were having moments to remember . . .'—you know, 'the day we tore the goalpost down,' stuff like that. I can't stand it, Melvy. The Bhagwan is driving me nuts. It's too hot here. I've lost my sex drive. And besides, I think all the people here have money. I don't have enough money to go take a lot of workshops that won't do me any good once I get back to the real world. I wish Meg would come save me."

MEG DID COME the following day. She came to take me away to Kashmir, where it would be cool and real and just us. But first I dragged her to see one of Rajneesh's talks. It was about the same old stuff, liberation from personal pain. Meg was not impressed. I was impressed by her lack of impression.

Meg and I had a farewell lunch with Melvy. Meg acted jealous of and threatened by Melvy and was very withholding. I didn't like Meg doing that, and for a moment I thought maybe I should stay there and not go.

Then Meg started telling me how we'd live on a houseboat up in Kashmir and relax. I longed for the coolness of the mountains. So we left Poona that day, returned to Bombay, and flew right up to Srinagar. As we stepped off that plane the cool air washed over me. What a relief.

We rented a houseboat on Dahl Lake. It was beautiful, but it wasn't enough just sitting there on the boat looking at those mountains. So one day not long after our arrival, we rented a gondola for a tour of the lake. The boatman put flowers around our necks and sat us up in the bow. Meg looked *great* with the wreath of jasmine around her neck. The lake was very still as the boatman poled us across. This was so much nicer than the Ganges, only we couldn't get the Ganges out of our minds because of the smell. Even the jasmine didn't overpower it. We couldn't figure out why the boatman didn't notice. We thought he must have grown used to it, or had just learned, like any good tour guide, how to ignore it. As we were passing through the mouth of a shallow inlet, I bent over the bow of the gondola and saw a bloated, decaying, drowned baby calf stuck on the bow, like some big, stupid death bumper.

All at once I was flying above it like a lake bird, looking down on the innocent boatman maneuvering us through the waterway with that dead calf stuck to the bow. I saw Meg trying to get her nose closer to her jasmine lei in order to wipe out that smell. And I loved her for that gesture then.

After that outing, Meg and I gave up on the lake and began to take tours of the rug factories. That was interesting but nothing to write home about. Meg was fascinated by it. And I was jealous of her, because I wanted something wholesome to take my interest. Meg would take the tour of each of those rug factories and then go to the sales room. I went with her because I was curious and I didn't have anything else to do. Although the rugs were beautiful, I was bored. Meg could see the patterns and workmanship in those rugs. She could see the story of how the rug was made, and it mattered to her. Meg wanted a rug to live with. She wanted to grow old with a rug. Things mattered to Meg, but not to me. I didn't want a rug. I didn't want to grow old, with a rug or anyone. I wanted an orgy. I wanted an endless orgy now.

Now that the weather was cooler my sex drive was coming back but Meg and I were having problems with our sex life—problems in the sense that the drive for each other was absent. It was there before we came to India, and then it just went away like the windy mystery that it is. Maybe all the sights of death had helped blow it away.

So the more Meg looked at rugs, the more I stood beside her and fantasized that I was back in Poona. Only in my fantasy the weather was cooler and I had at last decided to take one of the so-called Gestalt encounter groups. And I had taken on the orange, but it didn't matter, because the group leader made us take off our orange robes as soon as we came into the room. So in this fantasy there were twenty of us: ten very good-looking young women and ten real handsome men, me included. We were tan and lithe and languid. And the group leader was a German Gestalt therapist who had given up her few belongings in Frankfurt and come to Poona to live. And she comes into the room where we are and says, "Just do what I tell you to do and trust me, because what I'm going to tell you to do is going to feel good. I want you to take a risk to feel pleasure. I want all of us to pretend that we are here today just to experience pleasure." We're all standing on these mattresses as she's telling us this. The mattresses are covered with clean white cotton sheets that have just been hand-washed by a bunch of local Poona women. And the therapist, who I am now calling Hilda in my mind, Hilda says to us to please disrobe and hang our orange garments—raiments, I think she was calling them—on hooks that are all along the white wall to one side of the room. And as we all slowly slip out of our raiments, all kind of languid and humid, our muscles now completely relaxed by the warmth of the place, we look across the room and see that the whole wall is one big mirror. And Hilda hands us all some almond oil and asks us to begin rubbing each other's bodies in front of the mirror. I can feel hands going down between my crack and my hands are going down between other cracks, and everything's all oily and fluid, and as we stand there looking at ourselves naked in the mirror, Hilda adjusts the lights to a low amber and very relaxing Indian music begins to play. Hilda says in her German accent, "Come, people. Make a sitting circle in the center." We do as we are told, no problem, and it feels right. It feels good to do this. It feels all so perfectly right, as if there is no other place in the world to be. And then we sit there just gazing at each other's eyes, because we are still a little inhibited about looking at each other's body parts, even though we just rubbed them all with almond oil. Now Hilda pulls out a long wooden hash pipe and says, "Before we go any further, I just want everyone to take a big hit of my herbal medicine here. I promise it will help you relax even more." And she lights this pipe and passes it around the circle, filling the room with the sweet smell of hashish. The pipe keeps going around, and we all get real high and real mellow and real relaxed. I can feel the hash smoke go all the way down into my belly and fill up my balls. I can feel my balls begin to swell and roll. I can feel my lazy dick begin to sprout and peek out to see what's going on. And it's like Hilda is a great snake charmer who is gently bringing all the snakes out of their holes in search of new warm ones. And then Hilda gets up and says, "Now I'm going to turn the lights out, and I'm going out and I'm going to lock the door from the outside, and I'll be back in two hours. I want you all to go to town—do crazy things you've never done before. See if you can feel where heaven is. I want you to go to the Garden of Eden before you knew there was an apple tree. I want you to go to the Garden of Eden where the garden was only flesh, not flowers, when the landscape was you and not the earth, when your bodies were all the earth and the earth was your bodies, and there was no separation. Please go there. Please, please have the courage to go there just this once, so you will know pure pleasure before time and history, pure, pure, history-less pleasure." And she's saying all this wonderful stuff with a German accent as she turns out the lights and leaves us.

And what happens when she goes out of the room is so delicious that it stops time and wipes out death. Death is nowhere in the room. The room turns into a pure impenetrable fortress against death as we slowly begin to pant and touch. And Hilda has even turned off the music so the room is completely dark and without sound, except for the sound of all twenty of us turning into pure animal heat. All the body parts begin to feel like parts of one body as we link and couple in that room. Some gentle hand has found my cock and is guiding it into a warm wet hole, while I have found another kind of tighter hole with my finger, as all the oily bodies fit together. Someone wraps a thumb and finger around my balls and squeezes just so, and ooh, what's that? is that a tongue? and ooh, it's in my ass, and oh, we lie there humping and heaving until no body and no hole is unstopped. The holes and all the parts get miraculously connected like a great flesh puzzle linked up at last, and it's all done by sheer animal intuition. And everything gets filled up and satisfied, all the empty places get filled up. My ass is filled up solid with a cock and my cock is filled up solid with my blood and it fills up a waiting hole or mouth that a hand guides my cock to. And the whole room seethes and heaves and begins to fill with blue sparks that arch and jump around in the giant united body pile as everyone swells into a giant moan, watching the blue sparks fly in the mirror, and we all come in our various ways, in our various holes together. A bright blue Saint Elmo's fire outlines our bodies as we come together, we all come as one big panting river of flesh. And for just one glorious timeless time it's all one sound and one body. It is the Garden of Eden before the voice of God spoke to Adam. It is exactly that for all of us. And we know it, all at once, as we all come together and slowly collapse into a mindless, limp slumber, a slight river of drool and joy juice trickling from all the slack, satisfied cracks. And we just lie there in that timeless, absolutely satisfied body heap until at last Hilda opens the door and turns the lights up slightly so we can all look into each other's eyes again. And we do it—as brightly and innocently as a team of 1950s cheerleaders at a high school in the middle of America. "Hi, guys!" our eyes say. "Hi, gang!" our mouths say. "Wasn't that great?" "Yeah, that was far out!" "That was great!" "Let's do it again tomorrow!" And we don't even feel a hint of shame. Shame and guilt never enter that room. Of course we knew they were right outside the door. But we also knew we had consecrated a sacred place. We had created the Garden of Eden out of our bodies before the knowledge of good and evil. And we'd do it again next Wednesday. And the knowledge that we had the power to create that place, that it would be there for us again on Wednesday, made us able to live with the guilt and shame of the outside world. It purified us. And Hilda turned up the music real loud this time and it was Jamaican reggae, and we all danced naked, real happy, as we rubbed what was left of each other's juices onto our bodies to show we had been initiated into the brother- and sisterhood of pleasure: the Garden of Eden Club. Or the Eden Garden Club.

Now this fantasy was so strong that it played like a movie loop in my head. And the more it played, the more I wanted to return to Poona. In fact, I was beginning to get paralyzed by not knowing what was real and what was fantasy. I was afraid that if I went back I'd run into all the same barriers again. And I tried to calm myself by telling myself that I'd do it one day. I knew I loved Meg, but I also knew that I needed to get back to a place like the Garden of Eden Club. I had to get through the fantasy or it would turn on me and make me crazy.

You see, I was beginning to realize the mistake I made when I had my meeting with Rajneesh. I had been false. I had played some sacred and holy game with him instead of just coming out and telling him that all I really wanted was to get laid over and over again. I wanted to FUCK, and for some reason, perhaps because of the guilt I felt toward Meg, I needed his permission to do it. And here is the sad part: my fantasy workshop didn't even come into my mind until I was all the way up in Kashmir with Meg. I began to feel tortured. I could not accept the fact that I was torturing myself, so I began to blame it on the guru. I mean, I began to blame it on Rajneesh! I began to think he had power over me and was torturing me for not accepting him. And this began to frighten me and make me nuts. "Unfinished business, unfinished business!" was the phrase that kept running through my mind. I was playing around with madness when I could have taken a risk and gone mad in a safe way in Poona. I was about to poison myself with regret. I was beginning to torture myself with the idea that I had to go back there to Poona to do it right, to go to him and say, "I want to get laid. I need to get laid." Meg was not enough for me. I needed to lose myself and meld. I wanted to lose myself every morning and every evening in glorious, boundary-less sex.

I didn't realize how deeply I was into self-punishment, which, when you consider all the real hellish punishments in the world—well, you know, to punish yourself before the real ones get you has to be the ultimate system of control.

But Meg could see that I was obsessing. It was obvious because I couldn't keep my mouth shut and was spilling out all over the place. I think she felt the cure for it was to keep moving and see more, particularly places the average tourist had never seen. Meg wanted to go to a special, out-of-the-way place that had not been overly explored. It was her idea to travel to Ladakh, way up north of Kashmir on the Tibetan border. Meg made all the plans and arrangements to leave her rugs behind and rent a jeep with a driver who would take us on the three-day trip to Leh, the capital of Ladakh, which was buried way up in the Himalayas. Leh wasn't even a hip place to go in 1976. Nepal was still the hip place, and Ladakh was supposed to be one of those untouched places. The road there had only been open to tourists for one year. Until then it had been used for convoys taking the Indian army up to guard the border. What a preposterous idea, I thought, when we could go to Nepal and smoke hash and hang out with all the hippies! There was something frighteningly austere about Meg's idea to go to Ladakh.

As I look back at that very turbulent period, I see me, in my quest for a vacation, taking a very long fall from the top of the Himalayas all the way down into the bottom of the Grand Canyon. I fell from a place where I could look out over the surface of the planet to a place where I looked up at the vast layers of the inside of Mother Earth. It was a long and crazy fall that took a little over one year, almost ruined me, and finally ripped Meg and me apart. If you see any thread or meaning in it, so much the better. I'd have to call it some sort of penance. It was as though I felt compelled to create my own punishment, my own personal religion with its own sins and retributions. I was creating my own punishments for the fact that I hadn't saved my mother. I was attempting to put myself through what she had gone through—a fast and total disorientation of the senses.

So we rented a jeep and driver out of Srinagar, Kashmir. The driver was a very handsome Ladakhan, and either he spoke very little English or he was just the strong and silent type, but he didn't do much talking. Meg and I had very little to say, either, since we'd been with each other for so long. Before, we liked to talk about the different people we met on the trip, but now there were no people, only this driver who didn't speak. So we mostly looked at the landscape, while the driver slam-shifted through the five gears of that jeep like some sort of Buddhist cowboy.

As I gradually took in the miraculous landscape, I realized words were worthless here. I was hypnotized by the constantly changing, sweeping vistas, the swirling dark weather broken by rainbows arching over deep gorges. It was unlike any landscape I'd ever seen before— this vast, brown, rolling high desert, with patches of snow melting on the bare dirt hills. No wonder the driver was silent. He was, I was sure, just empty—not stupid, but empty and all eyes. For a time, which is perhaps the most we can ask for, that landscape cured me of thoughts of my past and future. Like the sea, it washed all thoughts out of my mind; but unlike the sea, it did not overstimulate me in that sensual way. It was a dry, motionless sea; those arid rolling hills rose into mountains like waves suspended. My body was crammed into that little jeep, but my head opened up to the outside. Far below the road there were flashes of rushing rivers or bright shocking patches of green at some cultivated little oasis that surrounded an adobe home. Up and up we went, climbing to the top of the world. I loved Meg then, the way that she looked at it all. When I wasn't looking at the landscape I was watching her. I was watching all the passion and wonder in her eyes as we went up up into this magic storybook place. We were on our way to heaven.

All that changed when we arrived at Kargil. It was a dumpy little town. We ended up at a ratty hotel for the night, had a dish for dinner called mok-mok, which was something like flavorless chow mein, and sat there eating across from a truly eccentric couple: a German man and his traveling companion, who looked like an Oriental transvestite. He or she wore a long red wig and was really quite beautiful.

The beds at the hotel were awful: mattresses stuffed with straw on ragged metal springs. I lay there rerunning images of the fantastic landscape that had filled our eyes, longing for the new day to come so that we could go out in it again.

The next day was both more tedious and more frightening. The tedious part came when we got stuck behind a long convoy of Indian army trucks bringing soldiers up to the border. If it wasn't for the view, it would have felt like being stuck in gridlock in lower Manhattan. But in order to forget our snail's pace, we looked out and down. That was where the frightening part came. There were no guard rails, and we were climbing higher and higher. I was sure that our driver believed in reincarnation, so that he drove with one eye on the road and the other on his next life. As I looked straight down, thousands of feet, to those rushing brown rivers below, he geared down, then geared up, trying to squeeze past that long convoy of army trucks.

On and on and up and up we went. Then, somewhere late into the second spectacular day, the jeep came to a choking, sputtering halt. Without so much as a swear word or any explanation at all, our driver got out and began poking around under the hood. Meg and I welcomed the stop because it meant we could get out and walk in the landscape instead of just looking at it. We decided to walk up the road a bit and let the driver pick us up when, or if, he got the jeep started again. As soon as we stepped out of the jeep, I knew that that was exactly what we needed.

Meg and I walked side by side, like bride and bridegroom, into a wedding of silence. When we stopped, the sharp reverberation of our feet on the gravel stopped and we stood in an absence of sound. No sound of stones or water falling, no sound of insects, no distant voices, no bird cry, no distant thunder or endless whine of new construction, no mechanical river of freeway sound, no jet trail overhead—nothing. And though for a while the memories of sound persisted, they too passed, and left us standing there in the most complete silence; a silence of mind and earth come together in perfect oneness.

I felt something go off in my heart, something like a small dam breaking, something that flowed into tears. Meg dove for me and latched tight into my arms, and I think we both knew at the time, although we didn't talk about it, that we were mourning the death of silence in our world below. Until that moment we hadn't known pure silence on this earth, and so we hadn't recognized that it had died.

We walked on together holding hands for a brief time and then we let go, and moved on like two astronauts floating into silence without a lifeline. The silence was only broken by the sound of our sandals on gravel, which seemed enormous. As we came up over a little knoll, we saw an old woman walking with a bundle of dried sticks on her back. The bundle looked twice the size of her, and she turned to us and smiled and called *"Julay!"* which we took to be some Ladakhan greeting. It wasn't so much her speaking that broke the silence, but her smile. Her smile was full and totally without cunning or fear. It was so incredibly open that for a moment I thought Meg and I had landed on a foreign planet. She was smiling at us with gold teeth. She was as old and beautiful and weathered as the landscape she smiled from. She was the landscape in motion, and that biblical phrase "from dust to dust" suddenly made sense to me. It was as though she had been shaped out of the very dust, clay, and rock that she walked in; and she was only a breath away from returning to it.

Meg and I stood there and watched the woman walk ahead of us without looking back until all we could see was a giant, slow-moving bundle of sticks on little sandal feet, inching up an endless road.

I have no idea how much time passed, because time there was only measured by the passing of light over rock. Perhaps it was the deeper, darker angle of shadow that made us both feel like Hansel and Gretel, in need of shelter for the night, and we decided we'd better head back to our driver and see what was going on.

Our driver made it clear to us that the fuel pump had broken and he had to hitchhike back to Kargil to look for a part. With no apparent problem, he had made arrangements for us to stay at a nearby house, an earthen structure growing out of the brown hills. It looked like an American Indian dwelling: a simple square structure made of adobe, with a few small slit windows here and there. Our driver, who by now had told us to call him Jun-yang, deposited us at the house like some sort of lost orphans. Jun-yang simply told us to stay there until he got back, and that was that. With no explanation or introduction, he left us in the care of two smiling Ladakhan women. One was as weathered and old as the woman with the bundle of sticks, smiling a similar smile of gold teeth. The other, who I took to be the older one's daughter, was younger and extremely beautiful. They both stood there smiling as I introduced myself and Meg. They stood there and smiled and then disappeared back into that labyrinth of dried mud, leaving us with the sunset on that sweeping, rolling, endless top-of-the-world landscape.

Meg and I had no idea what to do. We decided to go back down the mud steps that led to the main entrance of the house and go out for a twilight walk. I think we both wanted to walk in that silence again and refeel it. So we walked up one bare, brown hill and down another until we felt like we were strolling in the landscape of some storybook, perhaps *The Little Prince*. When we got back to the adobe house it was dusk, and climbing back up the dry mud front steps, we again came out onto the little terrace, where what looked like the man of the house was waiting. His hair was long and shiny black; his face had a beautiful round, full-moon, Mongolian look to it. He was stunning, dressed in black, his black jacket tied in six places with sky-blue velvet ribbons. He wore elegantly cut baggy black pants and soft suede boots with long, faded leather laces. His outfit was so individual and rare in design that it could have been the source of today's Comme des Garçons look. And what a carriage he had! There was nothing cocky or prideful about it. He was a humble black prince. "Welcome," he said in English as we came up the steps. "Welcome to our home. Call me Raymond. My Ladakhan name is too complicated and makes most Westerners frown. I go to college in Rishikesh, and they call me Raymond down there."

We introduced ourselves and Raymond gave us a tour of his house. First he took us to a little slit in one of the mud walls and showed us his mother and sister, who were now preparing what we hoped might be our supper. One at a time, Meg and I looked through this crack in the wall into a barren cavelike room, where the two women squatted beside a little fire of sticks, stirring the contents of the iron cauldron suspended over it. The only light came from the fire, which lit their faces from below in an eerie, witchy way. There seemed to be no door in or out of the room, and it looked like they had been created in there like a ship in a bottle and had never left that place from birth.

Then Raymond led us to what was to be our room for the night. It was all earth, a small square cave just like the room where his mother and sister were cooking, only without a fire. There were two straw mats on the floor and a little slit that looked out on the road to Leh below.

It was growing dark. Lighting a candle, Raymond led us to the toilet. Crossing the terrace we saw the first stars appear over the distant hills, and it looked like Bethlehem just after Jesus was born. I couldn't believe how clear and beautiful it was. Then that part of me, that dark, cynical part that wanted to withdraw from all beauty, got completely fascinated with the idea of the toilet, or what Raymond called the toilet, as we followed him by candlelight into the dark, dank, musty basement of the house.

Meg and I walked cautiously behind as Raymond held the candle high to light the earth floor beneath us, and there it was—dark and round, like the very asshole of the house itself, a dark tornado funnel going down into the earth. There was no seat over it and nothing around it. There was, of course, no toilet paper, just this deep, dark hole that went down into the earth. And this hole gave off a sweet, pungent, and not wholly unpleasant smell, something like a horse stable.

"This is the toilet," Raymond said, without a hint of shame or apology in his voice, as he held the candle over it. Both Meg and I looked at each other with the whimsical recognition that we were about to become very constipated.

Raymond led us back up onto the terrace again, and Meg and I looked up at the sky as if we were seeing the stars for the first time together. It was as vivid as that first LSD trip, only it was not seen through the medium of a drug. It was just seeing, and seeing was believing, and suddenly that enigmatic end to Keats's "Ode on a

Grecian Urn" made sense, as it crossed my mind like a little ticker tape:
" 'Beauty is truth, truth beauty,'—that is all/Ye know on earth, and
all ye need to know."

As a protection against too much love for the place, I started
poking around looking for imperfections, trying again to create them
before they arrived. Trying to build realistic boundaries again, trying
to ground myself in trivial conversation, I turned to Raymond and
asked him what the winters were like. He said the snow often got so
deep that no one could go out of their house for days.

I was stunned. What a horror! It would be one thing to be
snowbound in some cozy Vermont farmhouse with books and brandy
and canned goods and maybe a TV or a stereo, but to be snowbound
in this mud hole? How could one survive it? Remembering that
Vermont had one of the highest suicide rates in America, particularly
in winter, I turned to Raymond and without even thinking about it
I asked him, "Well, don't you have a lot of suicides here in the
winter?"

Raymond just looked back at me with a blank face and Meg
laughed. I made my hand into the shape of a pistol, aimed it at my
head, and, like some retarded Tonto, said "You know, suicide—bang,
bang, people kill self."

"No, no," Raymond laughed. "We have none." Before I could
question him further, Meg interrupted. She'd found the magic door
to the one room we hadn't seen yet. It was adjacent to the terrace and
had a beautiful hand-carved wooden latch on it. She asked Raymond
what was behind the door.

Raymond answered matter-of-factly that it was the household
shrine, and asked if we wanted to see it. Meg and I both nodded at
once and he led the way into a room that was as spectacular as the sky
above it. In contrast to those other bare rooms, this one was an ornate
jewel and at the same time splendid in its simplicity. There were two
simple hand-carved wooden benches facing a little royal-red Buddhist
altar with bells, paintings of Tibetan gods, and a small photo of some
smiling lama in a handmade silver frame.

Raymond told us this was the altar to which they prayed every
morning, and I realized in a sad flash that they had something going
there I had never encountered before: an in-house, all-purpose, con-

nected, working religion, complete and without doubt. No TV or telephone on snowbound winter days, but infinite connection of mind instead. No one worshiped in that room alone. They worshiped with all of the snowbound Ladakhans scattered in their mud abodes. It was a giant connection through ritual and prayer, and this is when I had my first big dose of loneliness, as I looked back on America and saw that we were only interconnected by machines now.

After a dinner of rice and potatoes, we went to sleep on the straw mats. But some time close to dawn, which felt like the middle of the night, I woke up to the voice of a man calling from below. I staggered to our slit of a window to see Jun-yang, our driver, waving up at me. He had been able to fix the fuel pump.

We were off again, with no breakfast. We were off, driving farther up into that landscape, and once again our eyes were so filled with the beauty of that place, we hardly noticed our empty stomachs. There was nothing to make us feel the lack of anything, just complete empty space and a delicious poverty of objects; no road stands, no billboards, no diners, no mileage signs to tell us how far we were from Leh, only spectacular mountains and deep ravines. Only landscape without stories.

It was as though some gods had planned special effects of nature as we entered the capital of Ladakh. We were now on the highest plateau of the desert, and we could see the snow-capped Himalayas all around us. Dark clouds whipped up and broke and gave way to glorious shafts of sunlight. Then out of nowhere it was hailing. Great golf balls were beating on the hood of our jeep. And when the hailstorm passed, it left a spectacular rainbow arched over the entrance to Leh, as though the city was a long-sought-after pot of gold.

"Is that it? Is that Leh?" I called out to Jun-yang, and he nodded and said, "Leh."

Entering Leh was like driving onto a movie set for an American western, only the town was filled with what looked like American Indians instead of cowboys. Leh was one dirt main street with little rickety shops and stores on either side. There were no movie theaters, opium dens, or strip joints. Yet there were soldiers everywhere. Most of the architecture was that British Colonial stuff we'd seen down in Kashmir: houses made of old wood and some brick. There were a few jeeps on Main Street, no cars, and all these incredibly gentle, handsome people walking hand in hand. Even the Indian soldiers, who had been sent up to guard the border, were walking hand in hand.

Jun-yang took us to a rooming house, where they boiled up some water so we could take the traditional bath, pouring water from buckets all over each other. The two of us were feeling like little naked kids again, having a cleansing water fight. After our bath, I was able to procure a bottle of the local brew, a milky, bitter Tibetan beer called Chang. That did the trick. Two sips of Chang and I felt complete again. Buddhists everywhere say that the essence of all reality is *dukhka,* which translates as "suffering through incompletion"—the idea that nothing is ever enough. I experience *dukhka* most acutely when I smoke hashish or marijuana; but when I drink liquor, particularly at that elevation, it seems to eliminate all the *dukhka* for a while.

I'm not going to go into a whole lot of detail about what Meg and I did up there in Ladakh or what we said to each other. I don't remember much of that anyway. What I do remember, though, is that I was suffering from scopophilia: I was caught in my eyes, looking and looking, looking at all these happy people everywhere, and I was getting very lonely because I knew that I was not one of them. Every morning all these happy people greeted me in the streets with their gold-tooth smiles, crying, *"Julay!"* They were not trying to hustle or sell me anything. They were just smiling, and they seemed to want nothing more than a smile in return. I think it would have been easier to give them money, the way we did in India. As they came at me that first morning, their simple beauty and innocence was almost too much to bear. Their hearty bodies were dressed in black, embroidered with beautiful reds and turquoises, framed by splashing clear snow water that played around them like liquid silver. They were coming at me out of the cobblestone street with their gold-tooth-spangled smiles, the glitter of snow water rushing by them, down ragged stone gutters, as they cried, *"Julay! Julay!"*

And all the time I had this dizzy vertigo feeling, like a kid on top of a giant globe about to teeter and fall. I had the feeling that we climbed to the top of the world just in order to slide down, to get enough momentum to roll all the way home, and because of this I was impatient to begin our return trip. That water rushing down at full speed out of the Himalayas was pulling me down with it; all that happiness in the people's faces was driving me away. The deprivation of the lowlands had made me feel fortunate, but the absolute abundance of joy here made me feel deprived.

When I wasn't out walking alone and feeding my scopophilia until my eyes felt full to the point of bursting, Meg and I would take tours to the various Tibetan monasteries in the area. They looked like the buildings in all the old photographs of Tibet. It wasn't entirely clear how the Buddhist monks felt about guided tours interrupting their services, but I wanted to sit in the middle of one and try to be a part of it.

Once we got past the wild dogs at the monastery gate, one of the head lamas would always lead us right through the service and into the back of the monastery to see some sacred icons or special gold Buddhas or intricate, dazzling wall paintings, but I really wanted to be with the monks while they were chanting. Meg was much better at dealing with what I call the museum factor, and she was fascinated by the wall paintings. At last, in the Tiksi monastery we got to sit and vibrate with the deep chants of the monks as they rolled off endless sutras and prayers from their prayer wheels. They would blow their long Tibetan horns and wink at us as they blew and then wink again between crashes of crazy cymbals. That was the best part—just sitting there vibrating with them. But the tourist guide moved us on to the next monastery and more savage dogs and another gold Buddha, and ancient leather-bound books in little libraries with the most incredible views that stopped time again. Everywhere we went, there were those gold-tooth smiles coming out at me from the glitter of snow water and that dizzy feeling would come over me again, of a child about to fall; and when this feeling came I would talk to Meg again about making plans for our descent. We had to set a date in order to get a seat on the bus, which left twice a week for Kashmir, and I knew that once I left Ladakh I would try to roll all the way down to New York City without getting caught up in any more diversions or temptations. You see, I had the feeling that in order to be happy anywhere I had to get back to America, to figure out what went wrong and why I couldn't smile in the streets of New York and say "Good day, good day" to all the people passing by there. Let the people in Ladakh carry on in their own happiness without me. I knew it was impossible to ever be a part of them.

At the time I had no idea that I would have to go through so much stupid confusion before I'd even begin to get to the other side; and in all of this confusion, water, without my knowing it, was really the ruling force. I wanted now to flow down with it, follow it down the mountain all the way to New York. I had no idea where it was leading me until I at last found myself at the bottom of the earth, lying naked in a cool stream. I had no idea about the long, dark, confusing route that would lead at last to the bottom of the Grand Canyon. Had I known ahead of time, I doubt that I would have gotten on that bus in Ladakh at all. But one day in late June, Meg and I got on the bus and we started down. We started home.

We were the only Westerners on that bus, and we sat in separate seats. Meg sat in the center and I sat in the back next to the emergency door, so I could jump if the bus started to go over a cliff. The only problem, as I saw it, and I saw it most vividly, was that my side of the bus was the side that was always toward the edge of those giant precipices, and if I were to open the door and jump, I would simply be falling independent of the bus and without Meg. And to make things worse, the bus was filled with Ladakhans—all those smiling people again, who, because of their belief in reincarnation, had little fear of dying. They looked like adults, but they acted like children in a jolly kindergarten. They were singing and laughing all the time, and calling out to the driver the whole trip as we followed that rushing silver snow water. Down, down, down we bounced and careened like we were part of some ridiculous children's storybook—like *The Little Engine That Could*, or *Couldn't*, or *The Little Bus That Flew*. Down, down we went, with those child-men who kept opening their windows to grab handfuls of fresh snow from the melting snow banks on the right side of the creeping bus. They'd make snowballs and throw them around the bus, laughing all the time, their gold teeth flashing. I crouched in the back, an uptight curmudgeon, saying over and over again to myself, "This too will pass." Then I will be sad and miss it, I thought.

As we went down, the melting snow banks turned into banks of green grass with the most spectacular profusion of spring wildflowers growing out of them. Down, down, down we went until at last we reached Kashmir, where Meg and I took the flight to Delhi, to the truly unbearably hot and humid flatlands, where the dark, moist clouds of the encroaching monsoon season gathered.

The heat of Delhi was impossible to deal with. It was 110 degrees and 100 percent humidity when we landed, so we went right to the air-conditioned Lodhi Hotel. I drank Indian whiskey and Indian beer, trying to calm myself and get ready for the big flight home, while all the time that old dark, vacillating *dukhka* part of me began to think maybe I should go up to Nepal since I was so close. But when I'd think about it I'd get afraid that Nepal would be too depressingly corrupt after that pure experience in Ladakh.

Meg wanted to stay for a while in Delhi and take a yoga class. I was incredulous. I couldn't imagine how Meg could do yoga in that heat, but she was disappointed that she'd come all this way to India and never once got to take any lessons in yoga. All she did was buy rugs. Until then I had been thinking of myself as the spiritual quester and Meg as the merchant, now that was changing.

So we were busy getting organized, Meg dealing with getting the rugs shipped out and trying to find the right yoga class and me trying to get a flight out to New York. I had no idea what I would do when I got there except try to figure out how to be happy. I was rolling down from the top of the world and running blindly for home base and couldn't stop until I got there. I wanted to be able just to stand still in some familiar place, like a New York City cocktail party, and say things like, "Well, I've been to India. Yes, I've seen the Taj."

I didn't know what Meg wanted. I didn't know what held us together anymore except that we were companions in motion. She was still a bright beacon counteracting my gloomy pessimism. I had no idea what I gave back to her.

I just wanted to get on that plane and fly alone to New York, to prove to myself that I could travel without Meg as my guide. I was shaking all over when we said goodbye at the Delhi airport. I felt like I would never see her again.

I NEVER STOPPED looking down onto that clear, clear day. It was as though a whole part of the earth had been swept free of clouds just for my view. I saw it all: the mountains of Pakistan; sweeping, endless desert; and then we were suddenly over the Pyramids. There they were! The pilot didn't even announce them. I could say I'd seen the Pyramids and I hadn't even been in Egypt. I craned my neck even more as my breath fogged up the window. Then we were over the Greek Islands. All of them! I was amazed at how barren they were, like scattered fragments of moon rock, broken and strewn in azure. As soon as I saw the islands, I wanted to go there. I wanted to be there. As soon as the plane lands, I thought, I will vacation in the Greek Islands. But before I could dwell on that, we were over the Swiss Alps, and then the lush plains of Belgium, and then slowly coming in low over the flatlands of Holland, and then *bump, bump,* and we were down. We had landed at the Schiphol airport in Amsterdam. I didn't want the flight to be over. Six hours had gone by like six minutes. That dizzy feeling of too much freedom came over me again, the feeling that I was no one and everyone everywhere, and that I could do anything I wanted, except there was hardly any "I" left to operate out of. Then, pulling away from the window, I realized that my head was locked to the right from having stared out that way for six hours.

I strolled into the almost empty Amsterdam airport with my head locked to the right, walked right past Dutch immigration officials, who all looked like stoned-out hippies in uniform, and it occurred to me that I could have been bringing in pounds of hashish and opium and it wouldn't have mattered to them.

Yes, Amsterdam felt like a little paradise of freedom, and all my plans to get on the next flight to New York City began to dissolve and crumble. "Why not spend one night in Amsterdam?" the little gremlin voice was saying in my ear. "Just one night." After all, what was the rush to get back to New York City in summer?

So I called Hans and Sonia and said, "Hi, it's Brewster. I'm just in from India and I'd love to come over and see you." It felt so exciting to be able to say "just in from India." Never in my life did I think I'd be able to utter a phrase quite as jet-setty as that.

"But of course," Sonia crackled in her thick Dutch accent. "What a surprise!"

I caught a cab and was off, sitting in the back trying to force my head to the left, overwhelmed by the large, hypertrophied prosperity of all I saw out the window. The wealth of that city! Never did I think Amsterdam would look so luxurious. The people in the streets were like great blown-up sex giants, strapping male towheads and butter-and-peach-cream-skinned women, coming and going on black Mary Poppins bicycles, their spines gloriously erect, their eyes straight ahead with the great purpose of life.

As my Mercedes cab wound through the narrow Dutch streets, I could see flashes of bright-colored, overflowing vegetable stands. After India, all the vegetables in Holland looked as though they had been blown up by bicycle pumps. That's about the time the fever came on me, just as I was looking at some particularly plump cauliflower. It was a cool, wet, beautiful Nordic day in June and everything was so fresh, but all at once I felt a chill creeping into my bones. I saw all the people again, all those Dutch people, and the realization crept into me, like the chill, that all of this had been going on without me: Amsterdam had been going on all this time, all this time that I was in India, all my life, and now I was just peeking in on it. Yes, all of Amsterdam—not to mention Frankfurt, Paris, Brussels, or London— had been going on without me. And no one cared whether I came or went, no one cared what I did or felt; so my newfound freedom was turning into a horror. No one even knew I was in that cab or who I was, much less how I perceived the cauliflower or the upright Dutch women on their black Mary Poppins bikes. No wonder so many people craved fame, I thought. It allowed you the grand illusion that you were someone. No wonder people need to pretend that God is watching them all the time. Any illusion would be better than this loneliness, this awareness of infinitesimal existence, this horrible disappearing. Thank God for Hans and Sonia, I thought. At least they'll recognize me.

By the time I got to Hans and Sonia's apartment I was shaking and sweating with fever and sure now that I'd come down with some exotic Indian disease. I couldn't believe how fast it had come over me, since I'd stepped off that damned plane.

Well, there they were, Sonia and Hans and Sonia's new baby, wee little Willie Winkie. And there I was with all my bags, wanting to collapse and not deal with anything. I had all my dirty laundry in a bag flung over my shoulder. I was suddenly very sick and needy, flinging my fevered body and laundry on their cozy Dutch hospitality.

"Come in, come in!" Sonia and Hans cried in their broken English.

"Stay away, stay away!" I cried back. "I think I'm very, very sick!" I said with my head still stuck ridiculously to the right, staring at the wall as I went up the stairs. "Just give me a bed to recuperate in. That's all I ask for." Then, seeing little Willie, I said, "Oh, what a lovely baby—but don't let me get close to him." The truth was that the baby, after what I'd seen in India, looked like he, too, had been blown up with a bicycle pump.

Hans took my fevered condition seriously and immediately showed me to the attic room above their apartment at the end of a very ancient winding stairway. The room was like a monk's chamber, just perfect for me, with a single bed, a little dresser, and one gabled window that looked down into three or four old Dutch backyards. I lay down, fully dressed, and Hans covered me over with layers of old grandmother quilts and the eiderdown. I fell fast into sweaty delirium, only to come to, wet and wasted, days later. Between the jet lag and this Indian fever, I was quite out of it, and thought I was back in bed as a child, with Mom, not Sonia, downstairs preparing vegetable soup.

At last I was back in the familiar land of the cool; and I realized that the great blessing of any illness like the one I had just gone through is that it leaves no room for neurosis, no room for regret, no room for the things I slowly began to feel upon waking. What I felt while in that fever I can only describe as spiritual, and this was a surprise to me, because I had expected to feel spiritual in India, not while suffering from a fever in Amsterdam. There in that attic looking out over cool, damp, green Holland in June, I felt a great renewal, combined with a melancholy that belonged to some other, lame, romantic time. I lay all damp and crusty under a pile of quilts, emptied out for the first time in a long time, and it was such a splendid feeling that I was even reluctant to open the door, lest I get filled again with the ten thousand things. I didn't want to have it all come in on me again. I even avoided going downstairs to the toilet by keeping an old Mason jar by my bed. I would empty it slowly, pouring it out over the slate roof that led to the ancient rusty gutter that carried my urine down to the garden far below. And as I poured, I looked out on all those Dutch backyards with their fresh laundry on the lines.

From my window I could see, as if framed in a storybook, great clouds billow, give off streaks of sun, then fold in on themselves. They would grow black and spit rain on the old irregular glass panes as I lay there cozy, thinking of that rain splashing on giant white fields of cauliflower, fields that spread near Dutch dikes, and beyond, the gray North Sea rolling in its late-spring chop. I was empty at last, empty of desire, content for the first time in months. I was content to live only in my imagination. It was purer, safer, sweeter. I'd seen enough to remember for the rest of my life, and I wanted to stay there under that quilt in that little room, just remembering.

Gradually I got better. I drank the mugs of homemade vegetable soup that Sonia brought up to me. As I got better I began to miss Meg a whole lot, and I tried to figure out when she would be passing through Amsterdam on her way to New York. I was sure she planned to spend twelve or fourteen days at that yoga school in Delhi, so I figured in twelve days' time I would have all the incoming flights from India paged at the airport.

On the third day of my recuperation I got curious about the books on the little shelf in my room. I pulled out a small paperback called *The Grammar of Living*, having no idea what a vulnerable state I was in, and how careful I should have been about what I filled my empty head with. Looking back on it now, I know it was the wrong book. I should have been reading my copy of *Zen Mind, Beginner's Mind*. I should have even carried that with me. Yes, that's why people carry Bibles with them: for when they get in dark places, places of temptation or sickness. Then they have a book to turn to, to guide their thoughts. Anyway, *The Grammar of Living* was filled with all these lusty, sexy sixties stories, told under the guise of teaching the reader how the nuclear family, with its accompanying Oedipal problems, had to be broken down and destroyed immediately, so we could all become free of guilt and experience liberating good sex. I lay there and swallowed it whole.

This guy Cooper would tell about how he was just hanging out at the local antifamily commune in London, hanging out tripping on pure Sandoz LSD, happy just to be there with no longings or desire, and then came this knock on the door. I mean, it wasn't even *his* door. It was just *the* door, because he was involved in this communal nonego, nonfamily door situation. So there was this knock, and there she was, this leggy Suzette, a long-torsoed, beautiful Frenchwoman from across the Channel. Without a word, the next thing Cooper knew, he was locked into some Kama Sutra Tantric pose with her—Cooper deep and hard into Suzette, and she with her long legs wrapped around him, swooning like a swan in blind lust. They were in the doorway just doing it in front of the whole commune, if they even cared, just doing it so the whole commune could observe and celebrate the end of the nuclear family. They were in what he called a deep sexual meditation, the unification of opposite poles, sex as a big France-and-England joy-juice spiritual thing. Pure sex with no words, no conditions, no apparent historical consequences, just dying to the moment.

Those stories put me in an almost unnatural state of desire and lust. I was so taken in by this damn book that I forgot to realize that this guy, this Cooper, had to have taken the time to write it all down and to get it edited and to get it published, which most likely meant that he must have rewritten it a number of times; but all of this didn't enter into my head then. I just kept seeing him as completely ecstatic in this state of ideal, pure, sanctioned, antifamily sex. I wanted some myself right away.

As I lay there in bed I began to have a big stirring notion that I could find what I needed down at the Dam, the main square in Amsterdam, where all the hippies hung out. And to make it even more perfect, Hans and Sonia were going away to the country for the whole month of July and they offered me their apartment for free! I could have it, I could stay there and do anything I wanted. I could smoke hash all day, or drink, or take LSD or read whatever books I wanted or indulge in Tantric sex.

I put down that damn provocative book and lay there in bed having elaborate fantasies of what I was going to do. I was going to pick up a young, dark, foreign woman—an Italian hippie who spoke no English, just enough for her to understand what I needed. I'd get her back to my little cozy Dutch apartment and get her in Tantric poses all over the apartment. It was about to become my new Garden of Eden. We would do it in the window, on the table, on the stairs, sliding down the banister in the open doorway and out onto the street. This was like a new fever, a fever in my brain.

I told Hans that I'd like to go down to just sort of look at the Dam, you know, from a distance. "You know," I said, "I'll take a nice little walk through Vondel Park, and then head on down to the Dam."

Hans said, "Well, please take my bike."

And I did. I took Hans's big black Mary Poppins bike and I had that sickening, dizzy freedom feeling yet again. I was wobbling all over on that bike, the wind blowing in my hair. I felt free and alive, and God what a scary place it was, what a wobbly, scary place. It was as though I suddenly found myself on a high wire doing a tightrope act without having had any practice, without any idea how I had gotten out there. I was in this scary, risky place that I felt could collapse at any moment into that dark, soft, destructive side of pleasure—the pain that feels so good, the masochism—or I could opt for the joyous, humorous side, which I really knew nothing about and had a feeling Mr. Tantric Cooper didn't, either.

The Dam was jammed with all sorts of hippies, hanging out, playing wooden flutes, dealing dope, selling their used VW buses. Everyone looked so fucking great, so beautiful, in their shaggy confidence, and so together, stoned and part of something that was beyond me. What was worse, no one even noticed me. No one noticed my incredible new skinny fresh-out-of-India body. No one noticed me in my raw-silk Nehru jacket riding high on my magic Mary Poppins bike. No one noticed me as I got off my bike and stood at the edge of it all, like a lame boy longingly gazing in at some glorious schoolyard playground at recess.

I thought maybe I should just go and have a beer and think all this over some more, go and make a few notes on the back of a napkin about what I just saw and try to put the puzzle together again. I could always come back to the Dam and pick someone up in a few hours.

But I was tortured by this new gnawing dark thought that this had been the history of my life: retreat. I'd never gone after what I wanted, because I'd never trusted that what I wanted was what I wanted. Everything always seemed like an illusion covering over another illusion, layers and layers of it.

I went to a bar for a beer anyway. At last back to the hops! The river of forgetfulness, I thought as I took my first slow sip. I knew I liked hops better than hash, because hops were grown in cooler climates and helped diffuse the flames of lust that were so often brought on by marijuana or hashish. Oh God, that wonderful Dutch beer was relaxing and smooth! But as soon as I'd get relaxed, all the ten thousand things would start entering my head again, the temptations that came like those wild and crazy birds flying at me, all those shoulds and woulds and coulds, which started now like an infernal engine in my head: shoulda-woulda-coulda. Maybe I should go to Bali, I thought, or maybe I would or could take a train down to Greece. Maybe I should go to Ireland. Then I'd order another beer to try to quench what now seemed like endless desire spinning in my head like a giant wheel of fortune. I sat there in that overripe place of desire and expectation, poised and teetering on the edge of a life not yet lived.

I ordered another big pint of slow, thick beer as Bali came back to my mind and then passed like those ever-changing Amsterdam clouds. I didn't even know what day it was now and I didn't care. I loved the lostness.

And so the days went. I would wake in my attic room, go downstairs and have sweet rolls and strong Dutch coffee with Hans and Sonia, then I'd play a little with Baby Willie. I'd talk obsessively of Bali. I think I was hoping that Hans or Sonia might tell me no, that was not the place to go. Although neither of them had ever been to Bali, they did have friends who had gone and reported back that it was very beautiful, that it was very, very beautiful. I would get very anxious, not wanting to think that I would be one who would flee from all that beauty to an ugly summer in New York City. I wanted to believe that I was one who, if he had the choice, would opt for beauty. What would be the sense of going home? I asked myself. This would set me off and I'd begin to think of that other home, not New

York or the bookstore in New Paltz, but my first home in Rhode
Island, and how shortly after I returned there would be the great
celebration—the Fourth of July, the big American bicentennial—and
there would be the parade in Bristol. I could imagine Meg and me at
the parade, holding hands, smiling and waving at the red fire trucks
and the Bristol Drum and Bugle Corps. I could imagine us eating cold
salmon and green peas with Dad and my stepmother, Babs, next to
their blue swimming pool on the Fourth of July, and I wanted it all.
I wanted to be there as well. I craved to be this little ubiquitous god.
I couldn't stand to give up something for anything else. I wanted to
be an endless, sensuous, conscious wind that blew here and there and
everywhere. I didn't have any idea at the time that I was designing my
own nervous breakdown.

I was on the brink of creating the very condition I'd seen take
Mom down. It never occurred to me that by not making a choice, I
was about to be acted upon. I was trying to make my life stand still
by taking no action, or by making stabs at action, little tentative stabs
that were never completed. I was there, flying high in Amsterdam,
flying high in this new lithe boy freedom unaware that I was soon to
be shot down to earth in the rudest of ways.

After I finished my Dutch breakfast of coffee and sweet rolls, I
would play at making a decision and say to Hans and Sonia, "Well,
I hate to say goodbye, but I've decided to take the two-o'clock flight
back to New York City." Because I had never unpacked my bags from
India, I was always ready to go. After making my announcement, I'd
go out for a last farewell look at that quaint and cozy city. But I would
always take just one more peek into the window of the travel agency
around the corner, see that poster of Bali, and get swept away all over
again, the sound of the sea crashing in my ears. It was as though I
thought I could walk into the poster like Alice through the looking
glass. I'd begin to treat it like a real place. After coming out of the
poster I would go inside the agency to talk with the travel agent,
hoping all the time that he would tell me that this was not the right
time to go to Bali because it was the rainy season or something like
that. But he always said, "Oh, you must go to Bali. It's temperate there.
It's never really hot. It's always perfect and very beautiful any time
of the year."

It turned out the agent was from Bali and had moved to Amsterdam in 1941, the year I was born. A coincidence like this no longer surprised me. I saw it as a sign that came from I knew not where, and it was my job to interpret it in order to get to the right place—as though there were some right fixed place, some safe harbor waiting somewhere to receive me. Did the sign mean that because I was born in 1941 I should now go to Bali to be reborn in 1976? Or was it a sign that I would be unborn—that is, die—if I went there? All the time I was thinking these things I was vaguely aware of how my regular old neurosis was edging its way toward full-blown psychosis; yet I still had faith in the signs, which never came out all that clear. I'd change my mind about flying to New York and go back to Hans and Sonia's. When I got there I would call the airline to cancel my reservation. They were always very polite and would always say, "Yes, Mr. North, anything you want. You have an open ticket. You can fly to New York anytime in the next year."

It became a routine: calling each morning right after breakfast to reserve a seat for the afternoon flight to New York, going out for a farewell walk and a few lunchtime beers, and then coming back and canceling again. After canceling I'd slip into the deep fantasy of what the KLM flight-information and reservations lady must be thinking about Mr. North. Was she thinking I was doing hot diamond deals? Was I having a wild affair? This would be followed by guilt and anxiety that I was not living up to the fantasies that I was having about her fantasy about me.

Eventually I developed a new plan—that I would get work in one of those live sex shows in the red-light district of Amsterdam and have a sort of guaranteed, sanctioned, and remunerative sexual activity. I'd get on Hans's big black Mary Poppins bike, and with great purpose and direction, not weaving or wobbling anymore, I would ride down into the red light district at midday, before the sex shows were open to the public, and make my rounds. I'd go to each sex show and make a rather formal request to the manager. To my amazement, they all treated me with respect and credulity. They were not unlike the flight-information and reservations lady. They told me that I would have to do three shows a night with a female partner and the shows would consist of some dancing, a lot of stripping, and then: *public sexual intercourse.* They said I didn't have to come three times a night, but I should be able to get erect and make a full-blown, obvious vaginal penetration in public. It struck me as a wonderful way to make money and have a good time. Like the New Leftists say, it would be true erogenous work; all the senses would be involved, and further- more, the porn-show managers said they were open to me creating my own show. But (and here was the big, show-stopping "but") I had to have a female partner. They did not supply the female partners. The first person that came to mind was the KLM Royal Dutch flight- information and reservations woman. But somehow I knew that was just a fantasy and out of the question.

Now I had a reason to go down to the Dam again. I would go to the Dam and try to find a partner. I was sure I could, but first I needed my lunchtime beers, and after two of them I was thinking of Bali again. I no longer had a will. I was being swept away by an endless succession of fantasy whims. My will had been eaten away, and I was blowing around like some weird wind.

The days came and went. Sleep in my little attic room was fitful and filled with strange dreams. My largest span of concentration was little more than five or six minutes. Then one fateful Saturday, while waiting for Bali or my live sex show partner to appear, I made the mistake—or perhaps it wasn't a mistake, who can really say?—that completed my division of self.

I was out for a walk and I found that I was standing outside The Tubs, the infamous gay baths of Amsterdam. I'd never seen the place before; I'd only heard of it. Without thinking I just walked right in. I'd never been in a gay bathhouse, and I was very curious just to have an anonymous look around. As I paid my four guilders, put my clothes in a locker, and walked naked into those steamy tubs, I thought, Curiosity may have killed the cat, but satisfaction brought him back. I hadn't realized that my time in India had feminized me. By that I mean it had activated a very passive, languid, and beautiful side of myself. It had always been there but India brought it to the surface.

I don't have to tell you that everyone is bisexual. That's an old story. It's just a whole lot easier to live in the world if you make a choice to go one way or the other. Trying to go both ways tears most people apart. I know because I got torn.

As soon as I walked in, I found myself surrounded by all this very active and aggressive European male energy, a whole lot of which got aimed at me. I didn't feel aggressive at all. I felt extremely passive, and I must have been giving off that vibe in a big way because guys kept coming on to me, and I was surprised to find I liked it. Before I went in there I was feeling that old lonely, disappearing feeling again. But I had arrived in the eyes of all these men. I was no longer looking; I was being looked at. This was the way I thought a woman must feel being eroticized by the eyes of her lover. I could feel the energy of eyes all over me. Being looked at made me alive and present: alive in proportion to the number of eyes that were gazing at me. My whole body was tingling as those eye beams reified it.

Not only were these guys looking, or "cruising," but they were also asking me to go upstairs with them. I would answer with these little throwaways like "Not now," "Maybe later," or "I'm just looking."

After a while, a young blond guy came up to me and in a very attractive British accent asked me if I would please go upstairs with him. He was very good-looking and about twenty-two years old, but he didn't seem to want me enough to just take me. He was too polite in that British way, with his little "please." If I was going to have any sort of sex (and I had no idea what that would be at that point), I did not want it to be polite. I wanted it as raw as that whole place felt—big and juicy and raw, like some giant overripe fruit. At the same time I was curious to see what was going on upstairs, so I said "Okay," and then he asked me to stay where I was because he had to go to the loo, which I thought was weird because the whole place felt like one big loo, but he said he had to go and he'd be right back. Well, just the thought of him and his male biology doing something human in the bathroom was a turn-off, but I stood there waiting, and no sooner did I see his naked body get swallowed up by all those others than I felt a tug on my right arm, which turned into a caveman yank, and I was off for the upstairs, being dragged now by a new stranger. He took me—oh, how he did take me. And this too, like the feeling of all those eyes, was a totally new sensation.

This strange naked guy pulled my skinny nude body upstairs, which was a darker dream version of the downstairs. I felt like Eurydice being led by Orpheus out from the underworld. We were in a long corridor with small chambers closed off by sinister black rubber curtains. There was very little light, and the whole place was filled with gruntings and moanings and the strangest of primordial smells. I'd never quite smelled anything like it before. It reminded me, and yet didn't remind me. It was not a bad smell, not like the smell of raw sewage or shit, but more like a smell of seaweed and algae rotting at the bottom of a pond. It was like the smell of flora and fauna mixed with mud and fresh horse plops. It was not the sweet-fishy, fresh-cheesy smell of heterosex, but a deeper, darker sump-pump smell of men probing men in the most forbidden ways.

It wasn't bad. It was only new, or maybe not so much new as it was tapping some deep recollection of how everything must have first smelled when I was squeezing out of Mom, that one and only time, and then just for a moment I had a flash of how incredible my birth had been, how I had been right down in it all. Dad had only put his cock in there, and maybe his tongue, but I and my brothers had actually lived inside that place, and we had swum out of it, squeezed out of it. We had the whole experience. And that, I thought, was where I remembered this smell from.

Then I was back again being tugged from weird sex chamber to weirder. This strange young man I was with kept yanking the rubber curtains back in search of an empty chamber, and as he did, I caught glimpses of great hurly-burly men in the wildest positions. Still, I couldn't say I was sexually turned on by them. It was feeling like a wide-eyed, innocent child that turned me on. I was more turned on by what I couldn't see than what I could. A large spotlight would have taken all the mystery right out of that place in a flash; but now, in this dark strangeness, it was hardly different from a dream.

I moved with the motion of this man who guided me with a willful roughness that was irresistible because it was like nothing I had ever remembered feeling before. At last, finding an unoccupied chamber, he pulled me in and threw me down on an empty bed, like a hospital bed with rubber sheets on it. The little room was deliciously repulsive. It was filled with the leftover smell of perpetual sex to the point that the room itself seemed exhausted and very close to death. But I never wondered what I was doing there. I know it sounds crazy to say, but that room felt like the right spot. I knew I was about to be initiated into something very, very old. I was about to have another innocent layer peeled off of me, and peel me he did. He made love to me like I was a ripe banana. He started with the skin, my largest organ, and worked his way down.

At first he knelt over me like some sort of hungry, drooling beast. Then he pressed his wet mouth flat against my left hip and began to gobble in the most intensely hungry way. The sensation of his tongue and his rough sandpaper beard against my tender skin made my entire body shudder and shiver, as I cried out with little sighs, then held my breath against all sound, in fear that I would sound like everyone else, but deep inside there was what we all have—a sigh, a moan, the sound that comes with surrender. I stretched long and held the metal bed, feeling like I was on some pleasure rack as this nameless beast-man now began to suck on all my lower parts with so much desire that I felt I'd just pop right there, just go off in his face.

Then he began to move up with his mouth defining and bringing every part of my body to life. I lay there thinking, how could anything that felt so good be bad? He was giving me a complete tongue bath; he began lapping my belly and then up along my ribs, sucking on my left breast, then my right, like a wild baby trying to draw milk. I could feel the waves of sensation go through my whole body with each awful foul touch of his mouth and sandpaper beard until at last his body was fully extended over mine. He was over me in push-up position like a wild animal about to go for the jugular. And all the time he was doing this, other older, grosser men were constantly parting the rubber curtains and coming into the room to stand over us and watch while they played with themselves. They stood there, these gray-haired, beer-bellied, obscene satyrs, with their inflamed cocks arching up, almost glowing in the semidark. I opened my eyes wider to try to see them as they moved around the bed like hungry ghosts of lust. It was like some fevered orgiastic nightmare. Five or six of them, all naked and erect, were stroking themselves or stroking each other as they watched us getting it on below them. I was sure that they would spurt all over us if someone didn't drive them out of there, but I didn't care. There wasn't an ounce of refusal left in my body or my mind.

In between all these various suckings on my body, my German

lover—I guess you could call him that—suddenly leapt up and in an erect, athletic bound dashed at those old voyeurs, driving them out of our sex chamber. They scrambled through that rubber curtain like a big white hairless pack of jackals driven away by this hungry German lion who wanted to devour his prey in peace. When the chamber was empty, back he came to devour me. By this time we were face to face and mouth to mouth, and that was the most difficult part for me to take because it meant I had to see his face and maybe even look him in the eyes and see him for the man he was, and I wanted so much to keep him as this faceless devouring creature. I wanted him to be both all men and myself; I wanted the fantasy of having myself as well as the feeling of being desired so much.

Now to avoid his face and eyes I closed my eyes as he kissed me and then rose up over me like some mighty lizard. At the same time he did this he entered me, and that was one of the most spectacularly confusing body sensations I'd ever experienced in my life. It was a strange combination of pleasure and pain and I quickly realized that the pleasure came when I let go and opened up and didn't try to hold on, and the pain of course came when I resisted and held on. I was amazed how we fit together, like man and woman. Up until then I assumed that the positions of sodomy had to be or feel somehow unnatural, but this felt completely natural. I felt my whole spine come alive under his thrusts. His prodding cock felt somehow connected to the base of my spine and was manipulating it. Then his cock and my spine became one and my entire body turned into a cock.

As I felt freer I began to feel like I could not open enough for him. I felt wide open as I wrapped my legs around his hot sweaty back, and then, grabbing my toes with both my hands, stretched my legs in a great V to the ceiling, and let him go at it, let him in all the way as I at last forgot myself, forgot myself completely, and we came together by some unspoken chance, or by some agreement that our bodies made together, all far beyond my understanding. He came into me and I shot off, feeling the space between our bellies. It was as though his cock had entered me and gone to the base of my cock and shot up through it.

He collapsed in a sweaty heap on me, but didn't linger. He didn't want to remain in any sort of languid, intimate contact. He just jumped up like the big athletic guy he was. "Well, I'm off. It's time for a shower and a sauna," he said in his German accent, leaving me feeling like a used sack of shit. I lay there thinking, how could something that felt so good now feel so bad? Now I know what a woman feels like when there is no tenderness after. I had a sense of that feeling of desertion, how it felt to be deserted by the man.

ONE DAY, SHORTLY after the bathhouse incident, Meg arrived in Amsterdam. Meg arrived to stay a few nights with Hans and Sonia. She showed up without even having been paged at the airport. She just decided to stop in Amsterdam as I did, to break her flight up between India and New York. At first I was as surprised to see her as she was to see me. Then I was sort of happy and relieved, and then, just as quickly as all that occurred, I didn't want her to be there, because I saw clearly how over the years I had made Meg into my conscience, my guide to a controlled and meaningful life. As I said before, things seemed to matter to Meg.

Meg arrived in a bustle of purpose and direction, with all her customs papers for her Kashmir rugs in order, and all her energy focused on getting back to New York to sell her rugs and get on with her life. The yoga retreat she stayed at in Delhi had not been a very successful event, but she didn't dwell on it, and more importantly, didn't have any regrets.

Over a much-appreciated steak dinner, Meg told me how the essence of the yoga program was forced vomiting. Each morning everyone was required to drink as much water as they could, until they were so full they felt they were about to burst, and then they all had to go throw up in a large communal vomit fountain in the main courtyard of the ashram. The thought of this great vomit fountain made me laugh out loud for the first time in months, and then Meg started to laugh and just for a moment we were laughing together. I suddenly felt this wonderful comic reunion and a fondness for our insane and chaotic shared history. We had survived India, almost. We had escaped the giant collective madness of that subcontinent and were safe and reunited in a cozy restaurant in Amsterdam. Everything felt warm and good and right. Meg and my history with Meg felt like the only thing there was, the only real thing in the world, and as I sat there that line from Matthew Arnold's poem sprang up in my mind, "Ah, love, let us be true to one another!" And laughter turned into tears that welled up in my eyes but didn't flow. The whole room shimmered as though I was seeing through Jell-O. And then the dam broke and the tears came down, drenching my rare steak, and Meg, like a magnet, leaped up from her chair, flew at me, and stuck. She didn't ask me what I was crying about, and I was glad, because I wasn't entirely sure. Meg just clung to me with her unconditional, passionate love.

We had a brief, cozy evening visit with Hans and Sonia. Meg, the radiant one in the center of it all, was telling about the vomit fountain and her rugs and at the same time playing and laughing with Baby Willie. We at last retired to the attic room. We had friendly, satisfying, comfortable sex and slept, Meg with her arm across my chest. I had forgotten that was what I had been missing even more than sex: Meg's arm at night across my heart.

In the morning Meg was torn between flying home and taking a day to go to the Van Gogh museum. My God, I thought, going into a mild panic of regret, how could I have been foolish enough to have forgotten about the Van Gogh museum? And now I had a new regret to dwell on: how I had wasted my life in negative indulgence.

Meg was perceiving that something had gone wrong in me, that I was more troubled than usual; and perhaps she made a mistake when she said, "I think you better come home with me to New York." That little statement put me in a mild panic, because I began to assume that she perceived there was something wrong with me, and that if she did, then there must be. After all, she knew me so well and she seemed to think it was important for me to go home with her. At the same time I kept ranting and raving to her about how I should really take the time to go Bali.

When I'd spin out too far in too many directions, Meg would always rein me in, pull me back with questions like "Do you think you'll find yourself in Bali, Brewster? Come back with me to New York, come back and find your roots there. We'll celebrate the Fourth of July in America."

So there I was in Amsterdam, packing my bags like some sort of lost robot. I didn't have any joy about the return trip. I was without joy and without satisfaction. I couldn't find the real world I was supposed to live in. It just didn't seem to exist out there for me, and I seemed unable to make it up inside myself. I was in limbo.

I felt like a little boy standing next to Meg with my bags in my hands saying goodbye to Hans and Sonia and Baby Willie, suddenly feeling remorse because I'd not really spent any quality time with them. God, I hadn't even gone to the Van Gogh museum. I had just run all around Amsterdam like a crazy, obsessed chicken. I knew it was because I had read the wrong book when I was sick, because I didn't have my copy of *Zen Mind* with me. Well, we said goodbye and I apologized and Hans and Sonia acted like I had nothing to apologize for. They said they were sorry that I didn't want to use their place for July. Oh God, that made me even more depressed, and I told them the thought of being alone at this point was just too much; it was out of the question. And we left and headed for the airport.

It was at the airport that it happened. That's where I think I finally snapped altogether.

Meg and I had checked our bags and her rugs in for the KLM Royal Dutch flight for New York, and we were wandering around the duty-free shops, or rather Meg was wandering in her purposeful way and I was like this robot dog-boy behind her. I couldn't help noticing that I didn't have the usual feeling I had in airports. I didn't feel nervous or anxious about the flight, and I didn't want to buy any duty-free booze, which is really weird. I didn't feel anything until we got close to the boarding gate, and then I had one very strong feeling, kind of an impulse: I didn't want to go. I did not want to get on that plane. I did not want to go back to New York. This feeling turned into a kind of nervous, neurotic twitch. As we stood there in the boarding line I began to groan, and when Meg asked me what was wrong, I simply told her I needed to get my bags off the plane. Worst of all, she didn't disagree with me. She didn't try to talk me out of it or stop me.

By now the flight attendant had noticed my distress and came over to ask what was wrong, and I said, "Please, please, I can't fly today. Get my bags off the plane."

Then, to my surprise, the flight attendant paid attention to what I was saying. She stopped and picked up her walkie-talkie and began acting like she was really going to do something about my demand, and I began to think that maybe she was the same lady I had been calling on the phone each morning to reserve and cancel my reservations to New York.

I said again, "Yes, please, please, get my bags off. Get my bags off the plane!" And then as quickly as I said that, I changed my mind. "No, no, I'm on, leave them on—I mean yes—I mean no—yes—no—I mean no." And then I just fell into a short circuit, "Yes, no, yes, no, yes, no," and I groaned, almost barking like a dog, between nos and yeses and nos, and Meg, who was in front of me, slowly turned and looked at me as though I were going completely mad. Then she began to move forward toward the plane without me, and when I saw that, I just said to the flight attendant, "No, leave the bags on the plane. Let my bags go back to New York. I'm staying here. For better or for worse, I'm staying here."

And she said, still very politely, as though she were dealing with a completely sane and responsible adult male, "But, Mr. North, I'm afraid that you can't do that. You must accompany your bags to New York. That's policy." By this time Meg had already boarded without me, and I stood there sweating and shaking in my self-created hell of confusion, then took one giant step and I was on. I got on the plane to accompany my bags to New York.

I took an empty seat by a window in the rear, in what I felt was the safest part of the plane. I didn't even try to find my proper seat next to Meg. And then, for the second time in my life, I took off in a plane without holding Meg's hand and this time Meg was on the same plane. I was surprised to find that I was not afraid. I was without fear. In fact I was without almost any feeling at all.

Not only was there no emotion, there was no sense of time passing. That seven-hour flight could have been seven minutes. I remember only seeing what I took to be the tip of Greenland and then descending toward New York. I also remember watching Meg from what felt like a great distance. I wondered if she was reading or sewing or crying or doing a crossword puzzle or crying on her crossword puzzle. At some point in what seemed like a seven-minute flight, I walked up and said hello to her, like a stranger. She seemed surprised to see me, and at first I thought she was acting, because I thought she knew me well enough to know that I couldn't stay in Amsterdam without her. I sat beside her and told her that I was scared because I'd never been on a plane before without being worried the whole time, and now I didn't care one way or the other about the plane crashing. And that made me think I didn't care if I lived or died. Meg just listened. She didn't try to make sense of it or throw any interpretation on it. She just listened as we came down into crazy, hot New York in that completely mad bicentennial summer of 1976, the year of the tall ships, the strangest year of my life.

GOD, MEG WAS organized. If I was chaos, she was all order and meaning. She got me through customs and had even made plans ahead of time for our friend Barney to pick us up at the airport.

A blast of hot, humid air slammed us as we walked out of the airport and onto the sidewalk. I don't know why I call it air. It was more like the fumes of summer. It was as though we were back in India, but without the exotic, pastoral vistas. There were no cows in the streets for taxis to weave around, no barefoot men running rickshaws. Only cars and more cars, buildings roaring with air conditioners and countless machines. There was nothing feminine or soft or inviting about New York City. My whole body and mind felt as if they had been thrown into the hellish jaws of a giant robot and were being chewed up by metal teeth. I felt like a robot being chewed by a robot. I wanted to go right back to India. If I could have just jumped on the back of a giant bird . . . and flown there it would have been fine, but I couldn't face another plane trip, another giant mechanical coffin with wings.

Barney rushed over to greet us. I tried in vain to hug him and get close, as though I were there, but my body had not caught up with me yet, and it all felt like the ridiculous abstract motions of a robot. Parts of me were scattered in the long wake of our travels. Pieces were still in India, The Tubs, and in that attic room in Amsterdam. New York City was too real.

Meg was so happy to see Barney. I watched it all like a crazy play going on at a great distance. It was as though I had died and was watching life go on without me. There was no homecoming feeling, no feeling of home, only absence. I listened to Barney's enthusiastic babble about the tall ships that had sailed into the New York harbor and about how someone was filming a remake of *King Kong* at the World Trade Center, and wouldn't we just love to drive by and see that giant ape wedged in between those twin towers? "No, please," I said. "I need a drink. We need to get home." Then, even worse, I realized we had no home.

Not thinking we would return this early, we had sublet our apartment until September, and we were going to have to stay at Barney's loft. I shuddered, beginning now to realize I had touched paradise and I had not taken it. It had slipped through my fingers. I couldn't be there or here or anywhere. I couldn't relax. That would be to let in more pain than I could bear. There was no way out, I thought, as I downed my beers in Barney's kitchen and tried to drown myself.

After five beers and the insertion of my earplugs, with Meg's arm across my chest, I at last eased into a welcome unconscious sleep, which was interrupted throughout the night by fire trucks and raving bums in the street below. I woke well before dawn and just lay there soaked in sweat, trying to get a grasp on where I was, what room I was in, who I was lying next to. I woke with all the dreadful feelings of a condemned man who was about to be executed at dawn.

I tried to count my blessings. I tried to tell myself that everything was all right. After all, I had Meg; I could see; I could walk; I could still enjoy beer. But was it enough? It was nowhere near enough. I didn't want merely to be a survivor. Merely to survive was a disgrace in America. We were doomed the day our forefathers had written "life, liberty, and the pursuit of happiness." Yes, "pursuit of happiness," I thought. Exactly. I saw Americans as a pack of mad grey-hounds, all with their tongues hanging out, speeding after some stuffed rabbit.

Meg tried to get me to gear down and focus. "First things first," she told me. "We must slowly and carefully rebuild our lives here and not overly complicate them with frantic fantasy."

I was afraid now to make any action out of fear of the multiplic-ity of crazy reactions it might cause, so I tried to follow Meg's plan. First we would take a bus out to her parents' house in New Jersey, where our van had been parked. Then we'd get the van back on the road and go to Rhode Island to visit my father and stepmother for the Fourth of July. That way we'd escape the madness. I didn't want to see any celebration. I didn't want to see fireworks or tall ships.

Everything was too overwhelming. The world was too filled with objects and people, and some of the people had to go, had to be condemned to death so that the productive ones could go on living and make the earth into the good and wonderful paradise it was meant to be in the first place, and should certainly have been by this bicenten-nial summer. And worst of all, I knew that I was one of those who should go. I should step aside for people like Meg, the protective rug merchants of the world, the blessed people with a plan and a will.

Meg's mother could see that I was very upset and overly thin. At the same time she was not given to indulgence. She came from one of those places where a nervous breakdown was viewed as weak and self-indulgent behavior. So on the whole she left me alone, and I spent my visit there draining endless cans of Budweiser, watching our great nation on TV prepare for its bicentennial summer: smiling faces eating pies and cakes all across America.

Meg cheered when the van started right up, and we were off for yet another joyless visit to another version of home in Rhode Island. Meg drove, and I sat there like the zombie I'd become, wondering how we would ever get through this season in hell together. By the time we got on the Connecticut Thruway, I was reading to Meg out loud from my well-underlined copy of Norman O. Brown's *Life Against Death*—perhaps the wrong book, but I kept feeling there was comfort in it somewhere, although I couldn't grasp it. I think I was trying to identify, embrace, at least understand what this dark force was in me,

this huge drive to return to nothing. I'd read a passage to myself and
have the fantasy that I understood it, and then I'd get all excited and
read it out loud to Meg. But I could see Meg didn't understand it, and
when she didn't understand it, it fell apart in my mind like gob-
bledygook, and nothing held together. I wanted that damn book to
save me by helping me forgive myself for being so neurotic. I was
hoping it would allow me to see myself as a fatality of civilization.

I thought that being with my father and my stepmother, Babs,
would be a good way to escape the bicentennial madness. It would
definitely be fuzzy and subdued, and I thought, Well, we'll just take
it easy and get drunk by the swimming pool, treat it like a vacation.
And maybe if they're interested, we'll show them a few of our slides
of India Meg had just gotten developed.

I had lingering fantasies of Mom being alive, standing at the gate
of the driveway, weeping with joy as her prodigal son came down the
road, home from the sea at last, with his round-the-world stories and
his duffel bag of dirty laundry thrown over his back. I was able, with
Meg's help, to realize that was a far-gone fantasy, but I still expected
Babs and Dad to be just a *little* bit excited about our trip to India.

We drove to Rhode Island on July third. The road up, at least
as far as New Haven, was like some insane, end-of-the-world *National
Lampoon* takeoff on the Fourth of July, only I wasn't laughing. I was
looking for, if not the answer, at least for some way to forgive it all.
I thought if I could figure out what Norman O. Brown was talking
about before we got to Rhode Island, I'd be saved. I wanted him to
tell me it was not my fault, and not Mom's fault, and if I had to find
fault to save myself, it was in the capitalistic culture I'd been born into.
I wanted him to tell me that my pain was real, that I was one of
civilization's discontents, and now I had to learn to be courageous and
live with it, and not leak out so much on everyone. I couldn't help
noticing how I had marked up all the pages of the book just like Mom
used to do while reading her weekly Christian Science lesson from
Science and Health.

I felt so alone and out of it, so unpatriotic, as giant breadbox-
shaped station wagons filled with large American families passed and
wove in front of us, cutting us off as they dragged hideous speedboats
and trailers behind them. There'd be a flash of three or four children

smiling idiotic sugar smiles out the back window of a station wagon as a giant semi truck moved up behind them, like a great mechanized whale about to devour them whole. After New Haven, the traffic thinned out some, but it still seemed like one big race to pleasure, everyone heading up the coast to get to the sea before that great bicentennial Fourth of July popped in their faces. And as we rode I had a dreadful sense of how that giant megalopolis was spreading like a great colorless cancer up the East Coast, and every time I heard that phrase "Northeast Corridor," I thought of cancer: Washington spreading into Baltimore, Baltimore bleeding into Wilmington, which crept into Philly, which overflowed into Trenton, then Newark, and New York, then on to Bridgeport and New Haven. It was one long, endless sprawl of tacky houses, factories, shopping malls, and multiplex cinemas. The desperate thought of it grinding in my mind made me search all the harder for the answer, the explanation, as I paged through that damned *Life Against Death* with shaking hands. Then, just before Connecticut turned into Rhode Island, there was a brief, beautiful stretch of highway where we could see some rolling hills and one or two working farms in the distance, and this, at last, led into the less populated region of Rhode Island where Dad and Babs lived, our weird sanctuary from that 1976 Fourth of July.

Dad and Babs had chosen that ranch house as a kind of pleasure dome where they could start a new life just down the road from their painful origins. They had bonded out of mutual pain and disaster. Shortly after Mom killed herself, Babs's husband drank himself to death. He'd started drinking in a big way the day the youngest of their three sons was killed in a marine training accident at Camp Pendleton, and he didn't stop until it killed him. Dad also started drinking in a big way after Mom died and Topher, Cole, and I fled what was left of the nest, and one night he woke up in a puddle of blood. He had made it as far as the telephone and was able to call the emergency unit, the same one that came so fast for Mom just a few months before, but he passed out before they arrived. Something inside Dad gave way, and there was blood everywhere, but they got him to the hospital before his entire life leaked out. I didn't go home to visit that time. I only called in each day to see how he was doing. Coleman didn't go home, either. Topher had moved to Providence and I'm not sure how often he checked in on Dad, if at all. But when Babs, who lived down the road, found out about Dad's condition, she began to visit him every day and some new bond was made.

Babs and Dad married less than a year after both their mates did themselves in. I didn't blame them for that. It must have been hell to live alone swamped in those painful memories. Babs's family was less tolerant of her new marriage, and her older son was acting like Hamlet when he complains about his mother getting married before the funeral meats were cold. He'd have nothing to do with Dad or Babs after the wedding. Her younger son was more demonstrative. He had just returned from Vietnam addicted to heroin and ended up burning down Babs's old farmhouse, with most of her antiques in it, when he was stoned and crashing there with a bunch of his Nam buddies. They got out before the fire got them, but the farmhouse was a total loss. By then, Dad and Babs had moved into their new home just down the road from the dark spot where Mom had died in the driveway. Such a history of pain. I went over it again to myself and out loud to Meg, who stared ahead into that holiday rush like a freaked-out fighter pilot trying to land her plane.

As we pulled in on that black asphalt driveway, we saw the whole yard as an immaculate stage setting that gave our eyes some rest, after the hectic highway. It was blessed order, perhaps the result of a fascist mind, but certainly the best part of it: the fresh-cut lawn, as well-kept as a golf course; the flagpole with the American flag fluttering slightly in a gentle southeasterly wind up from Narragansett Bay, which lay in the distance far below.

Dad and Babs must have been on the lookout for us (most likely their entire morning's activity), because as soon as Meg parked our van, they came out of the front door onto the flagstone terrace to greet us. Dad cried "Hi-ho, hi-ho!" in some strange parody of a party voice, like an actor who was standing close to you on stage but making his voice sound as if it was coming from far away.

"Hi, kids," Babs said, and Meg and I both delivered the obligatory pecks on Babs's weathered, leathery face with its rosy glow of ruptured capillaries. Then there was the obligatory bundle-of-wire hug with Dad, followed by his old quick pat on my back, his almost pleading signal for release from too much intimacy. We all backed away from each other. Meg and I had arrived.

As soon as I stepped into that house the panic began. I kept having flashes of India, Amsterdam, and fantasies of Bali. I kept thinking I could be in Bali now rather than here, and every time I thought that I'd realize I wasn't in either place. I wasn't in Rhode Island and I wasn't in Bali. I was stuck like some tortured ghost in a self-created limbo between a place I had seen too much of and a place I had never seen.

When I saw Dad's bright blue swimming pool out the living room window, it occurred to me that was exactly where I wanted to be. That was the reason I'd come home in the first place. I'd come home so I could swim in Dad's pool. I sensed the only thing that could bring me back into this world was to immerse myself in it, and I rushed to change into my Speedo swimsuit while Meg brought our bags into the guest room.

Babs went into the kitchen to start dinner and Dad followed me around the house asking me what I was doing, as I did the obvious, and then commented on it for him. "Now I'm changing into my swimsuit, Dad. Now I'm going for a swim in your pool, Dad. Don't worry about me, Dad, I won't drown."

Stepping into their backyard was like walking into a Kodachrome Hollywood postcard, a synthetic reality. The very unreality of it allowed me to be there, as I stepped out, a little chilled in my new slim, fatless body, the string of my Speedo Ocean Brief pulled tight to take up the slack.

Above the pool was a powder-blue sky with streaks of pink from the descending sun, and the sliver of a new moon could just be seen. Below this expanse of blue, framed by the high wooden fence that surrounded the back patio, was the other blue of the magnificent protected pool and its deck of dark green Astroturf. I could feel the turf's cool oily resilience under my bare feet as I moved toward that perfectly heated water and plunged. That dive and its mad splash, the facedown beating strokes that carried me from one end of the pool to the other, made me feel like I had arrived at last.

But that feeling was almost instantly broken by Dad's following me around the edge of the pool with his ongoing, chattering commentary about how he had measured the temperature at a steady seventy-six degrees all day, and didn't I want to have a look at his new automatic robot pool cleaner. It was also broken by Babs calling from the kitchen window, "My goodness, Brewster, we're going to have to put some fat on that body of yours! It looks like India has turned you two kids into skeletons." I was too excited by the fact that Babs had acknowledged our trip to India to care that she had broken my picture of perfection.

I was still swimming when my body sensed, as if participating in a kind of intuition of fluids and liquids, the encroaching cocktail hour. The cast of melancholy light breaking over the tops of distant elms and maples sent terns, sparrows, and swallows flying home to their night nests and left the sad, empty, lonely chirping of robins on distant lawns. All of this made the entire swimming pool feel like a giant dry martini, and gave me the sign that it was at last cocktail hour. I pulled myself out, wrapped up in one of Babs's big, fluffy, brightly colored bath towels, and went in to change.

As Meg and I passed through that dustless, posh, wall-to-wall–carpeted living room, we saw Babs nervously thumbing through *House and Garden,* waiting for Dad, who paced by one of the antique grandfather clocks, to give the official bartender's "okay." The clock said five of five and I could feel that familiar, tense anticipation grow in the room as the hands of the clock slowly moved round and struck: one, two, three, four, five; and all the tension of the day gave way as Dad said, at last, in that formal bartender's voice, "May I fix you a drink, Mrs. North?"

Babs put down her magazine as if she were surprised by this offer. She just sat there for a moment pretending to consider it, as if she might at any moment say no and order cranberry juice instead. And then in the most casual tone that she could deliver—and she delivered it as convincingly as any good actress might—Babs said, "Well, I don't mind if I do, Mr. North. Do you think you could fix me a dry vodka martini with three onions?"

And Mr. North answered, "Well, I don't know why not," and they were off for their glorious cocktail ritual, Babs going into the TV room to turn on the local news while Dad headed for the bar to begin his measuring and pouring. Soon the tinkle of ice against glass blended

with the local news and the Muzak that played in every room under
it all.

Before Mom died, and in the early years while we were growing
up, there was no formal cocktail hour in our home, perhaps because
Mom didn't drink, and Dad drank very little in those days. He kept
his bottles out of sight. When he opened the liquor cabinet in the
dining room, he always took out a bottle of bourbon and measured
it carefully. He used to make two tall bourbon-and-waters, which he
drank sequentially—just enough to relax.

But now that Dad had a wife who was also a drinking partner,
the bottles were proudly on display, sitting there on a fully equipped
bar with lots of cocktail accessories. It looked like a little altar.

Although Babs had a vision of herself as a gourmet cook, it was
not so easy for her to drink and cook a gourmet meal at the same time.
We were usually doomed to raw meat and oversteamed vegetables. For
some reason it never went the other way; we never ended up with raw
vegetables and overcooked meat. I guess that had to do with Dad's
needs. Only Dad knew how to cook a steak while completely high
on bourbon, and Dad wasn't cooking that night. He was waiting for
the Fourth to do his big barbecue.

That night Babs served us frozen frogs' legs. They came out on
a plate looking like the hairless amputated legs of Lilliputian Olympic
runners. Meg and I both rolled our eyes and looked across at each
other. It was funny how Babs's cooking was bringing Meg and me
closer; and as we looked at each other, Babs slipped those hairless little
legs, garnished with parsley, onto our TV tables somewhere in the
middle of a national news report about the tall ships.

Meg could hardly touch them, but I was drunk enough to eat
them whole and ask for seconds. After dinner and dessert, somewhere
in the middle of "The Odd Couple," Babs, with the help of Meg,
cleared all the dishes away and put them in the dishwasher, starting the
last annoying mechanical grind before Dad's white-noise box took
over to drown out the sound of night crickets.

Still without a word of inquiry about India, Dad and Babs began
to get ready for bed. Babs disappeared into their bedroom and Dad
performed his last evening rituals: checking the home weather unit for
wind velocity and barometric pressure; instructing me as to what lamps

not to touch or turn off because they were on automatic timers. Then he retired to Babs and his white-noise box.

Meg went to our guest room to read and I went for a welcome walk alone. I wandered in the warm night down the long country lane that led, if you followed it all the way, past the place of Mom's death and on to the charred remains of Babs's family farmhouse. Protected from fear and anxiety by the warm glow of alcohol, I wandered and staggered under the stars. Nothing could touch me now, and for a minute I even considered walking all the way to our old house at the end of Shady Lane to meditate on Mom, to try to see that night in July I had missed when I was in Mexico with Meg. But it was too far to walk and too painful to dwell on, so I decided instead to try to sneak into Dad's pool for a naked swim. I had a feeling I could pull it off if I was real quiet and didn't splash.

Taking my clothes off brought back the most delicious body memories from childhood, of running naked on summer nights under a full moon, running nude through the white statuary in the yard of the mansion across the street from my honeysuckle boyhood home. And I suddenly wanted to have myself and I rubbed my hands all over my warm naked body trying to surprise it with some foreign touch, some unexpected move.

I slipped into that heated pool and without a sound I swam on my back, looking up at the stars. At the same time I ran my hands down over my new body, my ass and thin thighs, as they opened and spread and pumped like some fully alive animation of those frog legs.

When I got to our bedroom I found Meg asleep with the light on. Her pixie haircut was still damp like a duck's tail from her shower, and she looked fresh and innocent on the cotton sheets. She was almost a child again in my eyes, except for that one troubled blue vein that was slightly raised on her forehead. I stood there wondering how she could still go on loving me when I seemed to be doing all I could to drive her away.

It was a miracle, but I was able to sleep the whole night through, and even woke in the morning to one glorious moment of forgetfulness when only the delicious sensation of being wrapped in those cotton sheets was real. Then the panic set in again as all the crazy images of India, Ladakh, and Amsterdam swept over me. As soon as

I felt that anxious bale-of-wire feeling in my legs, I thought the best thing for me to do was get into the pool and work it out.

Dad and Babs had already been up for a long time, puttering and muttering. "Hi-ho, hi-ho!" Dad cried in his pretend faraway voice. Babs was, as ever, in the kitchen, rinsing the breakfast dishes by hand as she stared out over the still blue pool, then stacking them, completely clean, into the dishwasher.

"Good morning, Brew," she said in her Rhode Island twang. I said good morning back to the both of them and staggered out to the pool, still slightly hung over and half asleep. Dad followed me out, asking, did I have the right towel? How did I sleep? What did I want for breakfast? Were Meg and I going to eat breakfast together? And did we want Babs to fix it for us? Did we want the bacon already made, in the warmer? This was followed by a numerical rundown of the morning readings of all the gauges in the house: air temperature, barometric pressure, wind velocity, and the temperature of the pool. Never once did he ask me what it was like to travel all the way to India and back. In fact, as I stood poised, about to dive, I realized that Dad and Babs still had not asked me one question about India.

A big splash and I was in the pool again, and for a moment I was also in the moment again. It was all just water and motion, and something I called "me" in motion in it. This was the only time I ever understood my boundaries, because the thing outside of me was so apparently different, so liquid, so other, so unlike those solid things, those people and lawns and cars and mountains and buildings and trees. It was such a great curative, this thrashing and splashing, and I wondered as I swam back and forth from one end of the pool to the other how would I survive back in New York City without a swimming pool.

The swim woke me up and brought me back to life and I managed to get through Dad's living room interrogations about water temperature without much problem. In the bedroom I peeled off my wet swimsuit, dried myself with one of Babs's prize fluffy pool towels, and slipped naked into bed beside Meg, who rolled over smiling, but when she saw my face hers took on a kind of worried look. She wanted to know what was wrong. I told her I'd just had a swim and felt fine;

but she knew that I was wired and hungry for relief through what she called manic sex.

"Please, Brewster," Meg begged, "I just don't feel turned on in your father's house. Don't you know that? Haven't you noticed that by now? Let's get up and do something productive. Let's go wash and simonize the van before we go to the beach."

"Oh, all right," I said, groaning slightly, as I reluctantly dragged myself, semierect, out of the bed. "We can wash the car, but we can't go to the beach because it's the Fourth of July and I don't want to see it. I just want to pretend this whole weekend doesn't exist."

Meg was in better spirits over breakfast, but I was groaning more. I was groaning between bites of toast and swallows of Babs's dreadful instant coffee and Dad was hovering around me, washing and drying every utensil I'd put down on the table for more than ten seconds. I'd pick it up again and find it to my surprise all clean. Meg was reading the paper, oblivious (she had a way of falling into the news). After all of this, and a couple of Babs's Camel regulars which made me cough and wheeze, Meg and I at last went out to try to wash and simonize the van.

Dad was out there, running the flag up the flagpole, and I knew what was driving me nuts. On holidays you were supposed to have a good time, and I felt under so much pressure to have one; but I didn't know how. I never had a good time on holidays. People were supposed to let loose and laugh, and they usually did, but I usually heard them at a distance, and it drove me nuts. Sure, they had been working real hard in jobs they hated, so they had something to unwind from. I was just some sort of postadolescent searcher-drifter, going from job to job, then falling through cracks into anxiety when I wasn't working. I didn't know how to have fun.

After the van was all simonized and clean and shiny, we stood back and looked at it. Meg smiled, enjoying the pleasure not only of a job well done, but also of the transformation of that van into something like a smiling green truck in a storybook. I stood and looked at Meg's face, enjoying her enjoyment; Meg, my go-between. The van was like a green toy on the black, slightly mud-stained asphalt, framed by a perfect green lawn under a luffing red, white, and blue American flag, and for a moment it all held together like some physical poem of itself, a poem of the real world captured. But that vision gave way to my internal films again: me in Bali hanging out in some expatriate hippie commune, me just hanging out in timeless splendor with some great interconnected unspoken agreement between man and woman. Doing what, I couldn't tell; just lying there stoned, looking up into the not-at-all-meaningful palm trees. And yet, I thought, in the face of meaningless death, it must take great courage to do nothing, to just do nothing at all.

The rest of the day was spent out by the pool waiting for the end of the day to come, waiting for cocktail hour. Meg and I lay in the white hot noonday limbo light, Meg reading Dad and Babs's endless collection of glossy magazines. She thumbed through them, seeming content to read almost anything. She could switch from *The Magic Mountain* to *House and Garden* without that concentrated expression on her face ever changing once. She concentrated on everything she did and I loved her and hated her for it. When I wasn't watching her concentrate, I was trying to concentrate, but I never was able to find the right object.

I was definitely stuck in what is called discursive mind, bouncing from association to association, reduced to moving in a triangle, going from reading and underlining *Life Against Death* to fantasies of Bali to my new obsession with saving drowning bugs from my father's swimming pool. By midday, my obsession with saving the drowning bugs had taken over.

Dad and Babs stayed indoors. They didn't lie in the sun for fear of skin cancer. From where I sat watching all those struggling bugs, I could hear Dad and Babs in their endless inane putterings: comforting background sounds, like white noise. Occasionally the puttering sounds would be broken by little flare-ups between them, when their random orbits collided or when Dad would need help finding the ice-cream maker that he had most likely hidden from himself in some boozy haze, and now, too ashamed to admit it, he was turning on Babs to accuse her of hiding it.

Meg was lost in *Yankee* magazine as I got up and discovered to my horror just how many different kinds of bugs were drowning in Dad's pool. I'd never seen so many and in such different stages of panic.

I didn't know the names of most of them, but I was able to identify one or two big, repulsive june bugs, some grasshoppers, a few Japanese beetles, houseflies, and, most important, one or two good-luck lady-bugs. At first I went after them with a broken branch I found at the edge of the house near Babs's rose garden; then I shifted to the pool-cleaning net in order to rescue more in one sweep. I spent most of the day pulling each and every bug out and placing it in a safe little dry place to dry out on the rubber edge of the AstroTurf. It gave me such a feeling of accomplishment to watch them dry off, slowly come back to life, and creep away over that green AstroTurf into the rose garden. And yes, a sense of meaning gradually crept over me as I thought, All those bugs were saved today because I didn't go to Bali. When I finally looked up from that siege of drowning bugs, I saw Meg asleep in the sun. Except for that raised blue vein in the center of her forehead, she looked at peace. I noticed that the sound of puttering in the house had come to a halt, capped off by Babs calling out the kitchen window, "Aren't you kids hungry for some lunch?"

I wanted a beer more than I wanted lunch, but I figured if I had lunch I could have the beer with it. Dad had nothing but those damned Miller Lites around, so I had four to relax me after all those traumatic bug rescues. All the time I was eating my tuna salad sandwich, though, I kept seeing more and more bugs step off that giant edge of the pool and fall in and struggle on their backs, until I had to put my sandwich down and go rescue them. I never got back to *Life Against Death* that day. I spent the day saving bugs.

At last for one glorious moment the pool was free of bugs, and I plunged in to refresh myself. I felt that fluid, liquid feeling, and in no time at all it was blessed cocktail hour again. We'd almost gotten through that day without the sound of a parade or one firecracker. What a blessing, I thought, as I did my frantic laps from one end of the blue pool to the other.

We showered and dressed. Both Meg and I dressed in white, me in my white cotton Indian pants, Meg in a white cotton dress, and we went back out to sit by the pool. We drank there together with Dad and Babs as the evening brought a coolness to our suntanned bodies under the white cotton. After I'd had many drinks—Lite beers with scotch poured in to beef them up—and bunches of light peanuts that tasted like Styrofoam, Dad lit the coals and brought out his bloody bicentennial slab of raw meat, which I could see was attracting small swarms of mosquitoes and flies. As soon as Babs noticed the flies and mosquitoes, she suggested that we eat indoors. That became the new overriding topic: should we eat out or in? Was it too cold out? Was it too hot in? Were there too many bugs? The sizzling steak smoke rose up like a cowboy's campfire, and Dad said that the steak smoke rising straight up like that was a sign of continuing good weather. As if it mattered: how would we all act any differently if it rained?

Dad and Babs got in a panic every time Meg or I opened the screen door, because they said we were letting the flies in. I kept thinking of all the flies in India and all the flies I had saved from drowning that very afternoon, which were probably the ones following me into the house to celebrate being saved.

In the middle of this holiday bedlam of steak smoke and flies, Babs, after about three and a half martinis, got out her antique fly gun and went after them. It was this old tin gun that was supposed to have once belonged to Roger Williams, and it was worth, I was sure, a small fortune. There was nothing to this little gun. It looked like a toy tin handgun painted barn red with a spatulalike device that bent back and hitched on to the little trigger, which, when pulled, released the spatula; and if you were at the proper distance from the fly, it smacked the bug dead. It was such a funny, simple, stupid little thing, but no one was laughing. Everyone was dead serious, and I wanted so much to laugh. But I couldn't laugh, I guess because I kept thinking, Gee, this is funny—I saved all these drowning flies just so they could be mashed by an antique fly gun that once belonged to Roger Williams. Dad didn't think it was funny. He kept yelling, "Put that damned thing down, Babs, and get yourself a proper fly swatter!" By now Meg was off reading a brief history of Providence Plantation in the last of the fading light.

The steak on our plates was rare, definitely rare. It was very, very rare, and the blood from that meat attracted the mosquitoes in droves. Finally, Dad got out his big bug bomb and set it off around our feet and we sat there with the poison steaming up around our ankles as we tore into our raw meat. I bit into my steak and all the juice and the blood immediately put me into a state of desire. The more I chewed, the more I wanted. The more I ate, the less satisfied I felt. It was all chew, chew, chew, angry chew, and then big gulps, swallow, wash down with more and more Lite beer. Meg couldn't eat it. It was too rare for her. She asked for a charred end piece with all the toasted fat on it. Dad drank the steak blood from a serving spoon. Babs killed flies. Meg rolled her eyes and I went back to Bali in my mind. I was lying naked in a hammock stretched between two palm trees under the stars and there were no bugs anywhere.

After dinner I tried to introduce something new by offering to give Babs and Dad a slide show of our trip to India, and to my amazement they were not completely closed to the idea. So while Babs and Meg cleared the dishes, I helped Dad set up the screen and slide projector. We set it up in the living room, which was a major project, and Dad was now groaning louder than I was groaning. For both of us, it seemed a joyless task. Then Meg got out the slides, which we were both very proud of, and we showed them, alternating our random comments as we traced our trip from Delhi to Kashmir up to Ladakh and back to Delhi again. It looked like a story of someone else's life. Meg and I looked like characters in someone else's movie.

Babs and Dad hardly reacted at all, and after the slide show was over, Babs said, "Well, you kids really had some trip, and you're lucky to be back, aren't you?" Neither Meg nor I responded to her rhetorical question. We just got up and made motions like Dad and Babs as they got ready for bed.

Everyone went to bed and I stayed in the den drinking Lite beer to ease me down from all the hectic relaxation of that day. Then I dug out the old family album and pored over those idyllic photos of Mom and Dad's courtship, those old pictures of them on a moose hunt in Maine, with Gramma North and her boyfriend, all of them standing on a big log with guns in hand, smiling. They looked like they were having such a great time. None of the faces in those photographs had the existential, puzzled, troubled look that my face had in our India slides. No, those moose-hunt photos radiated smiling, innocent hope and anticipation of a new bright world to come.

I went on slowly turning the pages, following Mom and Dad's

life through to me, their second son, who in early photos looked like a sour, disgruntled little prunehead. Why was I so sour so early on? I wondered. Was I born into the world that way? I got up to fetch another beer, but there were no more beers in the kitchen refrigerator. I would have to go into the basement to bring up a new six-pack from Dad's basement refrigerator. Switching on the basement light, I started down the stairs. Halfway down, I was seized with fear. At first I could not get an image of what was frightening me. And then I realized it was the fear that Mom's ghost was about to haunt me. I stood paralyzed on the stairs, afraid that I would see Mom in some semicremated state, the way they say an incinerating body looks as it sits up from the extreme heat, popping up and twisting like cooking slabs of bacon. I was afraid I would see her body now in my uncontrolled imagination the way I saw it in that vision in Mexico, when she appeared in the flames in Olaf's fireplace around the time that she had actually been cremated.

I didn't want to go into that basement, but I wanted, and really needed, another beer; so I moved fast. I felt Mom's deadly, yawning, dripping, burned, disturbed presence in every corner, and as I ran up the basement stairs with that six-pack of Miller Lite in my hand, I could feel her hissing demon breath tearing at my backside. I could feel the dark, charred spirit of Mom that had never, at least by me, been properly laid to rest.

By the time I got upstairs I was so upset that I had to drink three more beers just to calm down, and as I drank them I remembered another ghost of Mom, less fearful, but more depressing, more banal. It came to me in a recurring dream I had of Babs and Dad with Mom moving like an unseen ghost between them. Those dreams came just after Babs and Dad got married and moved into their new house. In the dream I would see Babs and Dad walking around their new kitchen trying out all their new electrical gadgets and appliances. In the middle of it all was Mom, a less substantial figure, dressed in a summer smock, drifting like a transparent ghost or hologram of herself through Babs and Dad, who didn't see her and just went on filling the dishwasher with already clean dishes and turning on the trash masher and the electric can opener.

WHEN WE GOT BACK to New York I asked Meg to take some photos of me so I would have a decent eight-by-ten black-and-white glossy to help me get into the movies. In addition to her other talents, Meg was also a good photographer. She had a great eye. I knew she'd do a good job. And she seemed enthusiastic about my new focus. When I became focused she became even more focused, as she moved the camera in on my face. She had almost stopped judging me and my crazy whims. Now she was happy if I could get through the day with five minutes' worth of focused time. And I think I did focus on her taking my picture. We spent a long time doing it. We shot all around Barney's loft. I noticed every time Meg aimed the camera at me, it seemed to calm me down, like in the old days when I used to do my modeling. Maybe that was why I was trying to break into films. It wasn't that I was trying to own the perfect swimming pool. If being in front of a camera was a calming event, then I wanted to be in front of a camera all the time.

But when Meg developed the film, I didn't like the face I saw. In fact, I was frightened by it. There was far too much sadness in it. I had no idea that I was that skinny and that sad. The cheekbones I inherited from Mom were starting to push through. There was no way I could be cast in a film with a face reflecting that much pain and sadness. When I saw those photos I saw the truth of something I couldn't face. I couldn't face my face, and that's when the rolling and groaning began again. All that crazy indecision began again.

I've lost the linear order of my memory, and so I'm assuming that I must have been very confused in that bicentennial summer. Up until now I've been telling you the events of that great fall from the top of the world to the bottom pretty much in the order I think they happened. But my memory gets muddled. I remember the trip to Rhode Island as a little break, the slightest respite from the continuous motion of hurtling down from the Himalayas to the bottom of the Grand Canyon.

So it was July 1976 and summer in New York City and I would start my days in the most agitated of states, just rolling on the floor and groaning. When I wasn't rolling on the floor and moaning, I was calling travel agents to get them to talk to me about their discount summer tours; and for just a little while their responsible voices on the phone would lull me into a calm state. She or he would give such a complete description of Greece or Bali that I felt I didn't have to go because I could see it so vividly, too vividly perhaps. It would become like a loop of Kodachrome film in my mind. After I got through all of that, I would go out and buy *Back Stage* and *Show Business* and look for film casting calls. I knew there was no way I could land a modeling job, because I couldn't stand still long enough. Barney thought I was nuts, although he didn't use the word "nuts," to be looking for film work in trade papers. Barney made his own art films. He made beautiful films for hardly any money at all with his little sixteen-millimeter camera and eventually showed them to a small but enthusiastic audience. When he was out of money he would go to work as a cameraman for the big guys. He told me that there was no way I would find work through the trade papers. I had to go out and get an agent and come at it all very slowly and professionally. I had to learn how to be patient and wait and hang out. I also had to learn how to become a part of the scene. Talent was at the bottom of the list. Looks helped. But my little book of traveler's checks was getting thinner and thinner and I needed a job right away. I couldn't imagine what I could do. All that occurred to me was that I could try to call my morning groanings and rollings some sort of experimental dance and sell tickets. I could have people come and see me roll on the floor of Barney's loft. When I told Meg and Barney that, they laughed, and I was happy that I made them laugh, but also sad that I was not laughing with them.

Some time during all of this I began to make plans to drive to Provincetown alone. It occurred to me that all my problems were the result of the fact that I had never made it to Provincetown that summer of 1963, when I'd made so many aborted attempts to escape from Mom.

But Meg and Barney and Barney's girlfriend, Sylvia, thought I'd better get to a psychiatrist real quick, before August, when they all went on vacation. Sylvia gave me the name of someone she said was a really good shrink on Central Park West. Not only was he good, she said, but he was smart and healthy. He was healthy in the head, which is a rarity, she said. He was in the business because he liked helping people. Sylvia had called him and prepared him for my visit.

I was nervous going up to Central Park West and could hardly sit still on the subway. I kept yelling out like a nervous bag lady, not words so much as crazy shouts, but no one paid any attention to me. Maybe if they had I would have calmed down, like when a camera was aimed on me. But it didn't happen. Maybe I was living in the wrong city, I thought. Maybe I had to move to San Francisco or Seattle, where people would notice me when I acted out and then I'd have to calm down and act like them.

This psychiatrist's office was not at all big or ostentatious for a Central Park West location, and I thought he seemed to be a nice, smart guy when I was able to sit still long enough to get a fix on him. But most of the time I was bouncing off the walls, bouncing from chair to chair, and pacing around his office. I figured he could see that I was pretty crazy, but he must be used to that. He stayed calm while I moved around, and I liked the fact that he was able to stay calm in the middle of all my agitation. He just sat there with his hands folded under his chin and spoke to me in a real calm, adult voice. It was one of the few groups of words that I remember clearly from that summer. I remembered a lot of other things, but not people's phrases and sentences. He treated me like a responsible adult. He said it in a kind of gentle, professorial tone, with only a hint of drama in his voice. He said, "Brewster, you are going through a severe manic-depressive episode, and right now you are locked into the manic mode. I understand that it's a painful state, but still it's sensational and very dramatic and therefore in a perverse way almost enjoyable, or at least something to hold on to. In that mode at least it feels like something is going on all the time. But I have to tell you, Brewster, that this manic state you are in now will pass in due course. It will turn into a depressive episode, and that, I can tell you, will not be fun. I have to be very frank with you. That episode will be very, very depressing."

"What are you—what are you saying?" I asked him without

looking at him, as I paced the floor in front of him. "All this 'episode' stuff makes me feel like I'm the star in my own soap opera. I just want to know how much it will cost to get fixed."

All the time I was saying this to him, I was in fact afraid, deep-down afraid, that I had inherited Mom's illness, that it had been there all the time and now it was surfacing at last.

He was as frank and straight with me about his price as he was about his diagnosis. He said, "I cost eighty dollars a session with no sliding scale, and I'm going to want you to come see me three times a week."

I was thunderstruck. I was so shocked that I was almost instantly cured. In fact, for a moment I thought it was some new form of shock therapy that he was using, like some sort of weird monetary Zen slap. I got even more nervous and told him it was impossible. There was no way I could afford to pay that kind of money. I told him it was simply out of the question, and then he said something that scared me even more. He told me that I had to look at this as major surgery. He told me that what I had was like a cancer that needed to be operated on immediately. He told me to ask my father for the money if I didn't have it. "After all," he said, "if you had cancer and needed an operation and didn't have the money, wouldn't you ask your father for it?" Well, he had me there, and I didn't argue. I didn't even ask him how he knew my father had the money to pay for therapy. I guess in spite of my madness I still had the look of a Boston Brahmin. I didn't tell him that I couldn't ask my father for the money because my father didn't believe in psychiatrists, because they'd done nothing to help Mom. I didn't tell him I couldn't ask for the money because Dad had spent thousands on Mom, and I didn't want to put him through that again. I didn't tell him that what I needed was a long sabbatical, a break from life. I needed someone to take me on as a special patient. I so badly wanted to be special, and not simply that person he had already labeled in his head as your basic manic-depressive. I didn't tell him any of this. I just walked out of the office, and when I got outside on that hot-as-India Central Park West sidewalk, I got so afraid that I almost disappeared, like the way people faint when they're in pain. I thought of Meg's sister, who when she was giving birth to her first child in a farmhouse upstate was in so much pain she cried out "I'm leaving!" as though she could jump up and leave her body there in bed to have the baby on its own, while some other part of her took a long walk in the woods.

After that visit I began to plead with Barney and Meg to please get me to a white room, a white room with solid ceilings and white right angles in some nice air-conditioned mental ward where I'd have a sabbatical to do nothing. I didn't want anything coming in any-more—no more input, please. I wanted to swing way out into the restful void for a bit, and then be able to swing back when I was ready and rested. So one hot day, perhaps toward the end of July, I don't know (I had lost all track of days), I asked them—no, pleaded with them—"Please take me to Bellevue." (What a crazy choice, looking back on it now. That must have been one of the signs that I'd gone mad, that I chose Bellevue.) And they did it. Barney and Meg drove me there in the van. I think they were at their wits' end and just didn't know how to deal with me anymore. They weren't getting any sleep because I couldn't calm down ever since that damn shrink told me I could expect to be that way for a while. I wanted to go to Bellevue and they took me there. The big hurly-burly doctor at the admissions desk told me I could have a room, a scholarship room. "All you have to do, Mr. North, is to sign this paper and you'll be in and we'll take care of you. You'll have a room of your own and everything will be taken care of, but you must commit yourself by signing this paper." Well, I can tell you, that's when I realized I had a real commitment problem.

I didn't like the sound or thought of "commitment" at all, and I began to pace around the room groaning, while Meg cried in Barney's arms in the corner. When I looked over and saw how much I was hurting Meg I thought I'd better sign my name. So I went over to the desk and looked at that big official form with the small print. It bounced around in my eyes as I tried to read it. I got all freaked out again and began to pace and groan. Seeing how disturbed I was and how upset my friends were, the admitting doctor, this hurly-burly, bearded man, tried to calm me down by asking me some personal questions like "What do you do for a living, Mr. North?" I thought he meant "Who are you?" I knew that in New York City you are what you do first, and a person after that. I had a feeling this guy was trying to find out what I did for money, not who I was, and I got all confused because I was not a job. I was unemployed, but I didn't want to say that, so I got all confused and said, "I'm a model. . . . No, I mean . . . an actor. . . . No, not that. . . . I'm a . . . mmm . . ." I hesitated slightly and then spit it out: "I'm an artist." I wanted to tell him that I was a poet, only I hadn't written any poetry yet, but that was too confusing, so I told him I was an artist, which somehow felt right at the time. Without so much as a pause, he just smiled back at me and said, "Well, I can tell you, Mr. North, I understand you sensitive artist types, because I play the clarinet myself." And as soon as he said that, I knew I was not going to sign that admissions form. If he had said he played the oboe, well, maybe I might have signed; but when he said he played the clarinet, that was it. I just asked Barney and Meg to please take me home.

A T   B A R N E Y ' S   something happened that I read as a sort of sign, a synchronicity, the kind of thing I was on the lookout for all the time—a sign to guide me through that dark night of the soul. Barney got a call offering him a job as a cameraman on a porn movie. Soon he was coming back to the loft at night with all these stories about how he had to film women doing all sorts of crazy things with cucumbers and squashes. I could tell he was not happy in this new work, that it was just a job; but at the same time he seemed to be fascinated by all of it and couldn't stop telling stories. The more he talked about the movie, the more I wanted to be in it.

Now I was just operating on impulse, grabbing at anything that took my fancy as I rolled down and down in that constant motion that hadn't stopped since Ladakh. My plan was that I would act in one or two porn films and use the money to take a long bus trip to San Francisco, where I would stay with friends and be away from Meg to give her a rest and a chance to deal with her rugs. Then I'd come back all cooled out and we'd start out fresh again. I equated the West Coast with health and thought I could get better there. I thought San Francisco would be healthier than Bellevue.

Barney said it was a crazy idea, and Meg had pretty much given up trying to advise me. Her sister, Diane—the one who owned the bookstore with Joe and who tried to get out of bed when she was having a baby—said it all; she said, "Brewster, why do you want to turn everything into shit? Where's your self-esteem?"

I convinced Barney to give me the address of the porn film casting office and I was off. I got all dressed up in my white cotton pants and raw silk Nehru jacket I'd had made in India and went up to an office on West Fifty-seventh Street. I even took along one of the photos Meg had taken of me. I was a little embarrassed to find a woman was doing the central casting, but she put me at ease with her totally professional attitude.

"So, Mr. North, you want to act in X-rated films?" she asked. "That's all well and good, but do you have a partner?" Oh no, I thought, it's going to be like the live show in Amsterdam: they won't take me without a partner. And just as I was thinking that the jig was up, one of the porn film directors came into her office hoping to pick up some new talent. He had come in to go through her file of photos, and it took him no time at all to see he had a live one right there. His name was Bernie and he was a balding, sleazy guy who wore silver reflecting sunglasses. He was a big, fat, sweaty man who wore a leather coat, even though it was summer, and a lot of gold sex chains around his neck. He started right in asking me about my credentials—you know, my career—where I'd worked in porn films before and stuff like that. So I just started making up a history, and the more I did that the better I felt. My whole body took on a kind of confident, cocky attitude. I told him I'd been working in Amsterdam in live shows and doing porn films in Copenhagen for the past few years. I told them how I liked it in Europe because the women had "super bods," and the directors were more artistic, more sensitive in their approach. Then I told him a death in the family had brought me back to the States, and now I wanted to pick up a little work before heading back to continue my career in Europe. Bernie seemed to listen, responding with appropriate grunts here and there at the mention of the women's "bods" in Copenhagen. As for the stuff about the sensitive directors and the death in the family, that just reflected off his glasses and came back at me.

Bernie didn't ask me any embarrassing questions about cock size and stuff like that, or how long I could hold out without coming, things I had expected him to ask. He just told me to show up the following day at a penthouse on East Eighty-sixth Street, and we'd take it from there.

When I got back to the loft, Meg and Barney were amazed to see how focused and excited I was. At last I was going to be on camera. At last, for a moment at least, my life was going to mean something.

I slept the night through and woke up without groaning. Meg was so relieved. Now she could begin to sort out her rugs and try to get her business going. I was amazed that she didn't seem to judge what I was doing. She seemed happy just to have me out of the house and off the streets, like I was a child she had finally been able to get into day care. I was so excited that I arrived early, before the crew had set up. I felt like a new man as I strolled out on that penthouse terrace and chatted with the camera crew.

After Bernie and everyone else arrived, the shot was set up, and all the actors were herded back into a small bedroom which served as a waiting room.

We were all piled up in this little side bedroom, a mixture of men and women, just waiting to be called in to do whatever we were asked, in whatever combinations. I don't think anyone even knew what the film was about. It wasn't as though anyone was reading scripts or studying lines in there. We were just hanging out. No one was even reading a book. There was a strange and somewhat perverse quality of privacy among us. The actors and actresses didn't talk dirty, as you might imagine. They were all very discreet and proper, at least when it came to talking about what they did when they left the room and went on camera. In a regular, nonpornographic film you might expect an actor or actress to come off camera all bubbly, talking about how the scene went; but here, the actors and actresses just came back with discreet little smirks on their faces and then lay around in states of semidress, hanging out until they were called again. It was weird.

But they were not at all private in the way they displayed

themselves, particularly the women. There was this one actress who drove me to distraction. She'd come back into our waiting room after she did whatever she did and roll what she called a "spliff," a little marijuana mixed in with cigarette tobacco rolled into a cigarette, and then she'd just lounge back in that peach-colored satin robe, cross her legs, and bounce one foot until the robe slowly fell away to reveal a fantastic thigh and a nicely pruned bush. Then she'd let her robe fall open at the chest while she talked about her boyfriend and how he was a total grump when he didn't have his marijuana. "Just a big old grump," she said. She talked about some trip they'd taken to Hawaii together and how she thought it was going to be so spectacular, but her boyfriend was a total grump because he couldn't score any grass until their last day there. I just sat there like a dumbstruck ten-year-old in a candy store. The sight of that woman made me crazy. I wanted to touch her all over. I wanted to be her slave. I kept hoping that I'd somehow get paired up with her, but I figured that the chances were slim, real slim, because every time I caught a glimpse of myself in the mirror, my face looked so sad, so mad. I looked like Antonin Artaud in his last days. But I couldn't help making up my own porn film in my head about how this slinky lady would have me down on all fours with a dog collar around my neck, how she'd have me on a leash and command me to eat her all over. I was sure that to have her would be total satisfaction. But any attempt at conversation with her just fell between the beds, so I ended up talking to this guy named Gary.

Gary was about my age and was nice enough. He had a female partner. That's the only reason, he said, that he was getting so much work in porn films. He was surprised to find that I had gotten work without a partner. Unless you're a porn star, it was difficult to get work without a partner. Gary's partner was named Janine, and she looked like the star-struck starlet type, only she was just slightly off. She didn't have the pretty commercial look that makes it big in the movies. There was too much going on in her face. You could see the doubt and the anger. She couldn't hide it well. She couldn't plastic it over, and I figured that sort of turned off the casting people in legitimate films. Janine and Gary were old friends and they trusted each other enough to have functional sex on camera. Gary said they even had a good time sometimes, but he didn't want to dwell on the good times too much because he didn't want to get too attached. He wanted to be able to leave the city when the time came.

I was curious about Janine's story, but before we could get to it, Bernie came in, still wearing those damned reflective sunglasses, and called me out to the living room. I was very nervous, not having any idea what I would be called upon to do; but both to my relief and to my disappointment, the task turned out to be absurdly simple. All I had to do was walk by a bare-breasted woman who was being whipped with a little leather cat-o'-nine-tails by a man dressed as a pirate. It wasn't a violent scene. He was barely hitting her. I had to stand there and watch him whip her three times, look down at my watch, which Props had just put on my wrist, then look up at the camera and say, "Oh, shiver my timbers. I do declare, three o'clock. Right on the old nose," then just stroll on through the room like some absentminded professor. By now they had me dressed in a very nice Palm Beach suit. Anyway, there was no discussion of character or plot or who I was supposed to be or anything like that. So I just decided to do my line reading as Woody Allen would have, and everyone laughed when I did it, and that made me feel real good. I felt like I'd accomplished something, like I was potent. I had brought a little more laughter into the world, and I liked the feeling of that.

After my scene, which was done in three quick takes, I got to hang out against the wall while they did a setup for the following shot, just long enough to find out a little of the movie plot before Bernie ordered me back into the bedroom.

One of the grips, who was real nice, told me that the film was about some sort of wrinkle-in-time situation in which a pirate ship comes out of the eighteenth century to land at Fulton Street in down-town Manhattan. These pirates have come to claim one of their crew, who is now a Wall Street stockbroker and has almost forgotten he was ever a pirate in the first place. All he knows is that he has a fascination with pirate ships and he gets an erection every time he sees a picture or a model of a pirate ship. In fact, this grip told me that the star of the film had to get a full engorged erection while the woman playing his secretary carried a clock shaped like a pirate ship through the room. They had just shot that scene, and he was able to get erect just at the

sight of that ship-shaped clock. The grip told me that the star was a
very good porn actor and much in demand because he never required
a fluffer, which was the name for a woman who was paid just to get
the men up for their scenes.

Before I could get any more information, Bernie drove me back
into the bedroom, where I fell into talking with Gary again until at
last Gary, Janine, and I were called up for a scene together. I was a
little surprised that the three of us were called together, but at this point
not a whole lot was surprising me. Once we got undressed, we were
led into another bedroom, where the camera crew was all set up and
waiting.

Without explaining how the scene fit into the plot of the movie,
as if he was shooting this for some other film, Bernie simply described
the shot to us. He told us that this was a shot he'd been thinking about
for a long time. It was to be of Gary and me, just lying on our backs,
all limp and naked and relaxed, and then Janine was to appear in the
doorway, where she would slowly slip off her robe as we gradually
grew erect. Then there was to be a shot of us, or rather of our cocks
becoming erect "like two giant red asparagus growing out of a field
of pubic hair." That's the way Bernie described it, and his description
surprised me because it was so unlike him, so poetic. After they got
the shot of the two erections, Janine was to move in and we were to
have this glorious ménage à trois, where Gary fucks Janine in the ass
while she blows me at the same time. This was definitely not poetic,
and I had no idea how we were going to accomplish this rather
intimate and complicated act in front of all those sound- and cameramen, not to mention Bernie in his god-awful reflective sunglasses. I
think both Gary and I were hoping that some workable fantasy would
take over when the time came to get erect. But it didn't. Nothing
happened to either of our cocks when Janine came through the door.
They just lay there limp. I felt like I was on an operating table rather
than on a bed in what was supposed to be an erotic situation.

There were no fluffers available, so Janine was asked to please try
to fluff us up first, then run to the door and make her grand entrance.
So the work, and I mean *work,* began. Janine came over to the bed
dressed only in her robe and, while Bernie paced on the side like a
basketball coach and the cameramen adjusted their lenses and the boom

men fiddled with their booms, Janine began to fiddle and fluff with Gary and me. She started sucking on Gary's cock while she stroked mine with her hand. Soon Gary was erect, but nothing was happening for me. I was numb. There was nothing and no one in that room that was turning me on.

After Janine got Gary hard, she began to suck on me, which seemed to help, but while she was doing that, Gary went soft, so for a while there it was back and forth and up and down, like a sexual seesaw, one cock getting hard while the other went soft. Bernie continued to pace impatiently on the sidelines. I just lay there like a little kid with my mouth tight, trying not to scream. I just lay there getting done and watching this once-important part of me inflate and deflate again and again.

At last Bernie had the good sense to clear the room so Janine could work on us in private. So, leaving the cameras and booms set up, the whole crew left. Gary was to call them back when the task of dual erections was accomplished.

Janine began to work on us again, and somehow she was able to get both cocks up at the same time. By now it all seemed like something going on far away, something I hardly felt a part of. Gary called for Bernie and the crew and they all came running back in. But by the time they got set up again, Gary and I had begun to wither, and all they got were two rather wilted dicks that were mostly held up by our own hands. They looked more like display specimens in some medical journal than like erotic male members.

The next shot was not an unusual shot. If you've seen any porn films or any porn magazines, you'd recognize the shot immediately. It was an old demeaning classic—demeaning, that is, for the woman who was getting used at both ends. Janine was instructed to get on all fours, Gary was instructed to kneel behind her and fuck her in the ass while she sucked my cock. I was glad that I was the passive one in all of this.

As soon as Janine heard that there was to be anal intercourse in the shot, she called for her contract. Bernie's assistant came running with it and held it steady on the bed while Janine, naked, on all fours, signed the anal intercourse clause, which provided exactly for a thirty-seven-dollar bonus.

Once again the room was cleared for us to work in private. Janine, Gary, and I got this whole interconnected machine and all its parts working away, and then Gary yelled "Okay!" and the crew came running. Bernie was running up and down the sidelines like a coach for the winning team, crying out, "Oh, that's good!" Then to me: "Move around more, North. Make it look like you're enjoying it. Make some sounds, North—make some sounds, boy!" and I could feel myself going limp as soon as he used that word "boy." In order to counteract it, I went into my memory bank to try to come up with some useful fantasy. I went somewhere else in my head. I went back to the Dam Square in Amsterdam and found that young Italian girl and brought her back to Hans's house and at last did it there in the attic room, and that's where I was when Bernie called for the cum shot. Because there was only one camera, Gary came first, shooting his warm wad onto Janine's back, rubbing it in with his hand for the close-up, a standard porn film technique he'd learned in the past. Then it was my turn. Bernie yelled "Cum shot!" and Janine pulled her mouth away and I shot into the air. This left me with a very sad, empty feeling. Then it was over. Just like that, it was over. We were done for the day. In fact, we were done with that film altogether. I was handed two crisp fifty-dollar bills in an envelope and sent home.

That day I was certain of one thing, which was the first sense of certainty I'd had in some time. I was certain my career in porn films was over. I hadn't earned enough money to take a trip across the country, but I had earned enough to go to Provincetown at last. Maybe that would be enough of a trip to make me feel like I had left Meg, and allow me to return to her, at last a triumphant man. To make that short odyssey might be enough for now. I had to learn how to hang out on my own and spend my money without being self-destructive. I needed a vacation. I needed to relax and learn how to laugh alone. I needed to learn how to enjoy without needing a witness. I had no trouble crying. My tears came out at random like gushing streams in the spring. Had the film been about a man crying at the slightest cue instead of getting erect, I would have become an overnight star.

I could cry, but I couldn't laugh. My laughter was always short-circuited by an instant report on the event. It was as though I saw all the things that could make me laugh coming at me in slow motion, so that I had plenty of time to analyze them before they got to me. Then by the time they hit, by the time they got there, it was always, yes, yes, I see, I see, that's funny, yes, I understand, oh yes, I see why you're laughing now. Although that old loneliness was still there, I wanted to be laughing at it as well as crying.

HOW STRANGELY familiar it all was, like an old recurring dream, to be gathering things to take to Provincetown, only this time it was not my father's meat or Mom's Metrecal. It was just a yoga mat for the back of the van and a sleeping bag. I loaded up the next morning and was at last off on my trip to the tip of the mighty Cape.

As soon as I got on the road I fell into a perpetual-motion trance and was saved from time by motion. I drove as if on automatic through Fall River, past New Bedford to the open Cape highway, until the bright green van was rolling along like some pure and simple storybook creation.

In no time at all a uniform row of white bungalows flashed along on my left, marking the entrance to the old Provincetown highway. I could see the mighty arm of the Cape curl around into a fist which sheltered the beautiful harbor. And Provincetown was visible, an old fishing town in the distance; but as soon as I got close to the town it got thick and ugly with traffic and people all walking and gawking. There was a great line of Winnebagos, jeeps and overheating station wagons. The whole thing looked like a giant *Mad* magazine. It was disgusting, and the worst of it was, it was swallowing me up and causing me to feel like one of the horde. Just because I drove a green Dodge van, this did not absolve me from contributing to this piggish confusion. It was a classic lemming situation. The sea had drawn all these people to drive to it, only to be overwhelmed and end up circling in confusion. Around and around the town they drove, holding up traffic while they parked and ejected squads of little monsters to devour hot dogs, clam rolls, and saltwater taffy.

As soon as I got there I wanted to leave; but I had to see the sea first. It was late afternoon, and after sitting in traffic mumbling to myself a compulsive list of regrets—I could be in Amsterdam, Nepal, Ireland, or India now—I made it to the public beach and found a parking place; but much as I wanted to be in the ocean, I couldn't seem to leave the van. I was frantic-manic by now and I kept circling it, catching wide-angle views of myself in the hubcaps. Then I would kick the tires and mumble lists of places I'd rather be and then get back in the van and sit, and then get out and walk around it again. This pattern got tighter and faster and more and more like an old-time movie being played over and over. I became more and more like those automatic Amish automatons I had seen in my fevered sleep the day I arrived home from Mexico, but I couldn't seem to help myself. I was a full-blown, out-of-control compulsion on the loose.

What finally jerked me out of it was the arrival of the local police, who pulled up in a cruiser beside me. Two of them jumped out of their car and got me up against my van and said, "Hold still, boy." That word "boy" made me hostile. "What's up?" the big fat one asked. "Can't make up your mind today or what?"

They studied the pupils of my eyes and then let me go with a warning. "Don't let me see you out here looking at your hubcaps like that again. Never again."

I drove into town, found a metered parking space on the pier, and headed down that crowded main street. When I got in front of the town hall I decided to beg. Just like that. It came to me like a voice saying, "Why not beg for your money?" so I went back to my van to fetch my Tibetan prayer cymbals. I had been carrying them around with me to act as a calming agent. At night I would strike them and follow the sound into silence, which was the only prayer I could conceive of then.

Once I got the cymbals, I sat cross-legged on the sidewalk in front of the town hall. I folded one of my pastel-pink Indian T-shirts into a neat square in front of me and I began to ring the cymbals and chant and to my instant amazement people started dropping money onto my T-shirt. I was absolutely amazed how quickly people responded; but what they were responding to I didn't know. A few people even put down dollar bills. Everything was going fine until those same damned cops came along and busted me. They said one more time and they would lock me up. But I got to keep the money. I headed off to a local bar to celebrate the fact that I was able to pass for a real beggar.

I went to an old fisherman's bar for drinks, but there weren't any fishermen there, only tourists. I drank draft beers and ate peanuts in the shell. Those beers calmed me down. They always did. They were, I thought, still my cozy ally.

After enough beer to relax me and put me on the edge of drunkenness, I went out in search of food. I went to the foot-long-hot-dog stand on the main pier. I wanted to buy a lobster roll, but they were too expensive, so I went for two foot-longs with everything on them. While I was waiting for the woman to bring them I tucked my shirt in. All I did was unbutton the top of my pants and tuck my shirt in and then I buttoned right up again. But when the woman brought me my two foot-longs she acted real strange and real put-off, like I smelled bad or something.

Just as I was taking my first bite out of one of the foot-longs that damn police car pulled up again and the big fat one said, "Get in the car." He was real pissed, and I didn't know why until they took me to the police station and locked me up for exposing myself to the foot-long lady. That was their charge—exposing myself. I was incredulous, and once I was all booked and behind bars I started yelling, "She's out of her mind. She's been handling those foot-longs too long. She needs a rest." But they were gone.

In the morning they gave me back my wallet and keys and told me to get out of town forever.

WHEN I GOT BACK to New York City the other side of my manicness set in. That fearful depressive state I'd been warned about, combined with the August heat, just did me in. I fell into a dreamless, Rip Van Winkle sleep. I can't say it was a relief, because it was so unconscious. It was just nothing. It was what I suppose death is finally like: a giant absence of me, an end to all memory. It was only a relief in relation to the panic I felt when I woke up and realized I had been asleep for sixteen hours. I couldn't bear the fact that I'd been unconscious all that time. Meg tried to help me accept it as part of some sort of healing process. Although she didn't say it, I'm sure it was a great relief to her to have me asleep.

I slept like Rip Van Winkle through the month of August, only waking up to eat a little something and then pass out again. In no time it was September, which meant that Meg and I could move back into our apartment, provided Barney and Meg could keep me awake long enough to get me over there. Meg was sure that the return to our nest would completely heal me. As for herself, she couldn't wait to get there. She was a real nester and had been living out of a suitcase way too long.

Meg was ecstatic to be back in our apartment and busied herself with puttering and cleaning and unpacking and putting everything in order as she sang that Ezio Pinza song "Welcome home said the door" over and over again. She laid down her Kashmir rugs and raved to me about them while I nodded off again like some A-train junkie.

The world was now a soft blur around me, like it was in my old childhood days when I'd pretend to be sick and stay home, dozing to the radio soap operas "Ma Perkins" and "Stella Dallas," the distant sounds from my grade school playground seeping into my sleep.

It would go like this: I would wake up and try to act as though I was a normal sort of guy, facing another normal day, and Meg would fix breakfast and I would eat it, and then after a few cups of coffee I'd say, "Well, I'm just going to lie down for a minute and take a little rest." Then in no time at all I'd wake up to the evening news, have a bite of dinner, watch as much of "The Honeymooners" reruns as I could stay awake for, then conk out again, not even making it to bed. I'd just fall asleep right on the couch.

Meg was very patient with all of this and kept encouraging me to sleep as much as I felt I needed, but I was very frightened and tried to combat the sleep by undertaking meaningful activities like going shopping at the Grand Union. I'd end up nodding out while waiting in the checkout line, so I pretty much stayed indoors. Any outside input was too much, too terrifying. It kept reminding me that the world was constantly going on without me, that I could sleep for sixteen hours and not even be missed. It made me feel expendable.

During my three or four waking hours I was doing a lot of groaning and letting out little shouts and crazy sounds, like I had a giant nervous tic in my diaphragm. Those sounds were disturbing to some people in the streets, not to mention in the Grand Union, but on the whole I noticed that most of the people ignored me. They just treated me like another crazy New Yorker.

After a while it began to occur to me that this behavior might be the new condition of my life, a permanent condition, and I began to think about suicide as an alternative. Up until then I had never contemplated suicide, except for that silly time in the summer when I was young and I told Coleman I was going to jump out the window like Milton Berle's wife. I had always felt that my mom had made a giant mistake by doing herself in, but now I wasn't so sure. Perhaps it was the only way out of this endless sleep and those waking states that were so painful, except for when I watched "The Honeymooners." Those nightly reruns on Channel Eleven (which was then nicknamed "Eleven Alive") were my only thirty minutes of graceful pleasure, and somewhere I knew that if I could still respond to Ralph, Norton, Alice, and Trixie, I would not kill myself. They even made me laugh once or twice. They were all I lived for, and that was also terrifying, because I knew that if I lost interest in "The Honeymooners," or if they went off the air, I would surely die.

Then one day, while shouting and groaning my way up West Broadway to buy some chicken hearts at the Grand Union, I ran into an old friend who asked me how I was. I just turned to her and said, "Crazy! I'm crazy!" and then I went on shouting my way up the street. Well, this friend, Helen, who was a dancer and into all sorts of New Age diets and healing stuff like that, called Meg and suggested that I take a glucose tolerance test to find out if I was hypoglycemic. "Hypo *what?*" I groaned. "I never heard of such a thing." Meg explained that it was a condition of low blood sugar and could make people act crazy. Meg tried to get me to go for the test, but I was afraid I wouldn't be able to stay awake long enough to go through it. It was supposed to be something like six hours long, so I kept putting it off. I had good intentions. I wanted to take the test, but I kept falling asleep before I could get out of the house.

Other friends also tried to be helpful and gave me books to read about depression, but I got depressed reading them or fell asleep with them over my face. I remember one called *From Sad to Glad,* which was just the right weight and size to keep cracked over my face while I slept. The weight and smell of that book were very comforting.

The content, however, was not. I was able to get up to page 9, where the author writes, "There are a host of symptoms that help us identify the affliction. Not all of these symptoms are found in every case, but together they make up a classic syndrome. Please note that it is unusual for all of them to be present in a particular case." And then came the horrible list:

1. Reduced enjoyment and pleasure
2. Poor concentration
3. Fatigue
4. Insomnia
5. Remorse
6. Guilt
7. Indecision
8. Financial concern
9. Reduced sexual activity
10. Decreased love and affection
11. General loss of interest
12. Anxiety
13. Irritability
14. Suicidal thoughts
15. Unusual thoughts and urges
16. Concern about dying

To my horror I realized that I had every symptom but insomnia. I had the classic syndrome. I *was* the classic syndrome, and recognizing that, I suddenly experienced fifteen out of sixteen symptoms and passed out again on the couch with *From Sad to Glad* over my face, glaring at Meg all day like some insane advertisement.

Things were definitely not going well, and I think the only reason I didn't try to kill myself was that I simply was not awake long enough to do it. I also knew, somewhere in the back of my addled, panicked mind, that I was very lucky to have Meg as a nurse and that she cared for me deeply and was watching over me as I slept. It was in her eyes that I continued to exist.

With Meg's help, I was finally able to stay awake long enough to take that dreadful glucose tolerance test, and it showed that I was extremely hypoglycemic. This led me into the megavitamin therapy program at the Fryer Research Center, where I went once a week for giant syringe doses of vitamin B complex and niacin. I also had to take large doses of liquid vitamin B and liquid niacin at home. I was told to immediately give up all sugar, alcohol, and caffeine, which was an enormous shock to my already depressed system. I was put on a very strict, very boring protein diet. I had to eat five small protein meals a day in order to keep my blood sugar stable and stop my body's overproduction of adrenaline, which had been going off like a fire alarm ever since India. This, the doctors told me, had kept me in my perpetual hyper state, which had finally reversed itself into all that sleeping.

When I ran out of ideas for protein and got bored with fish, eggs, and meat (no milk because of lactose), I resorted to swigging from a plastic bottle of flavored animal collagen (melted intestine), which came in three flavors: orange, cherry, and grapefruit. It was sweetened with saccharine and tasted horrid, but it did the trick; it stabilized my blood sugar, though in the most unpleasurable way. I was now able to stay awake long enough to get uptown to see my new therapist, and that was important. I was even able to stay awake through the whole session.

A friend of Barney's had told me about a good therapist who worked on what they call a sliding scale, and said he might see me for only thirty dollars a session, which, unfortunately, was not sliding enough for me. Thirty dollars a session was an enormous amount considering I had no money coming in. Anyway, I'd talked with Dad about it and was amazed when he offered to pay for half of it. So by

November of 1976 I was on my way to some sort of slow recovery—
but recovery from what I was still not sure.

H ARRY BRILLSTEIN was a psychiatrist and not
just a psychotherapist. He was able to prescribe tranquilizers
for me, and he did that the first day I saw him. Harry worked
in a kind of classic Freudian mode. He never spoke first. He always
waited for me to speak, and if I didn't, we would go the whole session
in a tense, silent standoff, which he would usually end by saying,
"Well, I'm afraid our time is up. I'll see you next week, Brewster."
After a while Harry tried to get me to come in twice a week, which
I thought was odd because I wasn't doing all that much talking. I told
him I couldn't afford twice a week, because I was also paying for my
megavitamin therapy sessions. When I told Harry that, he said something that made me really distrust him and just lump him in with the
whole disgusting crowd of drug and medicine men, like the guy on
the admissions desk at Bellevue. Harry said, "Why are you taking all
those vitamins, Brewster? Is it because you're afraid of growing old?"

I had the feeling that Harry was probably a good man, and was
only saying those stupid manipulative things to provoke me; and I was
curious to see who he really was under that damned neutral mask. One
day I came into his office and saw a book on his desk. I wondered what
he was reading, so I just went over and tried to take a peek at the title.
Harry picked the book up, turned it over, and slammed it down on
his desk. Then he just stared at me with that damned neutral stare. I
didn't say a word. I thought it was weird. I just sat down and stared
back at him. I'd be damned if I was going to give in to his methods
of provocation.

Now, as I said before, this psychotherapy was coupled with
megavitamin therapy, and my new light protein diet, and slowly it all
began to come together and make me feel better. Slowly my horizons
broadened beyond "Honeymooners" reruns; and toward the end of
October I had a minor breakthrough with Harry.

It all happened one day in therapy when I was telling one of many stories about my family and how my brothers and I had longed for some sort of mystical transformation in my father. It was not so much that we wanted him to convert to Christian Science and be happy with Mom but, rather, we all wanted Dad to simply cop to the fact that there were forces larger than himself at work in the world, forces outside rational thought. In short, I think we all longed to blow Dad's mind. One night Coleman succeeded. I was in my bed and only heard it. I didn't see it, but I heard it, and I couldn't believe what I heard. I heard Dad in all sobriety crying out to Mom, "Katherine— Katherine, come quick! My slippers are flying! My slippers are flying!" I jumped up and ran in to witness what sounded like a great suburban miracle, but when I got to Mom and Dad's bedroom, the miracle had turned into a typical family fight. Dad was scolding Coleman for what he called his "weird behavior," and Mom was laughing in the bath-room doorway, laughing at Dad's confused rage. As usual she was laughing so hard she was wetting her pants, or in this case her nightgown.

When everything had calmed down and Dad was back in bed grumbling and pouting and trying to tune his radio into some relaxing mood Muzak, Mom took me into the bathroom and told me the story of the slippers. It seems that Coleman, who was then about fifteen years old, had crawled under Dad's bed some time before Dad came upstairs and just waited there. Every night Dad would go to his bed, usually in his blue pajamas and mahogany-colored L. L. Bean slippers. He'd arrange his slippers just so at the foot of the bed and then climb in to listen to his Muzak. But this particular night, Coleman reached out from under Dad's bed and tossed both of his slippers straight up into the air with such strength that they hit the ceiling, and Dad cried out, "Katherine, come quick! My slippers are flying! My slippers are fly-ing!" And for just a few split seconds, Coleman was able, to his eternal satisfaction, to witness Dad as a true believer.

Well, when I told this story to Harry, that whole neutral mask of his dissolved into laughter, and I felt good for the first time in his presence. I felt a kind of connection to my history. At last I felt Harry open up and let me in.

IT WAS a few sessions after he laughed that, in some simple pop-psychology way, I had an epiphany with Harry. I understood that the guilt I felt running away to the Alamo Theatre when Mom was in the throes of her nervous breakdown had inhibited and prevented me from fighting for the role of Konstantin Gavrilovich in that production of *The Sea Gull* years ago. I did not fight for what I wanted, and in a way I had been as depressed about that as I had been about Mom's suicide ever since. I understood that I couldn't bring Mom back from the dead, but I could perform *The Sea Gull* in my own way, and put some part of my history in order so that I could go on. I had flown the nest to become a successful actor and I had failed, and now I had to go back and succeed on my own terms. I had slipped into a postadolescent passive state of unproductive fantasy, which I'd not been able to come out of for years. I knew I had to stage my own version of *The Sea Gull*, and only when I did that would I be cured. Only now I decided to play not just the role of Konstantin Gavrilovich but all the other roles as well.

This decision was influenced by readings I'd done of Gestalt concepts about dreams in which the dreamer is an aspect of all the characters in his dream. I had had a very powerful dream at that time about Meg being pregnant, and in this dream Meg and I were both standing naked and her belly was very full, and I was standing there with my hand on her belly and I was all three of us. I was me and I was Meg and I was the child in her. I knew, too, that this dream meant I was to play all the characters in *The Sea Gull* and that Meg would direct it and we would be pregnant together with this play. I know this may sound like a big leap to you, but believe me, in my new clear megavitamin mind I was sure that I had to be directed by Meg in our experimental version of *The Sea Gull* to clear myself of the past.

So that was the next item on my agenda. I knew that I would be the actor and Meg would be the director. It was clear. Barney had an empty space in the back of his loft that he let us work in. I began by making a tape recording of the whole play, in which I read all the roles. Then I played the recording back through speakers set up around the loft. At one end of the loft I hung some dark curtains, so it was clear that I was backstage peeking out. The only props I had were a small tree that looked quite large when it was set in the loft and a whole bunch of old china plates and flatware that Meg and I had picked up at the Salvation Army. For a costume I had black pants, work boots, a sort of Russian peasant shirt, and a large faded-yellow stuffed sea gull that Meg and I had found in a taxidermy shop on the Lower East Side. I hung that around my neck. Then what I did mainly was move around the loft space, telling Meg, who acted as my audience, my personal history with that play. I told her what I remembered of the production at the Alamo Theatre. I demonstrated how I made the naturalistic party sounds with the dishes and flatware. I took a number of Konstantin's speeches and memorized them and then in a direct-address form spoke them out, interrupting them at different points to explain why I found it difficult to say certain lines in a truthful and honest way. I talked about how the translation felt antiquated and foolish to me at times. I told the story about eating the soybeans and how I gassed that carload of people, and about Mom's nervous breakdown, and about how a whole lot of young people were trying to get me to take LSD and go to Houston's first be-in. I told about all the offstage lives of the different actors and how the woman who played Nina would never go out of her apartment, and how the man who played Trigorin was having an affair with a wealthy art dealer in Houston, and how the actress who played Arkadina was knocked out by an overstrenuous character actor when their two heads bumped while making drunken love. Oh, it was a shameless production I was doing. It was as though I was doing a giant, scandalous, gossipy audition for the audience. I'd have to call it creative gossip. I even created a scene that never happened, where I at last confronted the director of the play and demanded that I have the role of Konstantin Gavrilovich.

It was definitely a deconstruction. For instance, I would focus on the speech Konstantin makes to his mother just days after he has tried to shoot himself in the head. His mother is sort of infantilizing him as she changes his head bandage. She says, "You won't play about with a gun again when I'm away, will you?" And Konstantin replies, "No, Mama. That was a moment of mad despair, when I had no control over myself. It won't happen again." Then there is a stage direction—"kisses her hands"—and Konstantin goes on to say, "You've got magic hands." And that was where I'd take my subtextual associative break and go into stories about my mom and her hands and how she touched me in two different specific ways: one to wash my uncircumcised penis when I was too young to do it myself, and the other to give me a back rub to put me to sleep. I followed that with a story of how at a family picnic just before I left for Houston, and just before Mom killed herself, I had seen Mom's hands as suddenly very old. I had said, "Mom, your hands look so very old." Then I went on to tell my "audience" how I knew I'd said it to hurt her as soon as it was out of my mouth. I just let these associations go on like that, at last ending up with the story of how when I once knocked myself out (hyperventilating) and burned my arm on a radiator, it was Dad and not Mom who changed my bandage every night. After I got all of this stuff out, I'd go back and say the speech. I'd say Konstantin's speech, and both Meg and I thought it would then have new meaning. That's what Meg said anyway, and I trusted her. She said there will certainly be people who will walk out on this production, this deconstruction of *The Sea Gull,* but there will also be people who come with a knowledge of the play who will appreciate it even more. Meg said we just had to look at it as a new kind of personal translation. And I agreed.

In the end, our production of *The Sea Gull* was a mad deconstruction, a rambling hodgepodge of mixed emotion, straightforward acting, and a lot of direct autobiographical address. Meg in her own ingenious ordering way had been able to help me frame it and put it all together. At first, only friends came to see it. Then, when the word of mouth was good, strangers came. The play—or "piece," as we called it—was entitled *A Personal History of "The Sea Gull,"* and it even got a favorable review in one of the downtown papers which read something like, "In this small downtown loft production, Brewster North explores the backside of a misguided *Sea Gull* in Texas." And the headline over that read, "Misadventures of Big Bird." It was, if nothing else, an interesting review, and it brought people in.

My life was suddenly coming together in an odd way. Meg and I were running this little theater in the back of Barney's loft and even pulling in enough money to pay half of Barney's rent. People were coming to see our crazy little play, and on those nights life had meaning. The rest of the time was spent mostly waiting to put on the play. It was as though Meg and I only lived for our newfound art. But as I got better at it, I began to want my life to be as full as the play, only I had no idea how to make it that way. The fullness only existed in fantasy, and the fantasy kept growing in what was left of my private mind. The fantasy was about me living somewhere on the West Coast, perhaps San Francisco or a small town north of there, with a wife and children in some very together community. I kept seeing myself as this man I made up. Brewster North would act the role of some man actually living his life.

I'D NOT HAD any drinks or drugs for several months and I was getting better, but my newfound health was almost boring. I'd wake up at six in the morning and not know what to do with all my energy, so I'd get up and go for an excessively speedy walk around Washington Square Park. I think I was one of the first speed walkers in my neighborhood. And it was on those walks that I'd be taken over by my fantasy of running away to the West Coast and becoming this new man. I had a very clear image of the woman I would meet and marry there. She was slim and had a boyish, athletic body and an absolutely extraordinary ass. She was beautiful, young, innocently sensual and wanted nothing more than to live in the present. She was intelligent enough to know that the United States of America was no longer united, and that it was rapidly going under, but she would also know that raising a family in a small-town community was our only salvation. We'd live in a tract house there and feel that we were blessed to be able to live out our days in a kind of sweet and sober peripheral harmony that could and would be possible, provided that we did not expose ourselves to too much information, and that we read only good old classics like *David Copperfield, Treasure Island,* and the *Zen Mind, Beginner's Mind.* We would have three children and no TV. I would get into my body and learn how to wind-surf, roller-skate, and hang-glide, and I would be able to do it all without a witness. I would at last live a witnessless life, in the present, not even asking or caring for God to see me. I would have the courage to disappear and drown in the eternal now. I would teach school for a living and on weekends I'd bike with my wife and kids and we'd explore the giant redwoods. As I was speed-walking around Washington Square in those early New York mornings, this fantasy would become as vivid as a movie. I was sure I had to have a wife and family in a small American community or I'd destroy myself. Acting *The Sea Gull* out was no longer enough. I wanted my whole life to be a successful play. I wanted to be "on" all the time.

I admit it occurred to me that pursuing my fantasy might be self-destructive, and that self-destruction was part of my construction. It was like my bite, or the arches in my feet; it was built-in.

In spite of all my West Coast family fantasies, when I saw Sherry hanging out in her earnestly flirtatious way after a performance of *A Personal History of "The Sea Gull,"* I sensed that my life was headed toward a new uncontrolled, massive addiction. My body was craving a new drug, and I was about to find out what that new drug was. It was sex.

It wasn't as though Meg and I didn't have a good sex life. We had a nice, balanced, comfortable one, but whenever I got balanced and comfortable, some little demon in me always rose up and pushed me over the edge.

Sherry was a theater student at Juilliard, and was nicely set up, I guess because there was money in the family, in a sweet little studio apartment on West Sixteenth Street. She gave me her address after *The Sea Gull.* She invited me for afternoon herbal tea. I hated herbal tea, but I was shaking all over at her invitation. I was shaking all over when she slipped me her address. It was such an obvious seduction. I could tell she wanted me as much as I wanted her, and that made good sense. I rang her bell at noon the following day. Her apartment was white, simple, and spare. It was a kind of neutral room, a place to work things out. It didn't reflect too much of her. It didn't overwhelm me with the details of real life. I had a feeling it would be all very safe and easy with Sherry, an exercise in pure, selfish pleasure. I hoped I was about to have that unbridled sex I'd searched for so hard in India. I hoped that Sherry was in a similar frame of mind.

On that first hot afternoon, we made the beast with two backs six sweating, ripping times. Our bodies flew together and stuck. Nothing I did seemed to embarrass her, although the sound of our bodies stuck together like two toilet plungers almost did me in. I must admit I blushed.

I did everything that first hot afternoon. I turned her upside down like an ice cream cone and tasted all her flavors, and she complied and sighed and cried. I shocked myself with the animal sounds that were coming out of me. They were foreign to my old Puritan ears. God, I thought, I was coming to real raw sex at such a late age. I was supposed to be nineteen when I was doing this. Well, better late than never.

We grunted and we groaned together and then we slumbered for a while, to awake only to grunt and groan again. These afternoon sex rituals quickly became a habit, a real big habit. I was hooked and so was Sherry. Sherry was hooked to the point of rescheduling all of her classes at Juilliard around our afternoon events. But strangely enough, my visits to Sherry did not cut down on my sex drive with Meg. It was as if my new diet had given me a potency that I never thought possible before. Sherry was Monday, Wednesday, and Friday, and Meg was randomly on the days in-between. It was as though I was re-creating Poona on my own terms.

And on the weekends I went on performing our deconstruction of *A Personal History of "The Sea Gull,"* which was playing to ever-growing audiences. Most nights were sold out, which wasn't saying a whole lot since we could only seat thirty, but still, both Meg and I were impressed. In short, my life seemed to be filling up.

I had found at last a precarious web of structure that was not only getting me through but helping me make a comeback. I was working with Meg on our *Sea Gull,* doing my megavitamin therapy and my regular psychotherapy, and best of all, balling with Sherry. That's what Sherry called sex—"balling." I got real turned on the first time she said the word. I thought, if Sherry called making love balling, then she was probably tough. That's what I thought. She was real tough and wouldn't go to pieces when I left her, because all the time I was balling with her I was thinking of leaving her. And, whenever I thought of leaving her, it made me want to do it to her more. It made it feel better. It always made it feel right on the edge of death, pretending that this was the end, this was the last time. I had this idea that I was going to run away soon, run away from "it," run away from it all, and step into that perfect West Coast situation of love that was not about human obfuscation and obsession.

Meg was very happy working with me in our new creative relationship. She had no idea about my discreet, steamy affair with Sherry. I think Harry Brillstein was the only one that knew, and I do remember him saying something like "Well, Brewster, are you thinking of trading one body in for another, is that it? Is that what you're after, Brewster?" Harry thought I was dealing in bodies. I thought what I was doing shouldn't be judged.

I got more and more focused on my performance in *The Sea Gull,* and when I was performing I was completely present. I never thought about the past or the future. The only other time that kind of presence took over was in Sherry's perfect sex den.

But in between these two events that damn shadow would fall again, all the real stuff, the constant condition of imperfection, and worse: the terrifying consciousness of NOTHING—the constant mind-boggling awareness of how we come from nothing and return to nothing. That awareness would lead me toward great performances in our little loft theater and equally great performances in bed with Sherry.

Meg was truly dedicated to helping me make inspired art. She would watch every performance of *A Personal History of "The Sea Gull"* and give me notes the following day, and the next night would often be better because of her notes. We were beginning to understand how to shape our strange and beautiful idiosyncratic theater form. There was nothing else around like it, and it wasn't dependent on reviews or outside responses as much as it was a necessary act to go through a personal ritual expressing publicly what we couldn't express between ourselves. It brought us to a full sense of satisfaction, but for whatever reasons it did not spread to the bed. The more innovative

and experimental our work became, the more traditional and perfunc-
tory our sex life became; and in reaction to that, the more experimental
my sex life with Sherry became.

Sex with Sherry was no longer confined to bed. I would do it
to her while she was cooking, while she was eating, while she was
talking to her mother on the telephone on Sundays. We never made
it in the streets, but we got pretty close by doing it fully lit at night
with all the shades up. We had a regular little audience, all framed in
various windows across the way. It was as though Sherry's white
apartment were a giant canvas and our bodies were the paint. We were
turning into great, gross, living Francis Bacon paintings.

Sherry's little Sunday-afternoon phone calls to her mother down
in Florida were remarkable. These were the calls in which she would
suck me and talk to her mother at the same time. She would suck on
me while she listened to her mother, and take my cock out of her
mouth just long enough to answer back or make a brief comment.
Luckily for me, her mother was a big talker. And somewhere toward
the end of the conversation I would have some new, strange, never-
before-dreamed-of climax. It was as though Sherry and I were equals
in our tendencies toward exhibitionism. We had a sort of unspoken
sexual charm together. If I hadn't already worked through my fantasies
of acting in porn films, I would surely have found a perfect porn
partner in Sherry.

By now I was thinking of myself as a Performance Artist, the new
prestigious, downtown term that, although it didn't bring in money,
certainly allowed for some very romantic and bohemian life-styles. I'd
meet Sherry two hours a day three days a week, and for those two solid
hours we would drown in each other. We would get lost in the
fingering, the endless exploring, the sucking and fucking and the
tasting of each other's parts. We didn't use drugs; we didn't need drugs.
We were each other's drugs. We only went outside together once, as
I remember, and that's when Sherry wanted to work out her new
fantasy with rubber Halloween masks. She wanted to stage her own
little porn show. Her mother had given her a new video camera, and
Sherry wanted to have some fun with it. She wanted the two of us
to go out and buy Halloween masks that we would wear while we
were fucking in front of the video camera. It was her idea; she was

only twenty-two years old, so I had to give her credit. I was amazed, shocked, and wondered what the hell was going on with these young people, but I went along with it, feeling it was good to get out on a nice fall day for a change, convincing myself I was getting a little bored with in-house sex, you know, stuff like that. Anyway, we went out to Forty-fifth Street and Broadway to a store that sold rubber masks. There were all sorts of masks: a Nixon mask, a Khrushchev mask, and a Kissinger mask, a Snow White and a Lassie mask, and a traditional, classic Frankenstein, all made from very realistic rubber molds. Well, as soon as I got there I told Sherry I wanted to buy the Nixon mask. And she said, "No way! It would never work." So I ended up with the Frankenstein mask and a pig mask, I mean a mask that really looked like a pig's head. We both had a deep, gut turn-on response to the pig mask. We got a feeling it would really work. Sherry took her time and picked out a Lassie mask and a lovely Snow White mask. I wanted to rape Snow White on the spot. And as we stood there, Sherry paying for it all, we both knew in our genitals that the Lassie and the pig would just do wonders together, wonders.

So when we got home, Sherry set up her new video camera, laughing and singing; she set it up on a tripod and we, as they say, went to town. We balled and balled, we laughed and we balled. It was ridiculous—all the different combinations: Frankenstein meets Lassie; Snow White meets the pig; Lassie and the pig. It was a lovely afternoon.

I have to say making our own homemade sex video was very exciting. It was as exciting as putting on *A Personal History of "The Sea Gull."* As much as *Sea Gull* gave me a personal identity, Lassie and the pig stole it all away and delivered me back to my body. The only thing that was missing was someone on the video camera to do close-ups, but neither of us had any idea who might do that job, so we were satisfied with the conventional side shot. After a while we got more elaborate and set the camera up closer, to shoot us at different angles. Then we got up again and moved it even closer. We just wanted shots of cunt and cock—no mask, no bodies, just the galloping, independent organs, like wild birds in a bush. That wild, wild animal stuff. Like those scenes I saw on the Zendo wall.

At last we had created this crazy, sometimes funny, sometimes very sexy home video that we'd watch together in order to turn ourselves on. Sometimes we'd even watch it while we had our regular sex workout without masks, so that we were surrounded by ourselves on the TV monitor, while at the same time being watched by the neighbors across the street. We couldn't seem to celebrate our new-found lust enough. We were on the edge of committing sexual suicide. It was as though we were trying to make ourselves disappear by eating each other up. We were both turning into greedy monster cannibals: Frankenstein eats Snow White, Lassie eats out the pig's ass, and other mindless and endless combinations of coupling animals. We never talked. We were in a state of either perpetual arousal or perpetual waiting for arousal. We had turned into what I could only call "rhythm pigs."

I had no idea what Sherry's redemptive outlets were. I had no idea if she had other, more transcendent elements to her life, and I didn't care. I had Meg and *The Sea Gull,* and I hoped Sherry had something so that we could continue our mutual rituals of sexual indulgence.

After a while I began to realize Sherry was trying to steal me away from Meg and that sex was her bait. She began to try to get me to stay overnight on the pretext that we could be better observed by the neighbors at later hours. Also, she said, her next-door neighbor, who was her best girlfriend, was home then and would like to be an ear-to-the-wall witness to our lust. I was really beginning to get frightened by this, and I longed somehow to get it all under one roof. I was also sure that by now Meg must be suspicious of my affair with Sherry. So one day, or rather one night, not being able to hold back anymore, I blurted it out to Meg. I just said, "I have to tell you, Meg, I'm having an affair." Meg just burst into tears, and as soon as she did I knew where my heart was because I could feel it again. I could feel it melt for Meg. I knew I loved her then with all my heart, but by then my heart and head and balls had all been divided and scattered. I felt like Humpty Dumpty, who had had a very great fall, and I could not imagine who or what could put me back together again. My heart and head seemed to be floating around the room with Meg, while my cock and balls were bouncing off the ceiling and walls at Sherry's place.

After Meg stopped crying, she gave me two weeks to break it

off with Sherry. That ultimatum only heated my lust up more, until at last the straws that were to break the camel's back showed up as Sherry's lusty scratch marks on my back. Sherry had left her brand on my back and shoulders to let Meg know that I no longer belonged only to her. The day Meg saw those scratch marks on me, she refused to sleep with me anymore, and then I realized that things had come to an end. It was time for a change. I knew I had to run away from it all and try to get to some abstinent and simple place of recovery. I couldn't afford a rest home, but I knew I needed something like that.

That's when I started to think about going to visit Wally, an old friend, in Santa Cruz, California. Wally had written me and had claimed to have found a simple, happy life there, working in a photography store. He was taking a lot of portraits of all the young hippie drifters, all those young and not-so-young people in motion, coming through town on their way up from Mexico to find work in Alaska. Their motion was the new escape, the way of relating to the world that was perishing right under their feet. To walk up and down on the earth seemed the only right way to celebrate it now, and mourn it while it was passing, all at the same time. I understood that and was drawn to it. I understood how Wally could find his center by taking still pictures of people in motion. He was trying to create a photographic book of the new American nomad.

And here I was about to make another move in my fall from the top of the world to the bottom. I decided not to tell Sherry this until I had one last fling with her, and then I would break it to her gently. That particular afternoon I decided to fuck her in all the positions we'd ever gone through, until I just couldn't come anymore. Then I would hold that memory in my mind, of at last being satiated by Sherry, and bring up that memory when I needed it to cancel out all those sexy obsessive images that ruled me.

So we did it and we did it until she was kneeling and I was reaming her from behind. I had a full erection, but at last it was numb and I couldn't come. After a while Sherry turned her head up and in the calmest, most centered voice I'd ever heard come out of her she said, "Are you having a good time?" I just pulled out and collapsed next to her and told her, just like that. I said, "Sherry, I'm going to California."

And she said, "Do you want me to come?"

"No, I've got to get away from it all. I've got to go it alone."

I was amazed at her strength. She didn't cry or protest. She must have known all the time what was going on, that she was involved in an exercise of brutal lust.

I CHOSE an old hippie bus called *The American Dream,* which cost sixty-nine dollars—a very sexy ticket price, I thought, as I dreamed about the cross-country orgies that would take place on it. *The American Dream* was to be leaving, as advertised, from the corner of Thirty-fourth Street and Eighth Avenue on June 30.

And on June 30, Meg went with me to see me off. It was there, just where they said it would be, an old converted Greyhound bus from the fifties, painted a chocolate brown, with its insides all converted from seats to beds.

The owners and drivers, Jacob and Floyd, had removed the seats and put in plywood platforms, which they filled with old mattresses covered with different colored patterns of paisley. With the exception of the paisley spreads, it looked like a mobile hospital. At first sight it was frightening to me, and I almost fled to the Greyhound station in search of a more conventional mode of travel. Being inside it made my head spin, made me dizzy and claustrophobic, made my eyes roll, made me grab Meg's hand in fear, made me say to myself, "Let this cup pass from my lips."

At last, after much procrastination, I kissed and hugged Meg and said goodbye, and I got on. Slowly the bus filled up with hippies, just as I dreamed it would. There were close to twenty-eight mattresses, and I huddled way in the back and watched, my terror mixed with curiosity. Then I had an awful heart pang as I saw Meg out the window for the last wave goodbye. Why, I wondered, was I putting myself through this? Why did I want to put myself in these constant situations of conflict? Why did I have to reject Meg to make me feel love for her? It was as though the only feeling I could feel was the sadness of separation.

Within an hour *The American Dream* was filled with a wild, merry, carefree bunch of hippies, all choosing their mattresses and unrolling their bedrolls. They seemed so confident and without doubt. They wore their life-style like a proud badge. Single guys were already trying to couple up with single girls as I huddled in the back of the bus with the only other two nonhippies, Heidi and Hanna, two phys-ed teachers from Norway.

Everyone cheered as Floyd and Jacob got on the bus and gave a peppy little speech about how they were our drivers and how they would be driving day and night, just under fifty-five miles an hour so as not to attract unnecessary attention. They went on to say that one of them would be sleeping in back, in what had once been the toilet when the bus belonged to Greyhound and now was a little bedroom for one of them to sleep in while the other drove. I peeked in from where I was sitting. The back of the bus was indeed a curious little boudoir. It looked like a miniature opium den or a very small Indian restaurant. The ceilings and walls and floor were all covered with paisley spreads. Because the bedroom had replaced the toilet, there was, of course, no toilet in the bus.

Jacob and Floyd assured us, though, that we would make numerous toilet stops. We would also make stops at health food stores that were off the main highway, where we could purchase alternative food like yogurt, sprouts, and almonds. There'd be no stops at Howard Johnson's or Stuckey's. Everyone cheered. There would be some stops for swimming. Everyone cheered again. At last we were off and everyone cheered a third time, twice as loud.

Then everyone started rolling joints and passing them around. I did the natural thing without thinking; I just reached up and took my first toke in almost a year, and everything went crazy. I suddenly had no idea where I was, and I propped myself up on my mattress on my elbows to try to get a sense of it all. I saw New York City from a strange, topsy-turvy, childlike view. I saw the city at wildly swinging angles as the bus made big sweeping turns and skyscrapers swung into view and then disappeared into sky. Then we plunged into the darkness

of the Lincoln Tunnel. Suddenly I relaxed. Suddenly nothing mattered. I abandoned myself to Jacob and Floyd and thought, Leave the
driving to them. Thank God I'm not driving this bus across America.

By dusk *The American Dream* had passed into the rolling hills of
Pennsylvania and everyone had slipped into a comfortable and con-
vivial mood. People began breaking out their little dinner treats: their
granola bars, their bean sprout sandwiches, their yogurt, their bananas,
their nuts. Music was playing constantly over the two little speakers
above Floyd's head as he drove. The song that I remember most
vividly, perhaps because it played over and over again like it was on
a loop, was "Only the Good Die Young," and I took that to be some
sort of message for the trip.

So there I was, way in the back of the bus with the two Norwegian phys-ed teachers. I was really terrified of taking out the nuts and
cheese I'd bought in public because I noticed that anytime anything
was passed around the bus, in traditional hippie sharing fashion, it
never came back to the owner. Of course I had to remember there was
really no "owner"; but whenever I'd see sunflower seeds go out or nuts
or even joints, they would all disappear before they came full circle.
I was afraid if I took out my bag of nuts, everyone would look at me
until I passed them around and then I wouldn't have enough to last
me for the trip.

The whole trip was one long drone that went on day and night
for four days, and the worst of it was that we were all condemned to
lying down, which in its own way is just as bad as having to sit up
for a whole cross-country trip. At times, particularly in the heat of the
day, I felt like a child sick in bed with fever, propped up on his elbows
looking out the window. Outside, everything looked like a flat dio-
rama that was being rolled by while the bus stood still. After about
three and a half days of this we were suddenly spat out of a tunnel
into Oz. There it was, San Francisco, bright white, peeking through
a blanket of rolling fog. The entrance over the Golden Gate was
spectacular; the fog was whipping across the bridge like a white
brushfire. The wind off the Pacific rocked *The American Dream* as we
crossed.

Beautiful as San Francisco was, I had had enough of cities and decided to hitchhike immediately to Santa Cruz. I had no problem getting rides.

As soon as I rolled into Santa Cruz, I knew it was the right town for me. I knew it as soon as I saw the clock in the clock tower in the center of town and was told how it had stopped years ago at ten past two, never to be started again. I knew it was the right place as soon as I saw that the town was small enough to walk around and that there was a big bookstore with a wonderful coffee shop named Purgalasi right behind it. It was the perfect place to learn to hang out, I was sure. If you didn't know how to hang out, the town would soon teach you.

I had called Wally from San Francisco to warn him that I was hitching down, and he told me to call him as soon as I got into town and he'd come pick me up and take me to his place, where he had an extra bedroom for me. And Wally did pick me up, in an outrageous car. It was a big pink two-door '54 Chevy, with large white polka dots all over it.

It was good to see Wally again. I hadn't seen him since he left New York City four years before. He looked the picture of health: slim, firm legs from obsessively riding his ten-speed bike; sun-bleached hair; red shorts; Hawaiian shirt; and most of all, a great, broad, natural smile, something I never remembered him having in New York. Oh, and then of course there were the Birkenstocks.

Wally's setup was perfect for me. He lived in an old Victorian house, not far from the center of town, which in the old days, when there were such things as large extended families, had served as a home for one. But now it was subdivided for single men like Wally, all bachelors, resisting growing up, perpetual boys of summer, all waiting to meet the right woman, and who, perhaps because there were so many available women, had not found her yet. It was as if the endless possibilities of women stunned these men into indecision.

The following day was Sunday. Sunday morning the entire communal kitchen at Wally's house was abuzz and filled with mellow and relaxed guys, all hanging out with their dates and live-ins. People were lounging, laughing, and eating French toast with fresh fruit and sipping mimosas and even passing around an after-breakfast joint. Why, I wondered, did such a relaxed gathering leave me so anxious?

I just wanted to have a bowl of granola and get out of there, go to the beach or something. But they all wanted to welcome me and initiate me into their pleasure dome. One of them, a real sweet guy in cut-offs, who worked in a bicycle shop on weekdays, offered Wally and me a teaspoon full of powdered psilocybin, just as a Sunday-morning brunch treat. I was surprised and demonstrably thankful, but Wally seemed even more surprised and told me to be flattered. "Frank," he said, "must have really taken to you, because he never gives his drugs away." "Then in that case," I said half jokingly, "do you think it's safe to take?" He just laughed at my paranoia. I decided not to take any drugs and just get out of there, go downtown to the Purgalasi to sit in the sun, sip a cappuccino, and read a little more Norman O. Brown.

I was trying at last to get to the end of the book and see how it resolved itself. But all the time I was reading Norman O. Brown's descriptions of polymorphous delight, I was watching what looked like the living example of it out of the corner of my eye. I kept watching this divine little blond six-year-old passing from table to table. When he got close to me I found that I was completely taken in by him—"mesmerized," I think would be the word. It was as if he were a living example of all that Norman O. Brown was theorizing about. There he was, this expansive, irresistible little Dionysian boy moving between tables like the spirit of eternal delight. He sat right down beside me and as soon as he sat down, I asked what he wanted. He said, "Cherry phosphate," just like that, all bright and decisive, and I thought I'd gone right back to the turn of the century. A cherry phosphate? What could that be? But I ordered it anyway and it came, cherry syrup in soda water, all stirred up into the most beautiful color. He put a straw in and went at it. He looked like a color drinking a color. He was barefoot and dressed in faded overalls and a yellow T-shirt. His face was a healthy pink framed by long blond hair. It was a wonderfully bright face which had a crazy devil-or-angel ambiguity combined with a great openness. It seemed he'd already seen a lot, but it had not harmed him or shut him down. He could not be an average six-year-old, I thought—and then again I wouldn't have known what that was, an average six-year-old, had one sat down on my lap.

We talked a little about his life and how he wasn't in school yet, but soon would be, because he and his mom had only just arrived in town and hadn't been able to work it out yet. When I asked him where he came from he told me that it was a real long, long way off, that he and his mom had hitchhiked for lots of days and nights to get there. As we were talking his mom came over and said, "Oh, I see you've met Shanti," and I said, "Oh, Shanti?"

And she said, "No, Om Shanti. That's my son, that's Om Shanti Karma." And she said it just like that, like it was one of the most common names in town. Perhaps it was.

"Come on, Shanti, we have to get going. Thank the nice man for the soda and let's head out," his mother said to him. Shanti jumped up without thanking me and ran to his mom and took her hand. She stood there, a woman about my age, with some premature graying hair like me. She just stood there, wearing her kung fu shoes and a full dark skirt and white blouse, and looked back at me. Her face was far from sweet or demure, like the other hippie mothers I'd seen there. Her face was very out of place there in that sunny outdoor coffee yard filled with clean and squeaky blondes with peach complexions, creatures you felt you could eat without washing or cooking, just eat them raw.

Shanti and his mother turned and started off, but Shanti stopped and looked back, melting me with one glance. Then he looked up at his mother and said, "Isn't someone coming with us, Mom?"

His mom turned to me and said, "Shanti wants to know if you're coming with us."

At that moment I wanted to drive them wherever they wanted to go, just so I could see Shanti's face when he saw that big, pink, foolish car. I said, "Do you need a ride anywhere?"

"Oh, that would be nice, wouldn't it, Shanti?" his mother said.

Shanti's face lit up just the way I hoped it would when he saw Big Pink sitting in among the generic Rabbits, hatchbacks, and fastbacks. We all piled into the front seat, Shanti between us, instantly and madly playing with the radio knobs as his mother asked me, pulling out her pack of Camel Regulars, if I minded if she smoked. That was another big surprise that made her, like me, not quite fit into the way things were in that town. She was the first person I'd seen smoke a cigarette since I arrived.

"Not at all," I said. "Smoke away," and smoke away she did, as I drove very slowly to the house they called home.

"By the way, my name is Mustang Sally," she said, taking another deep drag of her Camel, exhaling the smoke and with a fine finger removing a piece of tobacco from her thin lower lip.

"What's that?" I asked, and she said it again, "My name is Mustang Sally."

"Oh yes, of course," I replied. "But what should I call you?"

"Call me Mustang," she replied, taking another drag and exhaling the smoke straight up into the air.

In that short, slow drive to their little tract house she told me a bit of how they had come to be there, and I just tried to listen without judgment.

"Shanti and I are just staying with friends now until we can find the right place to pitch our teepee. We want to pitch it up in the Santa Cruz hills. We haven't found our spot yet, but it will come," she said, giving me a knowing look. "It will come in time."

Mustang Sally spoke with an educated East Coast accent, which I couldn't place, but it was definitely familiar to my ear. She went on to tell me how she and Shanti had hitchhiked down from Washington State with their teepee. "You mean you hitchhiked with a teepee? How did you ever get it into the cars?"

"Oh, no problem," Mustang said. "We got picked up by vans and trucks mostly, and with cars we just put it on the roof. People are still real open and nice, at least on Highway 1, and they even let us stay in their homes."

The house they were staying in was on a little side road not far from the beach. It was cozied in among a lot of other bungalows without much character or distinction. I pulled Big Pink up in front of the house and stopped. "Do you want to come in and smoke a joint?" Mustang asked. Her words went through me like an arrow. I wanted to do it and yet was afraid. Smoke a joint in the middle of the day? I'd only done such a thing once before, on *The American Dream*, and that had been so confusing. It had made me so anxious. I had felt very much out of control; but then again, here I was in a small little town with a car and Wally's safe haven waiting for me, so why not? I knew for the time there were no strings attached to me except in my memory, which I'd been able pretty much to beat off for the day. So why not go in and try to relax? If anything went wrong I could always just walk out and drive to the beach or go see Wally at work in his photography store. I was free. No one had any power over me, except perhaps Shanti; and besides, I wondered what it would be like to be stoned with Shanti and Mustang. But most of all I was not ready to say goodbye to Om Shanti Karma. I had fallen in love at first sight.

I did not like the feel, or "vibe," as they say, of that house. As soon as I got inside, it felt weird. It was dark and cluttered. The furniture was an odd collection of Ethan Allen, junk picked off the street or the dump, and a big Castro convertible couch. All the window shades were pulled down in the living room, and clothing was scattered everywhere. But the kitchen saved the day. The kitchen was big and bright and not too cluttered, although the dishes in the sink looked like they were beginning to grow a fine green moss.

Mustang put the kettle on for tea and got a plastic bag of marijuana out of the kitchen cupboard. Shanti sat at the kitchen table and beamed up at me like a bright shining light. He seemed to be the main source of light in that house, and I secretly hoped that he'd never burn out. He sat there playing with a pot holder and looking up at me with that outrageous and incredible trust, and he asked me where I came from. When I said, "New York City," Mustang responded by saying, "You remember New York City, Shanti. It was the place with all the big buildings."

"Oh, you've been there?" I asked, happy now that some shared history outside of Santa Cruz might be possible.

"Oh, yes," Mustang said. "Shanti and I hitchhiked there to visit his sisters once."

While Mustang was rolling our first joint, a tall, lanky, very tough-looking woman dressed in a dungaree outfit came into the kitchen and plopped down at the table between us. "Oh," Mustang cried with bravado, "let me introduce Ankh." Then Mustang struck a match and lit the joint. Holding her first toke deep in, she passed it to me and, after exhaling, said, "Ankh, this is . . . Oh, I'm sorry, I didn't get your name."

"Oh, it's Brewster . . . it's Brewster North," I said, almost embarrassed by the sound of 'it, or by the way it came out of me, so sort of uptight and preppy.

I took the joint from Mustang and took a deep drag. It was smooth, sweet, and mild and didn't make me cough. "Mmmm, good," I said, holding the smoke deep in. "Nice."

"Yeah, that's local stuff. It came down from the hills just outside of town," Mustang said, with a wry smile.

I passed the joint on to Ankh, who moved in slow motion to take it from my hand and then, lifting it to her lips, also took a very deep drag and, holding her breath, said, "What kind of name is Brewster?" The marijuana had already begun to confuse me, and I wasn't at all sure what she meant by "what kind of name." But I just played along and said, "Well, I guess it's English. It's really a family name," I said.

"Oh, yeah, well, sure, but what does it mean?" Ankh asked, holding her breath to keep the marijuana smoke in her lungs, sounding like she was about to explode. "So what kind of name is it? What does it mean?" she said, now at last exploding all over the place and blowing marijuana smoke out over Shanti's head while he looked up, glowing.

"Well, I'm not really sure," I said. "But if you sort of break it down, I guess it's obvious what with the word 'brew' in 'Brewster,' that it must have come down from a long line of English brewers or something like that. As for 'North,' I guess it just means the direction on the compass, so I guess quite simply 'Brewster North' means brewers from northern England—that's the most I can make of it," I said, now almost confusing myself.

This crazy, chatty explanation of my name made both Ankh and Mustang laugh in that kind of manic, inappropriate marijuana response, something that started in a laugh and then went into a raunchy cough and finished with a real long stretched out, "Oh, wowww, toooooo much! This guy is toooooo much!"

Shanti glowed right beside me, happy, perhaps at his mom's acceptance of me, or maybe because he saw that I felt at ease enough in their presence not only to make them laugh, but allow them to laugh at me. It never occurred to me to ask what the name "Ankh" meant or "Mustang" or "Shanti" for that matter, although at the time I remember the names all struck me—or at least "Ankh" struck me—as something Turkish.

"Ankh used to be named Bernice, and then I renamed her," Mustang said, to try to clear up my obvious confusion.

"Oh, really?" I said, more curious now. "What on earth for?" And both Mustang and Ankh let out with another one of those hacking bursts of laughter which was followed by another big "Oh wow, oh wow"; then they said, "Oh wow, he got it!"

"Yeah, right," said Ankh. "He got it, he got the 'what on earth' exactly. You are a very tuned-in individual, Mr. Brew," Ankh said with a great stoned grin.

"Ankh is the earth sign," Mustang said. "Ankh is the ancient Egyptian symbol of life."

"Earth sign?" I asked.

"Yeah, you know, the figure eight. Show it to him," Mustang said, and Ankh reached down her black T-shirt and pulled out a silver-plated figure eight that was on a chain around her neck. "You see," Mustang said, as she passed the joint to me again, "Ankh—" Then she broke off, stopped, and turned to Ankh and asked, "You don't mind if I tell him, do you? You don't mind if I tell him how you got your name?"

"No, no," Ankh laughed, "tell away, tell him. I love to hear you tell it, babe."

"Well, anyway," Mustang went on, "it's really not such a big story. You see, Ankh used to be Bernice, and she used to also hang out with a lot of Angels."

"Angels?" I asked, somewhat stunned. And they both went into another round of long, hacking laughter, which was beginning to make me feel extremely lonely, or as innocent as Shanti, who still just sat there between us, not laughing, but radiating contentedness as he continued to watch, listen, and finger a ragged pot holder like it was his new security blanket.

"You know—'Angels' as in 'Hell's Angels,' " Mustang said, after she managed to stop laughing.

"Oh yeah, of course," I said. "And then what? Did they give her the name?" This question of mine made them both start laughing again, and Ankh, who now seemed almost unable to breathe, said to Mustang, "Can you imagine Bobby Giraffe knowing what the Egyptian earth sign was?" and then they both laughed some more.

By this time I was beginning to feel a little uneasy, and I wanted to ask if I could excuse myself and take Shanti home with me, or just take him out to the backyard to play; but then Mustang, who was really quite observant, noticed my discomfort and went on with the story, which I thought was actually very short and could have been told without all this laughter.

"No, no," she said, "it was just because of Bobby Giraffe that Ankh paced so much, and I couldn't stand her pacing. She'd get nervous or pissed off at Bobby and would go into this frantic pacing back and forth, and I thought if I changed her name to Ankh, she might begin to move in a more graceful figure eight." At the moment I thought of saying, "Why not change her name to V-8 Juice?" but I held my tongue. I thought only Shanti would have appreciated it. "Anyway," Mustang said, "it worked."

And now, without laughter, like a weird dancer, Ankh, who was once Bernice, got up and demonstrated her figure-eight movement right there in the kitchen, while Mustang applauded and Shanti glowed, tearing small pieces of the pot holder off in his hand.

Well, I liked the story, but I was still a little nervous and had a feeling that I would be more relaxed with Shanti if the two of us could be alone. I stood up and stretched and felt the marijuana rush throughout my whole body; and then, without saying a word, because I figured they'd understand this kind of behavior, I just walked right out to the living room, and Shanti followed, just as I hoped he would. Shanti followed me like he'd been waiting for this move all afternoon. As soon as we got in the living room, Shanti plunked himself right down on the Castro convertible couch. As soon as his bum hit the couch a big, fuzzy puff of dust came up around him, and filled the shafts of sunlight leaking through the Venetian blinds. He laughed for no reason at all, or because of the dust. I laughed at him sitting there in that yellow dust, on that big gold-speckled couch, looking up at me as if to ask, "Well, what's next?"

I intuitively knew that whatever was coming next had to be physical, exuberant, and overflowing in that Dionysian sort of way. I reached down and took the pillow that Shanti was sitting on and lifted him up from the couch real high and held him there, as if he were flying on a magic carpet, then I let go of the pillow and dropped him.

Shanti squealed and let out with a wild laugh as he and the pillow hit the floor and bounced; and then, making an immediate recovery, Shanti jumped back on the pillow and cried out, "Do it again!" And so I did. I did it again, and I did it again and again and again. I decided I would do it until Shanti no longer cried "Do it again!" I made up my mind right away to try to totally satisfy him so that perhaps for once in his life at an early age, he would know the condition of complete indulgence and satisfaction. He would have no leftover longings; at least for this day he'd be cured of the longing for the event that never happened. Shanti would be king for a day, and I made up my mind that I would be his servant as long as it took me to fully satisfy him with this new magic-flying-pillow routine. And all the time I lifted him and dropped him, Ankh and Mustang looked on from the kitchen with strange expressions on their faces, sometimes laughing, sometimes crying, "Oh wow!" and sometimes just zonked out and staring, until at last Shanti rolled off the pillow and said, "I want a Popsicle." So we were off to the next indulgence.

Mustang called after us as we escaped together out the front door, calling, "Bring me a pack of Camel Regulars."

Shanti and I climbed into Big Pink and we were off to the local deli, with Shanti giving me directions. I drove the Chevy at a creeping fifteen miles an hour while Shanti tuned the radio in to Frank Sinatra singing "My Way," and the whole world fell into place.

Shanti and I took our time in the deli. He picked up and examined every kind of sweet item in his reach, while I slowly examined all the different beers until I found my favorite, Anchor Steam. Then at last, when we were both completely satisfied by our individual choices, we made our way to the counter for the Camels, and I paid for it all. Shanti had a packet of Black Jack gum, a roll of Necco wafers, and an orange Popsicle. I had a six-pack of Anchor Steam and Mustang's Camels.

When I got in Big Pink, with Shanti close beside me, I really just wanted to run away with him. I wanted to kidnap him. I'd never had a feeling like that before. I was totally in love with this little kid.

Everything he did refreshed me, delighted me, and brought me new life. But I didn't kidnap him. Instead I drove him back to the house he called home.

As we pulled up in front of the house some adult attitude came over me and I turned to Shanti, who was glowing at my side. A strange, older, responsible voice, something like my father's, came out of me and said, "Aren't you going to thank me, Shanti?" Shanti stopped glowing for a moment. My heart sank. He turned to me and held up each newly bought item, each slightly eaten newly bought item, and with orange Popsicle stain around his mouth and loose Necco Wafers raining everywhere, he said in an equally cool imitation adult voice, as he held up each item one at a time in my face, "Thank you for this, thank you for this, thank you for this, thank you, thank you, thank you." Then, returning to the glowing child again, he worked to try to open the car door, that big, resistant car door; and in the midst of it all he turned to me and said, "Oh my God! It's like an elephant!"

Inside the house Ankh was walking in her figure eight while Mustang was cleaning and straining a large quantity of marijuana. I gave her the Camels and said goodbye, and as soon as I said that I could see Shanti wither out of the corner of my eye, so I added, "But I will come again. I will see you all soon again, and that includes you too, Shanti."

"Oh yes," Mustang said. "Even better, let's all have a big picnic together tomorrow. Shanti and I know the best nude beach in town, don't we, Shanti?" she said, drawing him into her, so that the two of them now looked like one organism. Shanti, smiling out from between her legs, nodded yes.

I opened an Anchor Steam and sipped it while I drove. The marijuana had made my head very busy, almost too busy for such a simple, beautiful setting. I kept thinking I had all the answers and kept searching the glove compartment for a pen and a piece of scrap paper to jot them down, but no luck; so I had to memorize them, and every time I thought I had a grasp on one, it would float by me like the boxes I saw floating downstream when I was on LSD. I was watching all these boxes flowing downstream again as I drove Big Pink and sipped Anchor Steam and thought, Oh, I've come to the last place at last. I've come to the best place: Santa Cruz.

HEN I RETURNED the next day, Shanti ran to
Big Pink like a delighted puppet being drawn on a string,
and Mustang followed him, looking like some perverse and
demented suburban housewife, struggling out of her little tract house
with her beach bag filled with towels and picnic items. Shanti slid in
the car, beside me, still glowing as much as the day before, and
immediately started tuning the radio.

It was miraculous how quickly we were out of town and bullet-
ing north on Highway 1 through rough brown hills and rolling fields
of high dried grass with the giant Pacific Ocean sweeping and swelling
on our left. The air smelled sweet and good. No suburbia to contend
with, just open country on the edge of town. Shanti was still beside
me tuning the radio, and Mustang looked fine.

Fifteen minutes out of town we passed a bunch of parked cars,
four-wheel vehicles, jeeps and vans, and Mustang told me to pull over.
We parked, stepped over some old dusty railroad tracks, and started
down a very steep dirt slope which led, at last, after much slipping and
sliding, to a beautiful little nook, a beautiful sandy beach tucked away
in a horseshoe of rock cliffs that rose up over a hundred feet.

The beach was busy but not too full. Naked people romped and
cavorted here and there, making the place look like a cartoon of itself.
In between those hundred-foot-high cliffs and that vast ocean which
no one was swimming in, everyone seemed very small and vulnerable,
especially Shanti, who ran hopping and skipping ahead of Mustang and
me. We passed a nude volleyball game, which was rather odd because
of the way the men and women were jiggling. They were very tan;
the older ones looked all leathery, as though their skin had been cured
by a local tanner. There was nothing erotic about such well-tanned
flesh lit by the bright, flat light of that California sun. All the mystery
was burned away, leaving only biology. What a surprise, and what a
blessed relief, I thought, to be able to relax with nudity and not be
driven crazy by the grass-is-always-greener complex.

We settled down out of the wind, up against the cliffs between the volleyball game and a group of naked young people who were all sitting in a big circle playing flutes, recorders, guitars, and bongo drums. With the exception of two very hairy men who were playing an incessantly annoying game of paddleball at the ocean's edge, the place seemed like Paradise.

As soon as we spread our towels and blankets and settled down in our spot, Mustang and Shanti got completely undressed, and I just followed, feeling at first a little odd and embarrassed disrobing in front of these two strangers. But at the same time I welcomed the chance to be able to check out Mustang's body before I made any amorous advances. She was not what I would call robust in any way, not like those others, the ones playing flutes and beating balls back and forth. But Mustang's skin resembled the others' in that it had that deep, dark tan, as though she had gone native and her skin had changed its pigment permanently. It was not one of those glamorous tans you might encounter on Fifth Avenue at the end of March. Her skin was more weathered, like that of a fisherman or farmer, someone who made their living working out of doors. There was something shriveled and prunelike about her body. She looked like she needed a little puffing up, a little inflation. Her midsection looked more like a stomach than a belly, and her ass, like mine, was rather flat, but I tried not to scrutinize her. I tried to accept her for what she was, as I took small fleeting glances out of the corner of my eye. After all, I thought, she had given birth to a perfect son, and there he was dancing and glowing beside us like a little pink cherub flown down out of a clear, cloudless California sky. Shanti's body was like a delicious bowl of ripe fruit in motion, all the little perfect curves and fullnesses spouting and sprouting and fitting so perfectly together. He was a gem. There was no doubt about it. He looked like the model of undifferentiated id as he grabbed a piece of driftwood and spun around with it. Mustang called out to him "Be careful," and then "Shanti, please come over here now to me and let me put some suntan lotion on you." Then, turning to me as if she had to make an explanation, Mustang said, "Shanti is one of those fair ones who burn so easily."

I watched her put the suntan cream all over Shanti's body and thought how lucky she was to be able to touch him all over in a pragmatic, loving way, that simple mothering way. For a moment I found myself in such a complete state of empathetic ecstasy that I thought I could feel my body as Shanti's body as well as Mustang's hands as my hands. After she finished, Shanti was off, running down the beach by the great beating edge of the sea and then he ran further down the beach to make new friends or to make contacts with old friends.

Mustang rolled onto her stomach and I did the same, still a bit ashamed of my exposed front. The warm sun on my naked backside felt fantastic. I could feel it piercing my skin, and except for the rather awkward silence between us I would have been relaxed enough to just doze off and sleep. Then Mustang said, "Shanti is really a very social kid. He's never lonely. I think he may grow up to be the mayor of Santa Cruz—that is, if we stay long enough."

I made an un-thought-out, awkward response. I asked, "How long have you had him?"

Mustang looked at me with an arch smirk and said, "Had who?" And I said, "Shanti."

Mustang just looked at me like I was crazy, and said, "Ever since he came out of me six years ago." Then we both laughed, and after the laughter died down, I said, "But what happened to his father?" I guess the absence of Shanti's father had helped to foster the fantasy I had of him as a cherub fallen down out of a cloudless California sky.

"Well, that," Mustang said, as she cupped her hands around a match to light yet another Camel, "that is a rather long story."

"Oh," I said, "please tell it. I love long stories." I was suddenly very happy that Mustang had a story to tell because I had been not at all sure what we would do on that naked beach all day without anything to talk about. I was kind of afraid that Mustang would offer me some marijuana and I wouldn't be able to refuse it. But she didn't light a joint. She sucked on her Camel instead, and, resting on her stomach, she turned her head slightly toward me and with her wise, sardonic smirk that said, "So you think you really want to hear it? All right, Mr. Brewster, here goes—here goes the story," she told it to me. And I lay there listening, knowing that I'd most likely enjoy the story more than I would have relished the actual events from which it grew.

Mustang told me how she had grown up as Ellen Heath in what

she referred to as "a normal situation" in Columbus, Ohio, where she also got married and had three children. Then her husband read an article about free love in *Time* magazine and he began to experiment. This made her think she should too, and she ended up having an affair with her milkman, who also introduced her to LSD. After their first acid trip together she ran off to Washington State with him. They'd both realized on that first acid trip that the whole problem with their lives was that they were landlocked, and had to get to the sea, so they drove straight for it and came out on the Washington Coast. After they got there, they joined a commune where they lived in teepees and all practiced a far-out ritual called "King and Queen for a Day." Each week someone was chosen to be king or queen and they could rule the whole commune with whatever their fantasy was for that day. So Ellen, on her "queen for a day" day, would administer windowpane acid to the whole commune and then they would head out into the sea in rowboats pretending they were headed for the Bermuda Triangle.

After a while the commune broke up and the milkman headed off to Hawaii to harvest marijuana and Ellen, not yet Mustang, folded up her teepee and hitchhiked down to Santa Cruz, putting her teepee on the top of cars or in the back of pickup trucks. In Santa Cruz she met up with her brother, whom she hadn't seen in years. Shortly after their reunion her brother got involved in some sort of hit-and-run accident and decided to change his name. Seeing in the morning paper that the coldest place in the United States the previous day was Cheyenne, Wyoming, he changed his name to Cheyenne Shivers. That made Ellen decide to change her name as well; and wanting, as she said, to explore her "male energy," she changed her name to Edison Shivers. So it was Cheyenne and Edison, brother and sister. Shortly after the name change Cheyenne died in a motorcycle accident, and Edison wanted to change her name again but had no idea what it should be. Then one night while she was dancing to the music of Wilson Pickett, he played "Mustang Sally," and she knew that her new name had been given to her.

After the commune broke up, Mustang found that she was really missing her children she had left behind in Ohio, and knowing that she could never return to Columbus, she decided to have a love child in Santa Cruz. She found what she thought was the right father, a great blond hunk of a surfer, and promptly got pregnant. Everything was going fine until one day he came home and said he had heard that the singer Taj Mahal made his wife ask his permission before she spoke to another man. The father of Mustang's child said he liked that idea, he thought it was cool; so Mustang threw him out and had their love child on her own, and named him Om Shanti Karma.

And boom, I landed back on the beach, her story was over, just like that, just like she had taken me for a ride on her magic flying paisley carpet and then dropped me back down here on the beach, all solid and warm, just here. The only difference was I didn't say "Do it again." So here we were, very much here, and I wanted nothing more than to go run and romp with Shanti, and I told Mustang that and she made signs of understanding. I jumped up and felt the warm wind play all over me, and walked without shame in the sun, walked toward Shanti where he was playing a little bongo drum with all the other naked natives who sat in their sacred circle at the bottom of the great rock cliff. Seeing me approach, Shanti ran toward me and I swept him up in my arms and felt his glorious suntan-lotioned body slip and nuzzle against mine as we fit together like perfect pieces in a puzzle and I carried him squealing to the ocean's edge. We stood there together in the cold rushing foam with sea gulls screaming overhead, screams that mingled with Shanti's squeals, and I pressed his glorious young warm body close into mine until we almost melded. The only thing that separated us was the thought that it could be better, that perhaps we could be even closer. Then suddenly I was Mom and Shanti was me and we were on the edge of that other ocean so long ago and I knew then that it was Shanti I wanted and not Mustang. I wanted to be the mother of this child, and for a moment I was.

SOMETHING WAS COMPLETED in me that day on the beach with Shanti. After that I felt it was time to go, before I fell in too deep, got obsessive and couldn't live without that peaches-and-cream boy. I knew I couldn't love his mother the way I loved him, and that would soon become a problem, I was sure.

Also, I longed for some social order that would pull me out of that long and syrupy season of fantasy, that long fall from the top of the earth to the bottom. Meg and the old familiar East Coast represented that grounded reality for me. And I was running out of money. If I was going to get back east I needed to do it now.

Wally had a friend who needed a car driven across to New York. I volunteered. I had never driven myself across America before and was ready to give it a try. We worked out the details and I went to pick up my transport, a black 1967 Volkswagen Karmann-Ghia.

I called Mustang to tell her I was leaving and wanted to come over to say goodbye to Shanti and her before I took off. She didn't seem surprised and just responded with that sort of laid-back, go-with-the-flow, if-that's-the-way-it-is-babe-then-sure-go-with-it tone in her voice. She asked me for my time and place of birth because she wanted to do me up a little farewell present. And I was amazed that I remembered the information: June 5, 1941, 1:51 a.m., Providence, Rhode Island.

After I packed up the Karmann-Ghia with my few belongings, I drove over to say goodbye. Mustang came out of the house to greet me, and then Shanti came out, but sort of hid behind her and wouldn't look at me.

"Shanti doesn't like goodbyes," Mustang said, and then stepped forward to give me my farewell present. She had drawn up my astrological chart and wanted to tell me exactly what to look out for on my trip across the Mother (which was what she called the earth). I could hardly think of what was left of America as a mother, but for her sake I put on a smile and tried. The main thrust of Mustang's astrological reading was that I should be very careful to get involved with working for an institution or I would soon end up inside one. I laughed and scratched my head, having no idea how right her prediction was about to be. I thanked Mustang and said goodbye. It was easy to say goodbye to her, but not to Shanti, and I was glad that he had disappeared back into the house before I left. I knew then that I was like him. Goodbyes to people I loved were just too much.

WHAT IS THERE to tell about a cross-country trip? It's so monotonous. I had no idea how monotonous it was going to be. Had I known I probably never would have jumped in that car in the first place. The further I got away from one ocean, the more I just wanted to leap to the other. I felt as though I was simply racing from the Pacific to the Atlantic. I drove with the gas pedal mashed to the floor, hoping to make Las Vegas before nightfall.

I didn't want to stop to eat or break my pace. I wanted to get to Vegas fast, so I bought some Swiss cheese and a pack of Pall Mall cigarettes and nibbled and smoked as I drove straight out over that baking hot desert. The car was not air conditioned. I'd never experienced a blast of heat like that before; it was like driving through a great sauna. But as night came on it got cooler and beautiful beyond expectation. The clear, sharp angles of light highlighted hundreds of cactus, like those armies of cactus I'd seen fighting in Mexico, and gave a dark-line silhouette to the distant mountains as they met the clear orange and turquoise sunset colors above them.

Soon it was dark and there were only the stars and that little black Karmann-Ghia rambling along like a turtle on the ocean floor, being guided by a giant profusion of stars. Then in the distance I could see a glowing field of light like the landing pad for a giant space ship. It was, I realized, Las Vegas. I tuned my radio into Frank Sinatra singing "My Way" and headed straight for it.

I drove down the main drag strip, its blast of neon and glitz bringing me back from that hypnotic desert darkness. Vegas was such a contrast to Santa Cruz. There was so much more to be seen and done. I decided to quickly find a cheap motel and go out and do it all right away, maybe even hit the jackpot. I had no idea at the time that if you looked right—that is, like an average American on vacation—you could stay in a big fancy hotel for free, provided you gambled in the hotel casino. No one had told me that.

The motel I checked into was $29.95 a night. That was the best I could do in my rush to get to the gambling tables. My room had a vibrating bed in it. All I had to do was put a quarter in the slot and the bed went wild—just what I needed after my long trip across the desert. But I was too excited; I wanted to do it all. I took a hot shower with the Jacuzzi spray attachment, then lay on the bed, only to jump up in mid-vibration, dress, and run out to the casino, hoping to win and win again. I really believed that this was how I was going to make my next little nest egg to live off of.

I dressed up in my white cotton pants and brown raw silk Nehru jacket, left the black turtle parked safely in the parking lot, walked to the strip, and started down the row of casinos, one after another.

I'd always loved the look of roulette: the big, colorful table, the wooden ball dancing, and the blurred beauty of that big wheel spinning. I started safe, just playing red and even. I did not want to associate myself with black or odd—not yet, anyway. I saw those as the shadow and bad luck. I hadn't learned my lesson. Playing only red, I would slowly win a little, but it all seemed to keep balancing out, like life. I'd win a little and then I'd lose a little, and then in a very little time I was bored and started wandering around watching people play dice and fill up the slot machines. They looked like a bunch of compulsives to me, and I soon realized that I was not really attracted to anything there. It was like a big gaudy funeral parlor with a bunch of toys in it. As for the money to be won, it made me think of that old quote from Freud that I'd read in Norman O. Brown's book: "That is why wealth brings so little happiness; money is not an infantile wish."

After Santa Cruz, Las Vegas seemed so unhealthy. I began to feel a little depressed and longed to go to sleep in my vibrating bed, so I could get on the road bright and early the next morning and make it to the Grand Canyon before sunset.

Walking back to my motel, I realized that part of the reason I was feeling so spaced out was that I hadn't eaten. I'd missed my dinner. The initial excitement of the place had made me lose my appetite, and now it had come back in full force. So I found what looked like a regular restaurant and went in. I ordered a typical American meal: a cheeseburger, medium rare, and two Budweisers. The cheeseburger came well done and with very little cheese on it, something like

Velveeta, and when I got the bill, the price was so high that I was outraged. When I got to the cash register I found that no one was there. Fortified by the two beers, I decided to just walk out. The meal was certainly not worth paying for. I felt justified in not paying for it. I stuffed the check in my pocket and walked out and headed back to my motel. But before I got three blocks two police cars, each speeding from different directions, came to a screaming halt on either side of me. A cop jumped out of each car and came at me in the most threatening and aggressive way.

The one on my right said, "Okay, guy, let's see your ID," and that's when I realized that in my rush to get out of the motel, I had left it behind. So I said, "It's back in my motel," and the cop on my left said, "What's the name of your motel?"

Good question, I thought. I said, "I don't remember. I just checked in." Then he asked, "What's your name?" And for some reason, maybe because of the beers, I just politely said, "Why do you ask?" And I realized at that moment that it came out of me sounding rather snooty, and I hadn't meant it to sound that way. Then everything went real fast. The cop on the right said, "Where you coming from, boy?" And when I proudly answered "California," that did it.

The cop on the right said, "Well, we're going to teach you that you're not in California anymore," and they did. The next thing I knew I was down on my knees with my hands handcuffed behind me and the two cops were standing over me with their nightsticks vibrating just inches from my head. Then I was in the back of one of the police cruisers, and then I was emptying my pockets to a man behind a wire mesh screen, and then I was standing in a big room being told to take off my clothes, and then I was naked and someone was yelling, "Cover your eyes and mouth," as someone aimed a big gun at me that blew a great gusty cloud of DDT all over me, which made my skin itch and made me very quickly realize that I was indeed not in California anymore. I was in the Las Vegas, Nevada, jail. I was, just as Mustang had predicted, in an institution before I'd even had the chance to work for one.

After they sprayed me with the DDT, I was issued a gray prison jumpsuit that zipped up from the crotch to the neck, and I was led by two guards down the hall to some sort of holding tank, and I was locked in a twelve-foot-by-twelve-foot cell with about twenty men. There were nowhere near enough benches to accommodate everyone, so most of the men were lounging or lying on the floor in various states of rage, regression, and intoxication. I was told that I was allowed one phone call, but I had no idea who to call, and because I was so confused by what had taken place, as well as mesmerized by it, I think I went into a sort of mild dissociative shock and suddenly became an observer, a fly on the wall. It was as though some part of me was outside watching it all, watching this new stranger in a gray prison outfit, who, just moments before, had been Brewster North, all dressed up in white cotton pants and raw silk Nehru jacket. Now life had changed real fast and this same Brewster North was among what looked like a mob of soulless, hardened criminals, a bunch of losers, people arrested for all sorts of misbehavior, from jaywalking to attempted murder. A young man was talking to his father on a telephone the guards had passed through the bars to him, and he was bragging to his dad about how he had almost killed his brother in a fistfight, saying things like "Maybe I'm in the fucking slammer, but Jimmy got the worst of it. You should see his fucking face. He's unrecognizable," boasting in front of us all.

I was fascinated by this, by the level of depravity I found myself so suddenly in. It was much more interesting than the casino activity—I guess because it didn't have to do with money. Also I was surprised to find that something like that could happen so quickly, so fast, in America: that I could be Brewster North walking on the street, going home to my vibrating bed, and then suddenly be this prisoner, arrested for what I didn't know—for coming from California? And strange to say, it was not anger that took me over so much as it was a deep sense of curiosity.

After a few hours in the holding tank, a guard came and took me to another room to book me. It was there that they fingerprinted me and took my photograph. I expected to be taken back to the holding tank, where I would try to make my one phone call to Meg and ask her to help me. But instead the guard led me down a long battleship-gray metal corridor, past a series of dormitory cells. Then he opened two big gray iron-barred doors and pushed me into a very large room filled with bunks and about thirty men sitting and standing around in different positions all slowly turned and looked at me as though they'd been expecting me to come and join them.

The guard told me to choose a bunk. I took the first empty top bunk that I came to, then immediately lay down on it, covered my head with the stinky pillow, and softly cried for about twenty minutes. After crying, I came up more resigned to my new quarters. I looked around at my new home and all those very strange strangers in it, and I decided right then and there that I better start socializing and get to know them before they got to know me and noticed my New England accent and took me for a Boston Brahmin or, worse, a Harvard graduate, and crucified me at dawn.

So instead of talking to them, I just drifted among them, all through that large dormitory cell, trying to be as casual as possible, trying not to look like an educated weirdo they might want to crucify. As I did this I began to see that the men were sort of divided up into groups, or at least that's how I began to perceive it. I divided them all up into professionals, night people, poets, madmen, and, last of all, losers. I did not put myself in any category outside of the one that might be called "I alone have escaped to tell you."

The professionals were a very cautious and private group. They seemed to have consciously chosen a life of crime and were resigned to serving some time in jail as a consequence of that choice; it was their occupational hazard. They all seemed to be dealing with it like adults, without too much bitching or complaining. They had photos of their families and loved ones hanging on the walls beside their bunks. They were family men. They were dedicated criminal family men, and they spoke mainly in a rather dry legalese, a language that you might associate more with lawyers or lobbyists in Washington. They spoke without passion or imagination or love, and when I came too close to them, they'd just shut up and eye me with suspicion. After I moved on, they'd begin to talk again in low, secretive tones.

There were no windows to the outside world. It was a totally enclosed little world, with twenty-four-hour air conditioning belching down through a number of ceiling vents. At the back of the cell were two toilets without seats. They were completely exposed. There was no privacy. As I made my way around the cell I saw that some of the

prisoners who had bottom bunks had made their own privacy by
taking the one blanket that had been issued them off their beds and
hanging it from the top bunk, to make a little tentlike enclosure where
they hid out all day. I came to call the men who lived behind those
blankets the night people. That was their category. They were mostly
black and spent the whole day sleeping behind their blankets and the
whole night playing cards and gambling for push-ups. The lights of
the cell were never turned off; they were on twenty-four hours a day,
so the night people could play cards all night. And they were in great
shape, particularly the ones who lost all the time, because they had to
do the most push-ups.

There were really only two outstanding losers. The first was a
man who was originally from Weirs Beach, New Hampshire. He had
one of those consistently sad lives and had been in and out of jail since
he was busted for passing bum checks at age eighteen. That was the
same year his girlfriend was killed falling off the back of his motorcycle. After that he just kind of lost it and would spend his nights going
down to Weirs Beach, where he would shoot off the mortar he had
bought from a buddy who had brought it back from the Korean War.
Then he became a truck driver, and when he was stopped outside of
Vegas recently for a traffic violation, he gave the cop that stopped him
a lot of lip, so the cop roughed him up and tore his leather jacket off
him and threw it in a trash can, and when he told the cop to get it
out of the trash the cop refused and hit him with a blackjack. Then
he told the cop that if he hit him one more time he'd take the blackjack
away from him and hit him back, and he did. So that was that, and
he was in the slammer for a while. "I wish I had my fucking piece
under my seat where it usually is," he said. "I would have blown that
fucking cop away."

So this loser had been there on that bottom bunk for quite some
time waiting for his trial to come up, and while he was there he had
created a beautiful pencil mural on the wall behind his bunk. It was
a drawing of all the things he loved—a New Hampshire covered
bridge arching over a little stream, and bouncing like little cartoon
figures down a New Hampshire country road, all headed toward the
covered bridge, came his big semi truck, his old motorcycle, his mortar,
and his piece, which looked like a hefty .45. There they all were,

dancing toward the covered bridge. The mural had no people, not even the ghost of his dead girlfriend, just a bunch of guns and machines headed for a covered bridge somewhere in New Hampshire. This man was sad, and under his sadness I could sense a deep, deep anger.

As for the other loser, I hardly got to know him because he was in and out of there so fast. He was a dark, wiry guy, maybe Mexican-American, with a little dark mustache. Just after he was brought in I noticed him madly scraping something in the corner. He was giving off a kind of frantic energy, and at first I thought he had some kind of drug paraphernalia over there that he was fixing to shoot up with, because I could see he was unzipping his jumpsuit and beginning to expose his torso. Then he got up and walked over to the barred doors and, with his jumpsuit now hanging off his hips, he called to the guards. Just as the guards came running, he lifted into the air what I could now see was the well-sharpened end of a coat hanger and brought it down full force into his side. His crimson blood gushed and ran down his dark skin. The metal coat hanger was sticking out like the bolts that stick out of Frankenstein's head. The guards dragged him away, and then when they came back to check on the cell, one of the inmates said, "Did he die yet?" And the guard retorted, "If he hasn't, he should. That's the second time he's pulled that shit on us." Then everyone in the cell started yelling at the guards and calling them assholes, but the guards didn't even respond or pay attention. They knew who had the power; they knew who was in charge. They were blond and big and looked like pleasant, smiling astronauts or like captains of some football team. They knew who had the power.

As for the madmen, there were two that I remember most. The first was also of Mexican descent, and he just loved to steal transport vehicles of all sorts—the greater the variety, the better. He was not only into stealing cars; he had stolen an army jeep, an army truck, a Greyhound bus, and, at last, the vehicle that had landed him in jail: a police plane. He told me how the police all chased him in their planes, broadcasting over speakers behind him, "Land that plane. This is the police. Land that plane." His eyes lit up when he said, "Land that plane." His eyes lit up like Shanti's eyes when Shanti said, "Do it again." I could tell he had a real good time stealing that police plane and that he hadn't done it for the money, but for fun. His eyes shone in a bright devilish way, a way that made me like his more than any other eyes in that prison. While listening to his story I could clearly see the image of him hunched over the joystick of that police plane. His story was like a bright cartoon, lighting up that bleak gray prison cell.

The other madman was as regular as some odd cuckoo clock going off every day around cocktail hour. He always told the same story, and it always came just before dinner, after a whole day of lying on his top bunk with a blanket pulled over his head. He would suddenly tear the blanket off and sit up and cry out to everyone, who ignored him, "You want to know how I got here? Well, I'll tell you how I got here," and he'd proceed with this great rapid-fire diatribe that went so fast you could hardly catch it. His story started somewhere in the South Bronx as a teenager and moved its way through many turbulent years to that Vegas jail.

Then, last of all, the poet, who was this young, sensitive con man. I got closer to him than anyone else in that cell, in the sense of having a dialogue with him. He was maybe eighteen or nineteen years old and was really only into petty conning. He was also writing poetry and rock-and-roll songs on the side. His crimes were relatively innocent and somewhat creative, most likely not committed exclusively for the money, at least not yet. That was soon to come. For instance, he had made copies of credit cards from discarded carbons he'd found in dumpsters behind restaurants and then with these new counterfeit credit cards he made long-distance calls to China just for fun, just to see if anyone was there. Oh, sure, he would have bought hi-fi equipment and cameras and stuff like that if he had a place to put them, but he didn't. He was always on the move. He'd also do false setups, as he called them, to create parties. He loved parties, and no one could ever throw enough for him. He'd never had any as a kid. In fact, it was all for want of a party that he ended up in jail. He worked with his pretty sister and his buddy. That was their con team. His pretty sister would go into a casino bar and hang out until she was noticed by the owner or maître d'. She was pretty and hot, so she always got noticed real fast. When the owner started coming on to her, she let it all heat up real nice to the boiling point until the guy was about to make the big move. Then she'd give the cue to her brother and his buddy to enter, and they'd come in and put on this great show. She would start squealing and crying, "I don't believe it—it's Mickey! It's my long-lost brother, Mickey! What are you doing here? My God, I haven't seen you in ten years! Oh, lord save us, this is a miracle, a true miracle! What are you doing here in Vegas, Mickey?" Then she'd burst into tears. She'd actually break down and cry, and nine times out of ten the owner of the club would be so impressed and moved by this rare coincidence, this joyous chance family reunion, that he would order champagne for all, and more champagne, until a big party would take place. But one day, after a number of these parties, Mickey got busted for drinking underage.

It was strange, but a part of me was fascinated by everything that was going on in that jail, and that part kept me from demanding my one phone call, although each day I put in a written request, and each day I received no response. Once I got over the fear that I was going to be raped, beaten, or persecuted, I was more at ease there. People didn't seem to notice my New England accent, perhaps because I was listening more than I was talking. After all, I was in a prison suit just like everyone else, and I was even beginning to adopt a rather tough prison posture. At the same time, I really did want to get out, but for the first time in months I was experiencing a feeling of being centered. It was as though at last, because I was required to stay in one spot, I was able to enjoy it. I sensed that this was a necessary break from my perpetual motion. I now had a new order, a new force upon me. I'd been conscripted into a weird monastery in Las Vegas, and was being held there until all parts of me slowed down, stopped and grew into a stronger, calmer center. It was, I was sure, the daily, simple, ordering jail routine that did that.

They would wake us up at 5:30 a.m. Why so early I didn't know. It was not as if there was a whole busy and productive day ahead. Perhaps they just wanted us to be awake so we could contemplate our crimes and suffer more for them. Maybe that's what they meant by "doing time." They did time to you. They made you feel time. That was the punishment. I still had not been charged so I would meditate upon all the minor sins and crimes of my life as I staggered along that early-morning line down to breakfast, the first of the day's two meals. On the way down to the basement dining room, I would walk past the one window that we could look out of, and as I passed I would see all of Vegas still going full steam, spinning and flashing at 5:30 in the morning. And never once did I wish I was out there. I was surprisingly relieved to be in that air-conditioned prison where I could think freely about all the places I was not in.

All the jail's inmates were seated at breakfast at the same time, so that meant there were about two hundred and fifty men eating powdered scrambled eggs and grits and drinking very weak coffee together. After a rather subdued breakfast, we'd be herded back to our cells, where we would pace and smoke and sit and talk and pace and walk, never go out, maybe read an old tattered Ellery Queen paperback mystery book that came around on a little cart. It was as if every day was a rainy day in summer and we were all little kids shut inside, condemned to do our best to entertain ourselves until the sun came out again and Mom said we could go out and play.

But the thing that saved me the most from the monotony of those long lunchless days was writing letters. We were all allowed paper for letter writing and I took as much as I could get. I wrote one or two letters a day but never mailed them. Just writing them felt like enough, and besides, in most cases I didn't know the addresses of the people I was writing to. I wrote a letter to Mom asking her to forgive me for running off to the Alamo Theatre in her hours of need and then I ended the letter with my fart story. I knew she's find that funny, since she had a great history of it herself. I wrote Dad a letter thanking him for all his meat, all those great steak and roast beef dinners on Sunday and Monday nights. Then I thanked him for sending me to college and asked if he would lend me some money to pay my bail so I could get out of jail.

I wrote Rajneesh a letter telling him how he was wrong and Proust was right—there is no such thing as being in the present. I also mentioned I wished I'd stayed at his ashram longer—not for the sex, but to do the Primal Scream workshop, because I felt I could really use that now.

I wrote Meg asking her to forgive me for being so selfish and self-absorbed. I told her I would try harder not to be.

I wrote Sherry telling her just about the same thing I told Meg, except I told her how much I missed fucking her.

I wrote Norman O. Brown telling him how much I loved him, so would he please write a book I could read.

I wrote lots of letters, and last of all I wrote Shanti telling him how much I loved him and missed him and how I'd always keep him in my heart.

All those silly letters I wrote and never mailed saved me from total despair. I had never experienced anything like that before. Because I couldn't spell I had always been embarrassed to write, but now I was just spelling the words the way they sounded and that was fine because the letters were not being mailed. They were for me. No matter what was going on in that jail cell, I always felt better after a letter.

Some days, after I finished my letter-writing, we were offered group showers, which I did not participate in. The back of the cell, a large metal slab by the two toilets, slid away, revealing a dormitory shower room where you could take a group shower. Also, if I remember right, I think I was very constipated most of the time, because I don't remember ever squatting over that seatless toilet. While everyone else was showering and shitting, I was pacing, smoking, and waiting for dinnertime. Dinner was something like my old high-school hot-lunch program—mystery meat with mashed potatoes and overcooked vegetables, or mystery meat with red sauce, boiled potatoes, and canned cream corn. It was the height of white-trash cooking. It was gourmet white trash.

After dinner we'd be herded back to our cells again, and that's when the TV, which was hung from the ceiling at the front end of the cell, would be turned on full blast. It played only cop shows and it played them at top volume—sirens going, guns shooting. There wasn't much language or dialogue, just grunts and groans and "You do this" and "I'll do that." Some prisoners would sit gawking at this pale imitation of the world of crime they'd known since they were ten. Others would retreat to the rear of the cell and play cards and do other things—like the time two professionals, Vinnie and Frank, tried to make toast under my bunk. I thought the whole cell was on fire. After I found out what had really gone down, I got paranoid that it was directed at me. I suspected it all had begun when I showed too much enthusiasm over Vinnie's carrots.

That night at dinner Vinnie had offered to give his carrots away. Vinnie said, "Anyone want my fucking carrots?" But he said it with a tone that sounded more like "What asshole here likes carrots?" I jumped at his offer and said, "Oh sure, yeah, I love carrots," and at that moment I realized I was too enthusiastic. I had made myself into an individual. I was taking a stand by confessing my love for carrots. I was a carrot lover, and I had shown my weakness and my vulnerability. I was just a little bit too uncool. Up until that time Vinnie and Frank had never noticed me, but when Vinnie passed me his plate so I could scrape his carrots off it, the idea crossed my mind that nothing comes without consequences in any place, particularly that place. So I did not exactly eat Vinnie's carrots with relish; instead, I chewed each single soft, faded, tasteless piece about forty times before nearly choking as I swallowed. Vinnie and Frank eyed me all the time to see just how much I loved carrots.

Later that evening, some time around the second cops-and-robbers show, smoke, soot, and embers were floating up around my bunk, and I thought, My God, the whole place is on fire. I sat up in a panic and looked over the edge of my bunk, and there were Vinnie and Frank making a little campfire under the empty bunk below me. They were trying to toast some bread they had stolen from dinner. They had rolled up the mattress so that the metal surface of the bottom bunk was exposed, and then they had lit a whole roll of toilet paper under the bunk to heat it up. The spongy white bread was lying like some strange artwork entitled *Wonder Bread on Gray Metal,* while much smoke and a little flame lapped up around the edges of the bunk.

I was incredulous. I couldn't believe they were really trying to make toast. I thought they were harassing me instead, and I also could not understand how or why all the rest of the men in the cell would tolerate such a pollution of their atmosphere, as well as such demented selfishness. To smoke up the entire cell for two pieces of toast? It was outrageous. All that smoke and cinder had nowhere to go except into the air conditioner, where it got recycled and transformed into cool, smoky air for all of us to breathe.

I went to sleep that night angry, thinking I had to make a real effort to get the hell out of there. I had already been in four days and no charges had been brought against me. Also my buddy Mickey the con man was beginning to frighten me with his stories about how I was most likely being held on what they called a John Doe charge. He told me that because I had refused to give my name to the arresting officers, they could now refer to me as John Doe and spend years in search of my real name. "But," I protested to Mickey, "I did finally give my right name when they stripped me and took all my money. That's when I gave it to them." Mickey said that didn't matter. If you didn't give your right name when they first arrested you, you could be booked on a John Doe clause and disappear forever. "You've got no ID, right?" Mickey said. "And if they don't have no ID they don't got you. Without an ID you're lost forever." His voice was slightly sad, but also a bit sadistic.

Mickey's analysis was beginning to put me in a real panic. No one I knew on the outside world knew where I was. I could simply disappear. That was about the time I really began to press to make my one phone call. I was determined to get out of there, and it felt like one of the first times I'd been determined in years. I began thinking about a phrase I had read in *Life Against Death:* "All determination is negation." I began to get obsessed by all the things I had negated by being in that jail, and they came at me in vivid images. I was beginning to be aware of how my imagination was often more vivid and exciting than the actual experiences I had in the outside world, that the essence of my life was imagining the places I was not in. And here I was in a place where I could experience it in a dynamic way. It was not unlike my time in the Poconos Zendo. I could experience all these things that I hadn't done so vividly because all I had in that jail was my imagination. I would lie there on my top bunk imagining all the sunsets I was missing, and saw that I could imagine more places than one. If I was out in the world I could only be in one place with one sunset, but here I could skip from Provincetown to Santa Cruz to Alaska to India and follow the sun around the world. I could see the sun setting and rising over the Grand Canyon at the same time. The Grand Canyon—one of the places on my aborted trip I could have been but was not— became more alive than the place where I was. For the first time in years I felt a strange freedom. I felt incredibly free in the Las Vegas jail.

Another part of me was determined to get out. I managed to find out that my bail had been set at $285, and I thought if I could just get that information to Meg, I would have her send it to a bondsman in Vegas. On the fifth day, I was granted my one phone call. Two blond astronaut guards led me to the phone. Mildly shaking all over, I dialed Meg and waited with excited anticipation, my heart in my throat. I waited for Meg's responsible, all-saving, all-loving voice to come on the line. I got a busy signal. My heart sank. It was now that a very real feeling of fear set in as I pleaded with those smiling guards. "Oh, please," I said, "one more call? The line was busy. Let me have one more call, please?"

"Okay," the tall one said begrudgingly. "But make it snappy."

I called Barney and counted the rings, praying he would soon pick up. Fifteen rings later the guards made me hang up. They took me back to my cell, where I began to feel truly trapped. And I immediately made this deal with Mickey that if he got out first, he would call Meg and get her to send the bondsman the $285. Vinnie, the carrot man, in a more generous moment, had told me that that was how it was done—a piece of information I would have welcomed earlier, but didn't think to ask, because each day I'd been expecting to be released.

Every day just after breakfast, two or three astronaut guards would come into the cell and read a few names, followed by "Roll it up," which meant roll up your bedroll and get the hell out of there. I would sit on the edge of my top bunk and hear them call out, "Lombardo, roll it up—Crenshaw, roll it up—Allison, roll it up," and then that would be that. No one ever said, "North, roll it up." For the first few days I had felt like a bad schoolboy in afternoon detention, but now I was beginning to feel like a lifer. I gave Mickey Meg's phone number and told him, "Please, Mickey, if you get sprung first, give her a call."

Then at last, into my seventh day, the guard called, "Mickey Janis, roll it up," and Mickey smiled, gave me the power shake, and said, "You'll be out tomorrow, buddy boy—tomorrow we'll have a champagne toast together at the Sands," and he went out whistling. He went right out and called Meg and told her to send the $285 directly to him and he'd take care of it, he'd take care of everything. Only Meg was her old smart self. She didn't trust the way Mickey sounded on the phone. She did a little research and sent the money directly to a bondsman instead. So on the seventh day I heard "Brewster North, roll it up!" and I rushed to roll up my bedroll.

After getting dressed up in my white cotton pants and brown raw silk Nehru jacket, I was given a certificate with my trial date, which was set for two months later. I was given my money back in the form of a check. I didn't even have any cash to take a cab back to my motel.

At first I was very excited, and anticipated the great rush of freedom I would feel when I walked out of that prison door; but nothing happened. Instead I felt a rush of complications, as though I was entering another prison, a larger prison, the prison of the real world.

I hailed a cab and figured I would pay him with a traveler's check when I got back to my motel. I was beginning to learn the con system and didn't tell the cab driver until I got to my motel that I didn't have any cash, but I was able to put him at ease when I said I had traveler's checks in my room.

I was relieved to see the little black Karmann-Ghia getaway car still parked just where I'd left it, but I was surprised to find that my motel room had been emptied of all my luggage. I went to the front desk, where I found that the management was holding my bags until my return. "Where were you? Why didn't you call? We were going to report you to Missing Persons," the guy at the front desk said.

"I was in jail," I said, now with this light swagger, like at last I'd been initiated into the true ways of Las Vegas.

"Oh yeah," he said, "I figured as much. Too bad. A lot of people go that way. So here's your bill."

I got my traveler's checks out of my suitcase and paid the cab driver, then went back into the office to deal with my bill, which I was shocked to find was $240. "What!" I protested. "My room was empty. You could have rented it."

"No, no, not without you calling us first. We needed your permission. You had not checked out. You should have called. I would have checked you out."

I paid him off from my now-skinny traveler's check book and grabbed my bags and got the hell out of there. I got out of Vegas as fast as I could without breaking any speed limits. At last, back in that hot desert, I breathed a sigh of relief. I put the pedal to the metal and headed full speed straight for the Grand Canyon, completely ignoring the spectacular Grand Coulee Dam to my left.

I REACHED the Grand Canyon at sundown—perfect timing at last. I parked the car and ran straight to the edge, but when I got there, I could only see it as a beautiful flat backdrop. I saw it as a picture of itself. Too many postcards too early in life, I thought, as I stood there straining to see it for what it was. My imagined view of it in the Las Vegas jail had been more vivid than the real thing.

I checked into a log cabin motel right near the rim and vowed to climb to the bottom of the canyon in the morning, determined to penetrate it with my body and eyes; and feeling this new determination, at last I went to sleep again, and dreamed of the place I was not in, the Las Vegas jail.

Early the next morning I made my slow way down, deep into the bowels of Mother Earth at last. I was dressed only in my red shorts, and the hot, dry sun baked my newly freed body. I made my journey to the center of the earth with no provisions other than two oranges and three slices of Swiss cheese, which I carried in a plastic bag. Down, down, down I went. My knees shaking, I stopped every so often to look back up at the layered earth walls, then turned to go farther down into the crotch of the Mother, back down into her hot womb. Hours later, at last at the very bottom, I came upon a stream. It was crystal clear, a rushing transparency magnifying a bed of round, brown, glossy stones that lay beneath its glistening flow like a great nest of wet quail eggs.

I pulled off my red shorts and slipped into the stream. Its shocking coldness made all parts of me come together and immediately be there. Then some part of me surprised another part by yelling out, "Oh, my good Christ! Oh, shit! Oh, God! Oh, fuck, it's cold!" It came out in a he-man bellow that surprised and shook the fearful child within, that old child that lay deep in my bowels like an overgrown fetus, a sticky-shit, thumb-sucking fetus with cobwebs over its eyes. Too old to be innocent, too stubborn to be born.

Then some other part of me, a part that could clearly see how the man and the child were united in that complex of flesh, felt reconciliation. The feeling lasted only for a moment. It felt like that bright, sad, hopeful feeling, that comes when the sun suddenly bursts from behind a great dark cloud causing a momentary illumination and unification of a landscape of opposites.

As that reconciliation passed I became all body wrapped in a transparent cocoon of rushing water, lightly suspended, barely touching the fine moss on that bed of stone beneath. The stream was just deep enough to cover my body and leave my face out of the water. Then, relaxing and lowering my jaw, I began to let the water flow over my face and into my mouth, and taking small gulps, I could feel its cool transparency fill up my emptiness and quench me deep.

Then the stream turned into a fluid memory of all those other waters in my life that had in their way carried me to the place I was in now. And I felt them all, the crashing blue Atlantic, the vast Pacific, the ever-changing waters of Narragansett Bay, the LSD-blue waters flowing around me while I stood on those rocks in the heart of the Shawangunk Mountains, the dark brown Ganges crawling through India like a liquid beast, and last of all the snow waters of Ladakh flowing down from the top of the world.

I lay there looking up at the massive rock walls, the innumerable layers of eroded time that led to the canyon's rim. I knew my fall was completed. I was at the end of that long, crazy fit of perpetual motion. I had fallen from the top of the world to the bottom, from the Himalayan breast of the Mother to the deep, deep place of her canyon.

And here I could lay to rest a part of me, let my raging past soar up and out of me. A complex of emotions and personalities lifted and peeled off of me and like so many multicolored ghosts flew up and out of that grand Grand Canyon. And above me I saw all those ghosts dancing in a wild and crazy Matisse-like chain dance. They had grown out of those letters I had written in jail and now they were departing. I saw Mom in her sundress and saddle shoes, stomping. I saw Dad scattering her ashes over the bay. I saw Sherry barking in her Lassie mask and Meg flying among them all on a Kashmiri rug. I saw Bernie the porn king in his reflecting sunglasses holding hands with Rajneesh. I saw a bunch of Ladakhans crying *"Julay! Julay!"* as they pranced and danced with their black robes swinging. I saw Norman O. Brown; and Vinnie and Frank, the two toast-cooking jailbirds, come out together from under my bunk bed, squinting and smiling in the sun. I saw Uncle Jib sailing in the penguin's bathtub. And at last I saw Mustang and peachy, naked Shanti, joining hands with all the others and dancing a great boogie-woogie chain dance to heaven. And then they were gone like evaporating smoke in the wind, leaving me empty and free again.

Exhausted from the hike and washed clean by the stream, I was emptied of past and future, and everything came together in the present. For the first time in my life, I realized something did matter, something mattered to me. It was the sharing of this story, the story of all this, the true story of some of the things that happened to me while living on this earth. I wanted to go back to New York City and at last take the money Mom had left me to live on while I wrote it all down.

I was up and out of that Grand Canyon and on my way. And all the way across America I chanted "Right! I will write! Right! Right! I will write! I will write!" I would dare to remember my ghosts. Then maybe, after I captured them, I could take that vacation to Bali. I would have at last done some real work to take a vacation from.

At last I felt like I was driving home. I was driving straight for the Atlantic Ocean and I half dreamed and half remembered Mom's never-ending passion for the sea. We were all on our way to Gram's summer house in Sakonnet, Rhode Island, in our wooden-slatted '38 Ford beach wagon. What a car!